X X L - X S

NEW DIRECTIONS IN ECOLOGICAL DESIGN

MITCHELL JOACHIM

MIKE SILVER

Summary

Projects

Essays and interviews:

Acknowledgements

This book was supported by numerous grants from New York University Gallatin School of Individualized Study, the University of Buffalo Department of Architecture, and Cornell University. As the co-authors of XXL-XS, we wish to thank the publishers at Actar for believing in the project and supporting it to completion. We would also like to thank the writers, designers, artists, and architects who contributed their work and put up with our constant demands for updated material. A deep note of appreciation is in order for our copy editor, Irina Oryshkevich, without whose proofreading skills we would not have made it to the finish line. Finally, we would like to thank all of the students and teachers who directly inspired our thinking. We cannot sufficiently stress how much they contributed to the development of our ideas. It is our hope that an intensification of these dialogues will continue to open up new pathways in contemporary culture and its search for workable ecological design protocols.

Foreword

Michelle D. Addington

The numbers are omnipresent, the responsibility inescapable. Buildings consume more than 40% of the world's energy, and more than 70% of its electricity. Even these dire numbers underrepresent the true consequences of our buildings as many collateral impacts are not properly counted and attributed; for example, the embodied energy of buildings is currently charged to the industrial sector. And, of much greater concern, the rapid development taking place throughout the world will consume resources and energy at levels far beyond our capacity to manage greenhouse gas levels and the accompanying global temperature rise.

Certainly the profession of architecture has been active in regard to global energy and environmental concerns, and we need no longer champion those architects and practices whose early clarion calls to a greater environmental stewardship through sustainable design put them at odds with the rest of our professional community. Rather, our community is now in lock-step with the principles and procedures of those early adopters, while those few architects who continue to defend the autonomy of architecture as necessarily immune to the perceived determinism of sustainable design are considered as out-of-touch anachronisms.

Yet, this very mainstreaming may be at the heart of the stunning lack of effect that contemporary architectural practice has actually contributed to stemming the consequences of its actions. In startling contrast to the rapid and dramatic shift we have witnessed in our profession's commitment to environmental concerns, we have seen very little substantive change in the way that we do things. Indeed, in a world that has undergone enormous change in the last century, and

Future visions of Manhattan.
Bjarke Ingels, "Big U Plan"

which forecasts even greater changes for the next, architecture has remained curiously insensitive to these contextual pressures. Form is perhaps the one exception to this–the influence of computational representation and fabrication methods are readily manifest in our buildings–but this may well be because form is the only provenance in which architecture claims full ownership.

The constituency of sustainable design today, in spite of the heroic proclamations of the profession, is little more than a cobbled together collection of minor tweaks, and even these tweaks avoid addressing the major contributors to environmental impacts. We are willing to devote significant resources and effort to engineering the thermal properties of our facades and yet profoundly unwilling to curb the increasing bloat of our buildings. It is as if the field of architecture has assumed a defensive position, essentially doubling down on protecting the status quo from the trespasses of a messy and complicated world. By avoiding any specter of risk in our own quarters, we are increasing the risks borne by all of humanity. Sustainable design, as currently defined by the profession, has sidestepped the consequences of its relative inaction, and shielded itself from criticism by hiding behind a cloak of rhetoric. The field of architecture has not only ceded any leadership toward producing substantive change, but has denied itself the creative opportunities afforded by operating in an expanded field of contents and contexts.

The projects presented in this volume offer an alternative future, one in which architecture is inflected by the manifold influences of a rich and diverse planet, as well as one in which architecture extends its territory across multiple disciplines. By relinquishing authority, architecture gains agency.

Pieraccioli and Claudio Granato, "Human Heritage Site"

Design for a Planet in Peril

Mitchell Joachim and Mike Silver

Above: Deformed world map by Duncan Clark and Robin Houston showing the United States, India, and China as the largest producers of planet-warming CO_2.

Opposite: Mies van der Rohe's flooded Farnsworth House, the ultimate in levitating architecture realized at the expense of its usefulness.

"The first law of ecology: everything is related to everything else."[1]
Barry Commoner

In 2013, the United Nations reported that world measurements of atmospheric carbon dioxide had reached 400 parts per million (ppm), well above the safety limit set at 350 ppm by scientific consensus.[2] More alarmingly, by continuing the use of outdated technologies the developed world is actively accelerating the total amount of CO_2 pumped into the air each year. If we also consider expanding populations and regional conflicts over dwindling reserves,[3] it becomes clear that environmental problems identified as far back as the 1950s will likely become more difficult to endure in the near term. Despite these facts and the hopeful developments of the Paris Climate Agreement (COP21), active denial of human-induced climate change continues to be a serious problem. Provincial politics and shortsighted economic policies are dramatically slowing the progress that our society must make in order to avert a catastrophe.

Most scientists agree that many extreme weather events, like recent coastal cyclones, are the direct result of industrial activity. Some even suggest that climate change is already taking place in less exposed midland regions, such as the Great Lakes. In 2008 Tropical Storm Lowell and remnants of Hurricane

Left: Updated version of Robert Venturi's diagram for a monument. Right: The Gobi Desert encroaching on a Chinese farming village.

Ike passed through Wisconsin and Illinois, forcing the Fox River to overflow its banks. A famous causality of the deluge was Mies van der Rohe's iconic Farnsworth House, constructed in 1951 for a wealthy Chicago nephrologist. Although Mies designed his pristine steel and glass box to survive periodic flooding, unprecedented rainfall this time caused the river to surge well above the building's elevated interior. The half-submerged project is of course both a cautionary tale and an epigram of the dangers inherent in unregulated growth. Poor land-use policies in the surrounding county likely increased the amount of water flowing into the site. The near destruction of the house is also a sign of the long-term failures of 20th-century Modernism. Mies's drowning "duck,"[4] a bi-product of rampant industrialization with its crude and often poisonous technologies, suggests that architecture itself can both represent and contribute to the conditions of its own demise.

Toxic pollution, sea-level rise, species extinction and desertification, all seem to be the grim legacy of this energy-hungry aesthetic. But do the reactionary theories developed by postmodern architects like Robert Venturi fare any better? Do the appliqué signs promoted in *Learning from Las Vegas* provide us with any real alternatives? These might seem like odd questions to ask in an essay about global warming, but let's consider the shortcomings of current sustainability practices and how they support a strong disconnect between style and technology. Certainly, a LEED-certified (Leadership in Energy & Environmental Design) neoclassical library by Robert Stern and a LEED-certified ultramodern academic building by Thom Mayne[5] cannot both embody holistic solutions to large-scale ecological problems much less inspire a cogent discourse on the inseparable relationship between tectonics, ecology, and expression? Is the library more relevant because people can relate to its familiar imagery? Should new guidelines remain flexible enough to encourage variety and experimentation? And if so, what paradigm of sustainability is being showcased in contemporary structures that depend so heavily on ideas derived from earlier discourses like Deconstructivism and the Neo-Baroque, for which climate change and sea level rise were simply not driving concerns? While we prefer the bold aesthetics of Mayne's project, neither architect was able to implement viable ecological protocols in truly comprehensive ways. A relevant

architecture should not only be functionally green, but its formal, conceptual and material properties must also constitute a novel and tightly integrated whole, one that can relate to the larger world around it. Technique and form must be considered together, especially in buildings that serve shifting social, environmental, and global needs.

Complexity and Conservation

We like complexity and conservation in architecture, art, and urban design. We do not like over-articulation, retrofitted classicism, and the ad-hoc. Nor do we like the "precious intricacies"[6] of Neo-Expressionism or the Bio-Picturesque. Instead, we want to confront pressing ecological problems by inspiring the production of a rich, integrated and holistic art. We seek a complexity achieved through efficient means and minimal energy inputs. We prefer complexity without excess or waste. Today, the need to address constantly changing functions and widespread environmental destruction, even in a single building, has reached unimaginable levels of urgency.[7]

In opposition to the design methodologies of Buckminster Fuller, whose principle of synergy led to the creation of simple platonic structures such as domes and spheres, we are interested in the connection between variation and thrift, in the ability to do a lot more with sustainable materials and processes that simply did not exist in Fuller's day. A geodesic house made of standardized aluminum parts is never going to be complex or green enough. As a limited-use proto-

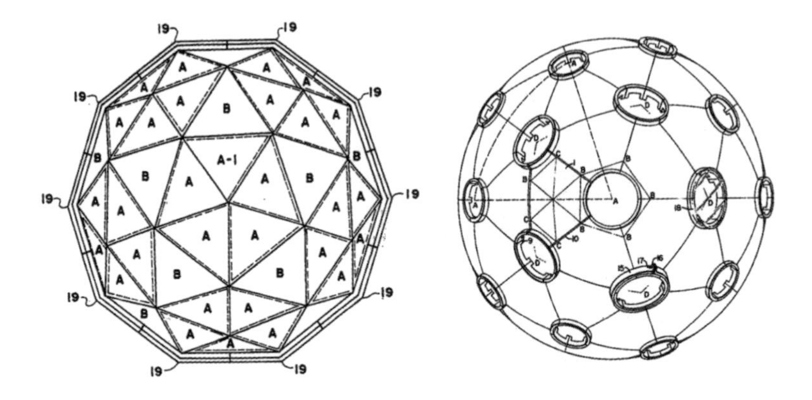

type, it has a hard time accommodating heterogeneous programs and adapting itself to increasingly challenging environmental pressures. Frank Gehry's Disney Concert Hall in Los Angeles and his Bilbao Museum in Basque, Spain are not viable models either. The informal, curvilinear massing of these buildings requires excessive amounts of steel to hold their shape. A better example for the future and one that escapes both inefficiency and over simplification can be found in composite windmill blades and boat hulls. Assembled using advanced robotic technologies and ultra-light, high-strength materials like fiber-reinforced plastics, these structures perfectly balance increased strength and surface complexity with the need to conserve resources.

If culture is to grow in a positive direction, it must produce higher, more integrated forms of innovation with greater economy and less waste. Architects (and developers) also need to recognize that the effects of their work are felt well beyond the borders of a typical building site. By definition, ecology involves the study and holistic understanding of interconnected systems that are not limited to a small set of isolated problems. Design must reach into the upper limits of our atmosphere all the way down to the deepest regions of nanoscopic space. By comparison, the main objective of today's sustainability movement has been the improvement of existing practices through numerous bland upgrades including passive cooling, low-flush toilets, and green roofs. The primary result has been uniform conventions, not organic assemblies. We consider such standards to be myopic. How can the broader design disciplines support cutting-edge work that responds intelligently to difficult environmental challenges? How can architects, engineers, urban planners, artists, and designers create stimulating, new, and rigorous works that improve the health and quality of global space? For this to happen our culture must learn from past mistakes and strike a dynamic balance between art, nature, and technology.

Left: Geodesic domes embody a workable synergy between structure and form, but both their parts and wholes consist of simple primitives. Right: The formal complexity of Frank Gehry's Disney Concert Hall necessitates the use of excessive amounts of steel.

Bottom: Composite structures such as this duckbill-shaped windmill blade employ strong, ultra-light materials to produce integrated forms of complexity with less waste.

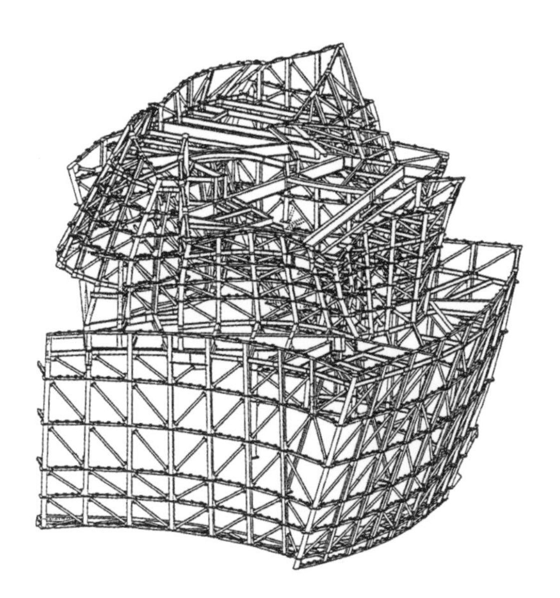

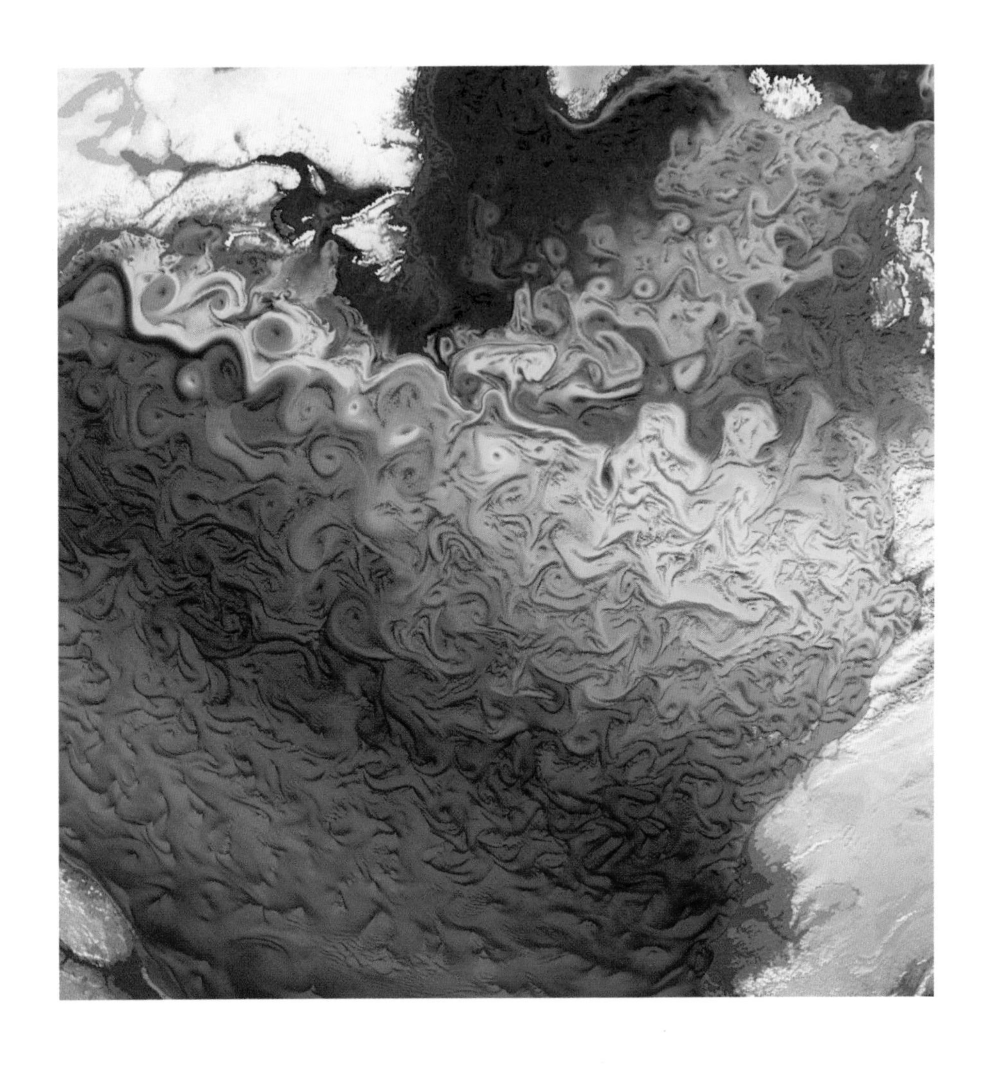

High-performance computer simulation of temperature flows in the Atlantic Ocean

Our thesis is therefore both global and performative in scope. We want an architecture that is more than just a constellation of digitally generated surface effects and conventional materials. We want a holistic architecture that uses the best techniques to connect directly with existing natural systems while creating a renewed ecology that can sustain itself well into the future. Along these lines, many of the projects featured in this book simply abandon the old tropes and construction processes of the past by creating numerous green alternatives that proliferate along unexpected pathways.

Both current and emerging technologies of representation can help us realize these goals. New mapping, sensing, and computer simulation techniques, for example, allow us to more accurately measure and predict the behavior of large and small systems. They offer new ways in which humans can steer complexity in directions that benefit all life. Consider, for example, how the active scanning systems used in driverless cars may increase our real-time situational awareness of urban and sub-urban sites. Linking high-resolution data sets with novel analysis and production tools will help us better understand our world.

XXL-XS

The disasters at Chernobyl and Fukushima demonstrated the far-reaching influence of local industry on worldwide environmental health. Effects of scale move constantly between the infinitesimal and the colossal. Globalization operates on many levels simultaneously. Its very nature implies incommensurable shifts in size, in which fixed and discretized phenomena lose their significance. As demonstrated in *The Powers of Ten*, written and produced by Charles and Ray Eames, scale is conveniently defined by discrete, numerically determined frames. The point of the film was to bridge different dimensions. Unfortunately, many interpret it as proof that uniform subdivisions of space are universal and real when in fact they are merely arbitrary. Although framing can help us understand the world, nothing in reality is isolated; at any particular moment things can blur and spill across boundaries.

The color theories of Isaac Newton and Wolfgang von Goethe, published more than a century apart, provide another instructive comparison. In his famous work on optics, Newton described color mathematically, in terms of absolute, numerically defined wavelengths and frequencies. In contrast, Goethe's *Theory of Colors*, written in 1810, pioneered a comprehensive theory of human vision, which described visual perception in relative terms. Goethe showed that no color could be reduced to a single, self-contained essence disengaged from its context. In other words, the experience of a particular shade of blue changes when it is seen next to red or yellow. This idea more clearly illustrates our thesis. The problem with design professionals today is that their thinking is Newtonian. Scale can be viewed in single, isolated snapshots, but it is best understood holistically, in a smooth space of interdependent values.

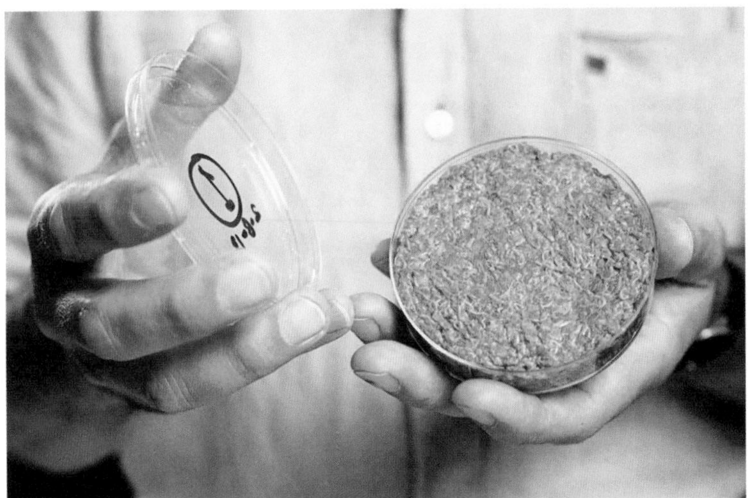

Above: Dirty, dangerous and difficult jobs can now be automated with co-robotic technologies that work alongside humans to do more work in less time. Bottom: Victimless materials such as this lab-grown hamburger are the precursors of genetically engineered products that may someday form self-healing skins for living buildings.

Right: Nano-scaled motors built from carefully assembled molecular components.

 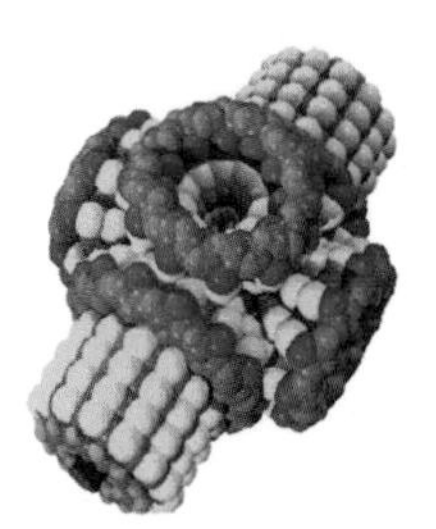 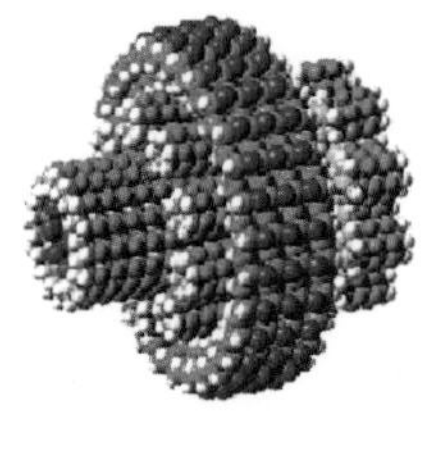 

Rem Koolhaas and Bruce Mau also emphasize the importance of size in *S,M,L,XL*, but their range is unnecessarily restricted. As a collection, the essays and projects in *XXL-XS* go well beyond Koolhaas and Mau and span a continuum from the extra, extra large to the extra small. Within this scaled framework, projects are grouped together into three primary phase states – solid, liquid, gas – and their associated terrestrial, aquatic, and atmospheric sites. (The book's contents form a circle, beginning and ending with two air-based projects.)

XXL-XS represents the emerging discipline of global design by assembling a wide range of innovators with diverse interests. Geo-engineering,[8] construction-site co-robotics, low-energy fabrication, up-cycling waste, minimally invasive design, biomaterials, and molecular self-assembly are just a few of the important advances explored in the book. At one extreme are massive public works, at the other, micro to nano-sized interventions that can have equally profound impacts on our world. From terraforming to bio-manufacturing, a whole new generation of designers is proposing unique ways of confronting the difficult challenges ahead. In this way design becomes a totality of relationships that affects all disciplines, which can no longer be thought of as self-contained fields, each handled separately by narrowly focused specialists. Globalization demands a restructuring of the profession as we know it. This requires a new breed of generalists who can work across fields and engage research on multiple sites around the globe. Today we need planetary designers versed in the art of integral design.

Notes:

1. Barry Commoner, "The Four Laws of Ecology," in *The Closing Circle: Man, Nature and Technology* (New York: Alfred Knopf, 1971), 16.
2. Retrieved on 8/11/15 from www.350.org/about/science
3. See Coral Davenport, "Pentagon Signals Security Risks of Climate Change," *The New York Times* (October 13, 2014).
4. See Robert Venturi, "The Duck and the Decorated Shed," in *Learning from Las Vegas* (Cambridge, MA: MIT Press, 1977), 90-91.
5. Jessie Reiser, "Keynote Address," New York University, Global Design NYU (http://places.designobserver.com/feature/new-york-university-hosts-global-design-event/26538/)
6. Robert Venturi, *Complexity and Contradiction in Architecture* (New York: The Museum of Modern Art, 1966), 16.
7. Ibid (paraphrase of the framework of the book's opening paragraph).
8. See Duncan Graham-Rowe, "Scrubbing CO_2 Cheaply," *MIT Technology Review* (March 9, 2009). Retrieved on 8/11/15 from http://www.technologyreview.com/news/412439/scrubbing-co^{2}-cheaply/

Inside of an advanced fusion reactor

Projects

Solitario Canyon
fault zone
pre-Prow Pass Tuff
volcanic rocks
Dune Wash
fault
pre-Prow Pass Tuff
volcanic rocks

Extraterritoriality Nexus
Melanie Fessel

Remnants, Resilience, and Resistance: Disturbances as Opportunity

We no longer map territories, but territories map us. Humanity is inscribing its vast impacts on the Earth's surface; these new engraved territories have no boundaries, they portray who we are, what we have done, and where we are moving.

Architecture and urban-planning disciplines have to be negotiated in the context of an increasingly globalized world, where immeasurable human impressions are so complexly woven that it is becoming increasingly difficult to maintain a distinction between nature, culture, and the built environment. Within these interrelations they uncover our ever-changing cities and landscapes. There are exceptions: fragmented geographically autonomous zones labeled as extraterritorial.

Extraterritoriality is a spatial system that crosses municipal, national, international, and geographical boundaries beyond the traditional sense of governance. Its zones are exempt from local legal jurisdiction and are often applied to military bases of foreign countries, refugee camps, military zones, and offices of the United Nations. Worldwide ownership treaties outline these extraterritorial zones and are defined as International Waters, International Seabed, Moon, Outer Space, International Zone, Antarctica, and Extraterrestrial Real Estate.

Extraterritorialities relate crucially to sustainable development because increasing ecological change creates more areas of instability without borders. Without applicable jurisdiction, these new zones of exception could provide explorative genealogies in terms of ecology for cross-national, transnational, and transcultural exchanges of large-scale connectivity. Spaces like ports and airports aspire to be worlds within themselves and provide vivid evidence of the remnants, resilience, and resistance that these territories carry. The hybridization of nature and society transforms extraterritorial spaces into long envisioned utopian places. Morphological and typological studies of these areas offer new readings of the changing conditions offered by the concept of extraterritoriality. Ultimately, they provide a new framework in which to nurture a discourse on sustainability in physical space.

Left: Our churning atmosphere, surgical geographies, and below-ground geophysical space form one contiguous design context. Territories in nature are never limited by national borders. This becomes increasingly difficult to ignore in a networked age.

WeatherField
Lateral Office and LCLA Office / Mason White and Lola Sheppard

WeatherField is a shape-shifting energy-generation park located on a strip of sandy beach in Abu Dhabi between Yas and Saadiyat Islands. The park is an open public space and is capable of harvesting abundant wind energy. As an economic sponsor, a visual or physical experience, and a source of information, the park offers a variety of ways through which to engage with climate and renewable energy. The Yas Island energy park is comprised of a field of 200 "para-kites," each equipped with a base station consisting of two flexible posts. Except for the posts that tether the para-kites, the ground and aquatic ecology is undisturbed. The para-kites use a parafoil system to remain aloft and a Windbelt™ system to harvest "flutter" energy from the wind. Each device is capable of generating 6220 kwh of power. Across the WeatherField, we calculate 1.24 GW annually, or about 620 energy-efficient homes. WeatherField offers three kinds of public experiences: a sponsoring resident may have free electricity and a free view of the Gulf from his or her home; a visitor may access views through a "periscope" embedded in every post on the park grounds; and an adventurous visitor may be harnessed to a para-kite to survey the site from the air. With such an abundance of wind, the Gulf has considerable potential to become the largest renewable energy field in the world and a model for future regional planning. Just as oil and gas operations have sought out invisible subterranean (geological) conditions for the harvest of dirty energy, so too WeatherField will seek out visible meteorological conditions for the harvest of clean energy. In order to transition symbolically from an oil-dependent to a weather-dependent energy state, WeatherField co-opts existing oil/gas field sites. The regional plan proposes to decommission a 20th-century industrial energy field across the Persian Gulf and transform it into a network of 21st-century public-energy parks.

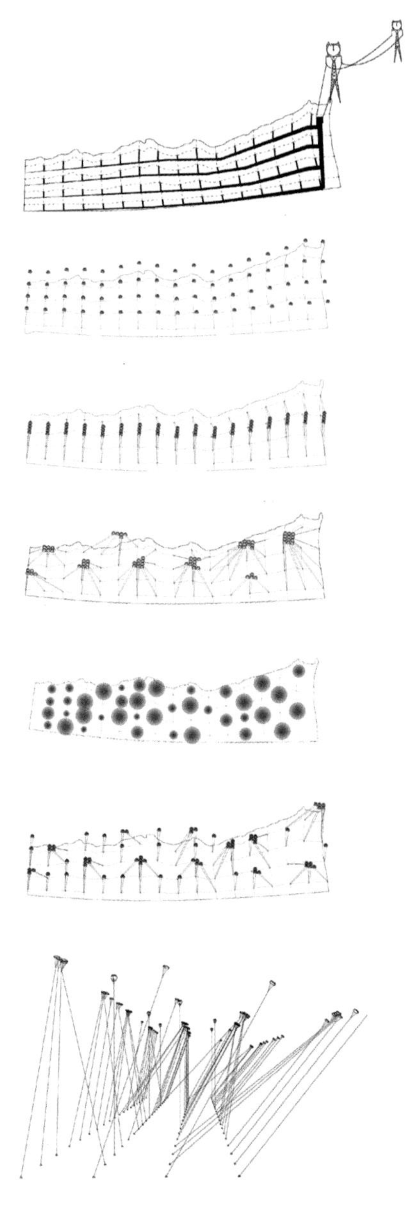

Smart, lightweight, air-based generators capture power from the sky. These para-kites can also be inhabited, offering visitors extraordinary views of their surroundings.

Amagerforbraending Waste Treatment Plant
BIG / Bjarke Ingels

Amagerforbraending is situated on an edge condition. Located on the outer rim of Copenhagen, it is currently being planned as a new center for recreational activities. Amagerforbraending divides the site in two: factories on one side, housing on the other. It is a place that people know from afar but seldom visit. The purpose of our project is to tie these opposing contexts together to form a new identity on the outskirts of the main city. Our principal objective is to transform Amagerforbraending into a desirable destination, a place in itself. Most of the recently built power plants in Denmark are simple, functional boxes, covered with expensive skins. In our projected intervention we have tried to construct more than a mere camouflage around an existing industrial building. Instead, we have added novel functions to the project's exterior. In our work the creation of value through new ecological programs is also offset by a desire for beauty, the creation of which we call hedonistic sustainability. In retrofitting Amagerforbraending, we pursued a both/and rather than an either/or design strategy to create a new breed of waste-to-energy production facilities, one that was economical, energy-efficient, and socially charged. Instead of considering Amagerforbraending as an isolated object, we intensified its relationship to the city by turning its roof and facades into a giant ski slope. At the top of the renovated plant is a large exhaust port that pipes out intermittent smoke-rings, which are clearly visible above the site and serve as reminders of the daily discharge of carbon dioxide caused by Copenhagen's continued use of non-renewable energy.

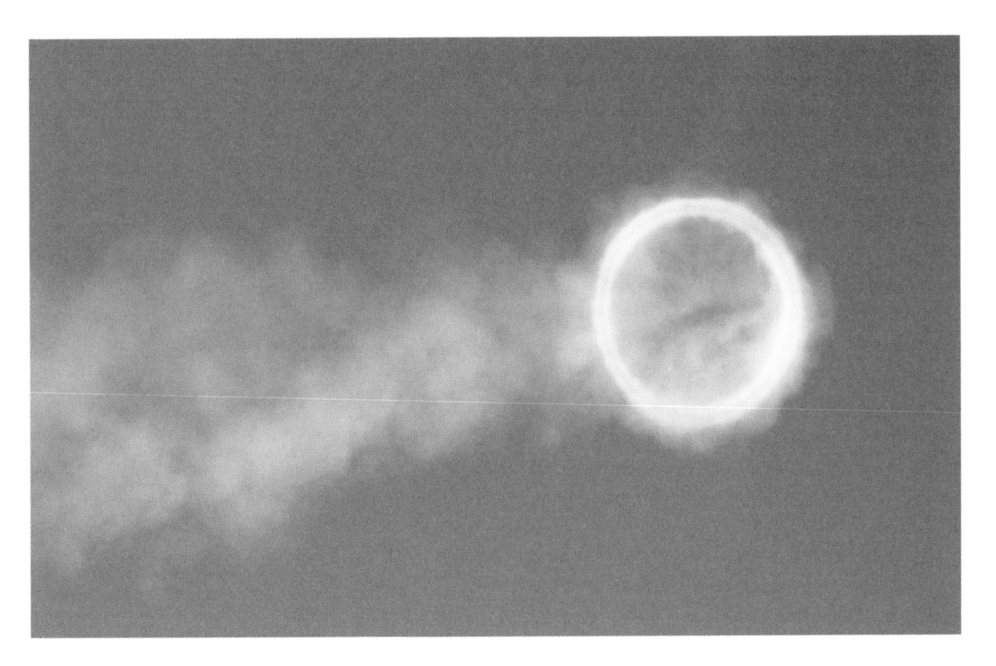

Left: The combined programs of recreation and waste-to-energy conversion create a monumental architecture in which green infrastructure is celebrated instead of marginalized or hidden.

Above: Rings of carbon pollution emitted from the plant become both an ambient public display and a dire warning.

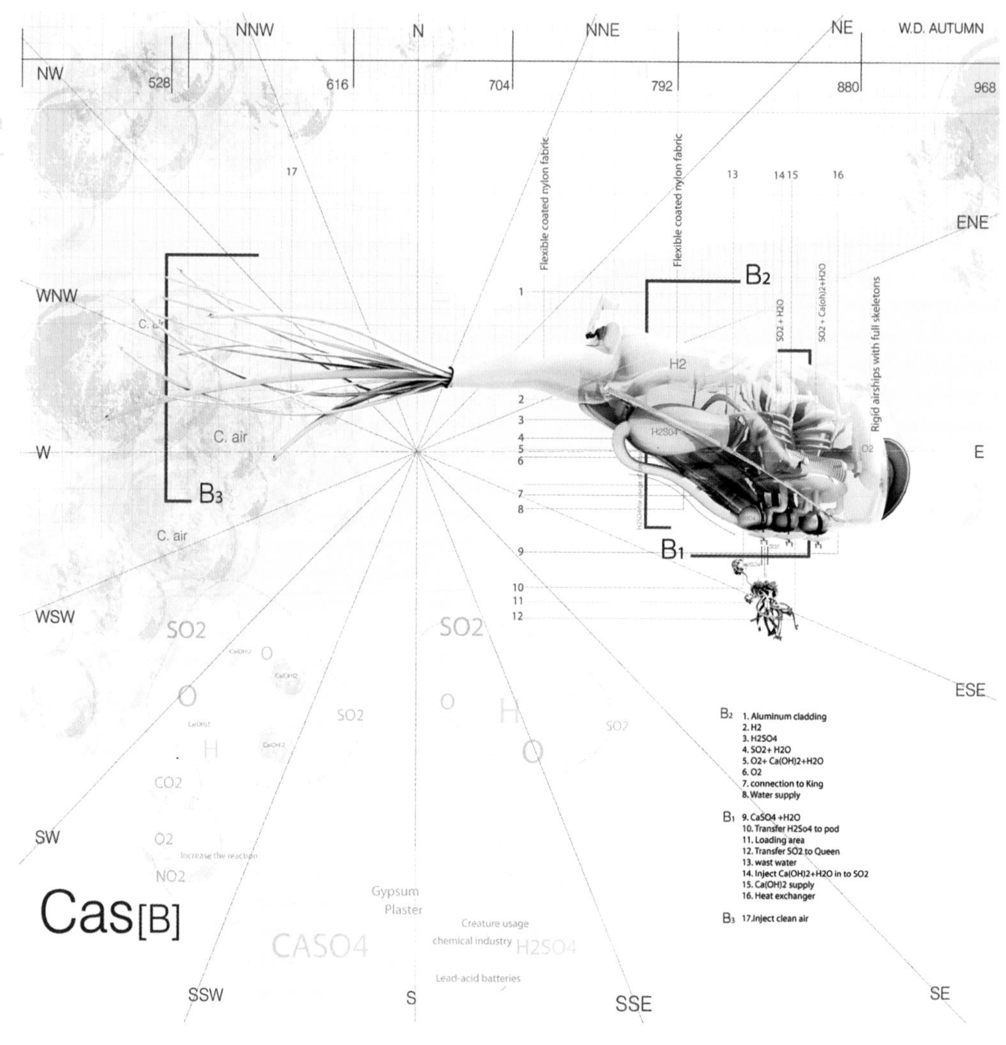

Cas[B]

Autonomous pollution-sucking robotic dirigibles scrubbing carbon from factory smoke stacks.

Clean
Azadeh Mohammadi

"There is no more throwing away... away has gone away." – *Gertrude Stein*

This project for an Ecotarium was produced as part of a graduate design studio directed by Mitchell Joachim at the University of Toronto School of Architecture in 2010. While speculative in nature, it envisions vast floating machines that roam the globe to seek out and consume toxic pollution produced by existing industrial infrastructure. Balloon-like vehicles use their vacuum tendrils to absorb waste fumes emitted from factory smokestacks. The design draws on technology not unlike that of the carbon-scrubbing machines and artificial trees proposed by Columbia University scientist Klaus Lackner. A functioning monument and public relations tool, the Ecotarium would become the visible counterpart of the more prosaic, ground-based remediation facilities imagined by Lackner.

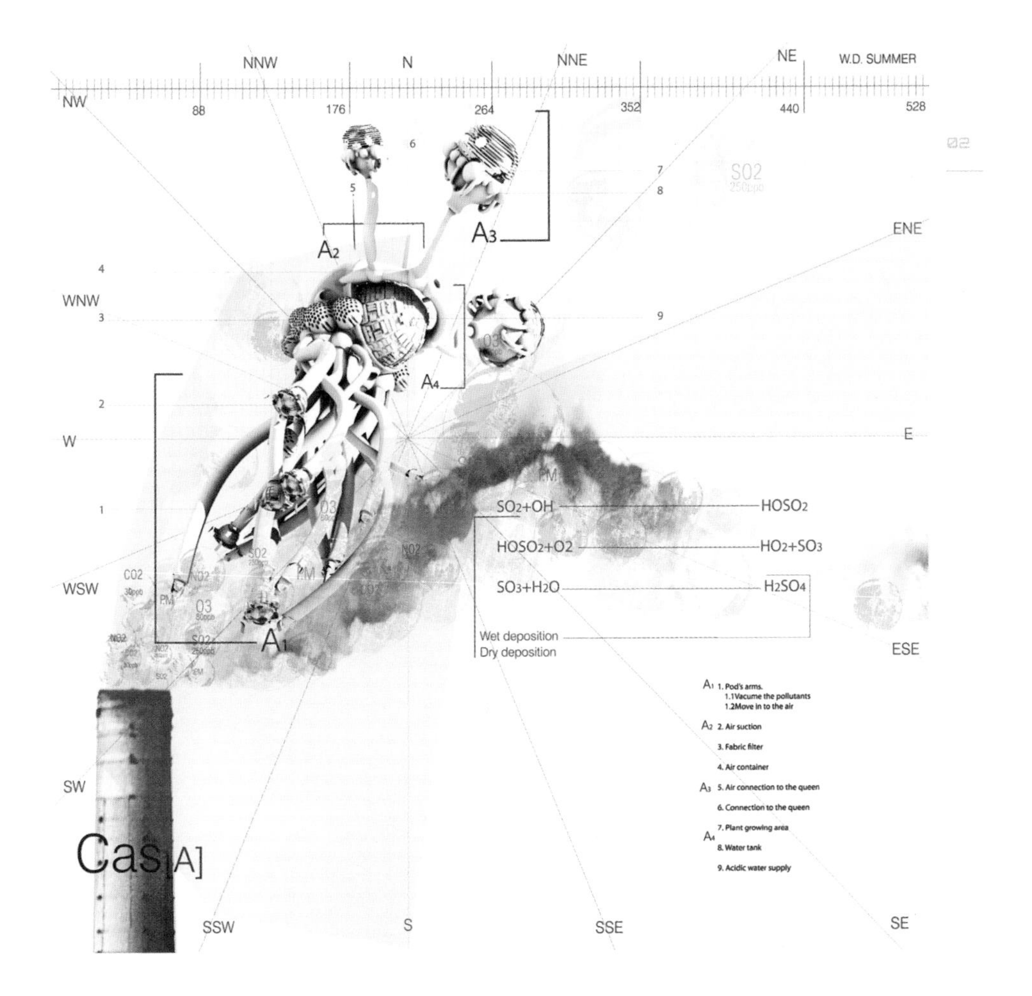

Future Venice
Rachel Armstrong

What would an architecture based on biotechnology look like? This is the question we have explored in our work with protocell technology, a chemically programmable, dynamic oil-in-water system that offers a radical alternative to contemporary construction technologies. In order to understand how protocols could change the way in which cities are designed, we need a test site that has ready access to water, faces continuous threats to its infrastructure, and is in urgent need of repair. Venice has weathered its site for over thirteen centuries but its unique architecture is constantly threatened by destruction. Some of its buildings have been literally digested into dust, and countless attempts to repair fist-sized holes with concrete, rubble, rubbish, even gum–are in evidence all around the city.

Along the watery edges of Venice is an indigenous ecology capable of constant renewal. Living organisms such as algae, shellfish, and bacteria have evolved fascinating ways of shaping their world by accreting, secreting, and sculpting available resources into suitable microenvironments. What if the resilience and adaptive capabilities of such living systems could be harnessed to enhance and preserve architecture? What if the city could develop a manageable, biologically-based way to repair itself? Could synthetic biology offer a solution? We believe that Venice can be saved by using protocells to grow artificial limestone reefs around its sinking foundations.

Photophobic protocells that shun sunlight could be engineered to seek shelter at the bottom of the Venetian lagoon. Once the protocells reach safety, a second metabolism would kick in and dissolve ambient carbon dioxide to create insoluble crystalline skins by using minerals in the water. These metabolic byproducts would form bone-hard surfaces. Over time an artificial reef would evolve and attract other indigenous marine life such as barnacles and clams. These organisms would make use of minerals produced by protocells and help synthesize an even more robust ecosystem. In this way the increased strength and expanded foundations of Venice would help prevent it from sinking. The preservation of the city is a complex challenge, but we believe that protocell technology could play a significant role. The ability to engineer specific species with programmable behaviors offers an entirely new way of designing eco-friendly architecture, one that remediates declining landscapes and reconnects us to the biosphere.

Left: Protocells are light sensitive and grow in dark waters around which they can petrify the rotting foundations of a sinking city. Over time this system could also produce a thriving marine ecosystem. Right: A proposal to save Venice by using artificial limestone reefs created with synthetic biology.

Aqualta
Clouds AO / Studio Lindfors

Studio Lindfors has released a new series of images called Aqualta–a play on "*acqua alta*," the ever higher tides flooding Venice–which visually explore what a coastal metropolis might feel like a hundred years from now due to rising sea levels. The images illustrate a cultural and financial epicenter–New York–adapting to, rather than resisting rising waters. City dwellers migrate to higher and dryer elevations as water levels gradually increase. Piers, boardwalks, and systems of navigable canals reestablish transportation networks lost below. Residents repurpose rooftops for farms and greenhouses. Wetland ecologies and oyster beds thrive and take root to better protect coasts from future storms. The city appears without combustion; engines, power plants, all emissions have been rendered obsolete, resulting in cleaner, quieter neighborhoods. Aqualta reveals an adaptable city infrastructure capable of acclimating to nature.

Left: Living with rising sea levels. New multi-tiered and overlapping infrastructure threaded into a flooded urban fabric. Cars and sidewalks are replaced by bridges, boats, dirigibles, waterways, and vertical farms.

Above: Nighttime view of Time Square with streets as waterways.

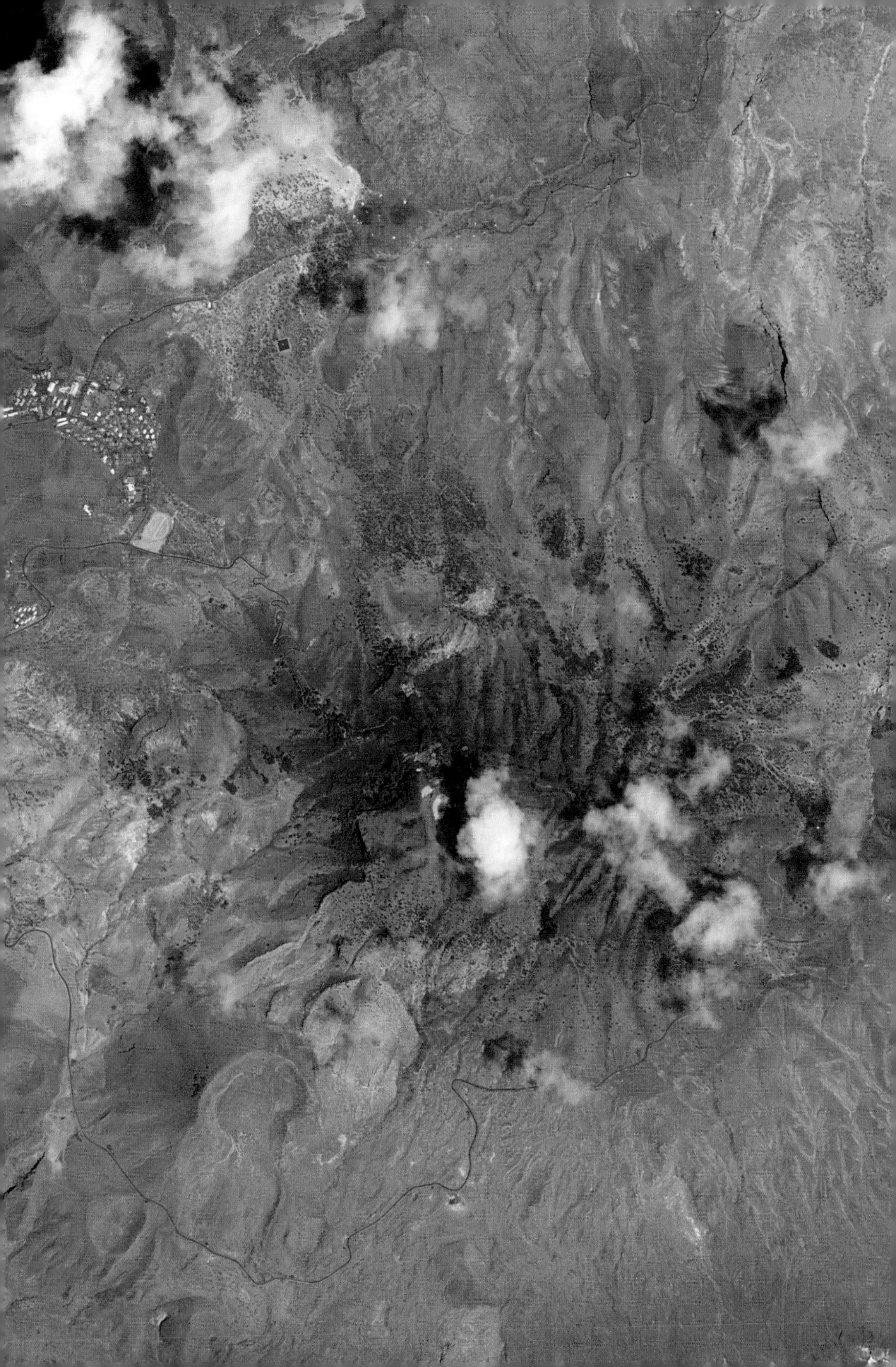

7°56'S - 14°22'W
Charles Darwin and Sir Joseph Hooker

Ascension Island, located in the Mid-South Atlantic 7°56 S-14°22 W, was once a completely barren volcanic rock. Today it is covered by an artificial rainforest planted in the 1850s by Sir Joseph Hooker and the British Navy, based on advice from evolutionary biologist Charles Darwin. Ascension Island is one of the largest and most successful geoengineering projects on the planet. Its trees produce their own self-sustaining water supply by capturing moisture from drifting clouds and sea mist. Were it not for its dense foliage, water from ocean storms would simply evaporate, making the island a lifeless, arid place.

Left: A large-scale geoengineering project realized with 19th-century technology.
Right: Sir Joseph Hooker, a disciple of Charles Darwin, turned a rocky and isolated desert island into a thriving rainforest.
Photo: David Catling

Very Large Structure
Zuloark / Manuel Dominínguez

"Very Large Structure" is a habitable megastructure with a high degree of independence. It exists in symbiosis with the physical environment that it traverses, and is physically able to manage it while in motion. Inside it, cargo is uploaded and downloaded, buildings are constructed and tested, and different territorial policies and infrastructures are designed, implemented, and managed with the aim of achieving the synergic updates and paradigmatic changes demanded by the twenty-first century.

VLS is a territorial manager, a synergistic machine within its environment. Its aim is to restore territory with essentially four policies, which are managed and implemented from the structure as it rolls along the plateau. Strategies for the synergic territorial restoration of Castle and Leon's plateau:

1. **Rural environment/range.** Exploitation of new rural environments. [a) reforestation of 30,000 Km²; b) managed and productive forests; c) promotion of natural spaces; d) rural, active environment industry tissue]
2. **Urban environment/range.** Castile and Leon's township network for restitution and real estate responsibility [a) reversible constructions; b) restoration; c) rehabilitation of urban plans of the last decade; d) development of physical and virtual connections between villages]
3. **Energy Production.** Association of producers. [a) multi-scale wind; b) local and territorial solar; c) biomass production and consumption; d) hydrogen-battery technology related to hydrolysis]
4. **Waste Management.** Territorial waste management and profit. Synergy between matter and energy. [a) liquid waste management (A1. integral water recycling and treatment process; A2. protection and promotion of natural water reserves); b) solid waste management (B1. pick-up and treatment of non-organic waste; B2. pick-up and composting of organic waste)]

Very Large Structure VLS – Mobile Test-Grid Platform for Territorial Management and Choreography.

04

CV08
Andrew Maynard

The suburb grew out of human dependence on cars. With peak oil production nearing its end, the epoch of the automobile will soon draw to a close and with it, that of the Australian suburb. Where will people live when there is no way to commute home? What will they do with the abandoned and decaying infrastructure left behind? And most importantly, what will happen to all those unhealthy Australians who have grown overweight due to their dependence on cars and a sedentary lifestyle? Well, Andrew Maynard Architects has the answer: CV08, a robot that consumes abandoned buildings with its two front legs. Processing these materials, it fires compact missiles to awaiting recycling plants. CV080's legs and feet also terraform the newly reclaimed earth with native flora and fauna. A large collection of the plants and animals stored within the robot's body will be set free on what was previously suburban wasteland.

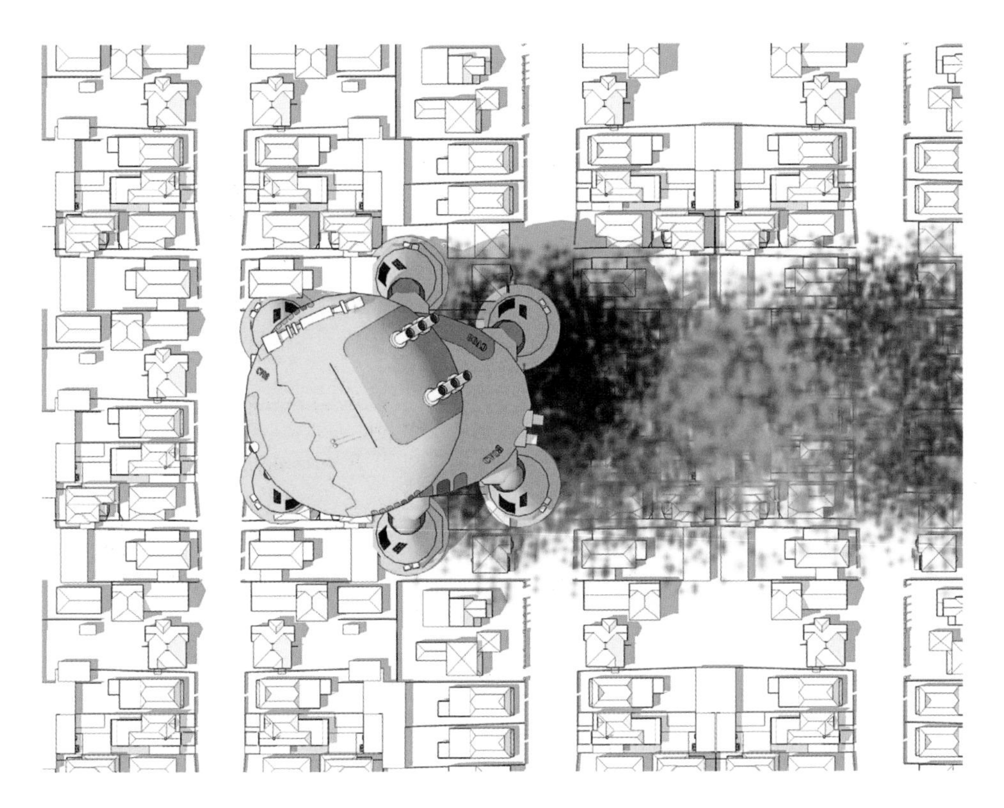

An extreme way of mitigating suburban sprawl. Colossal robots eating suburbs while turning their waste into forests.

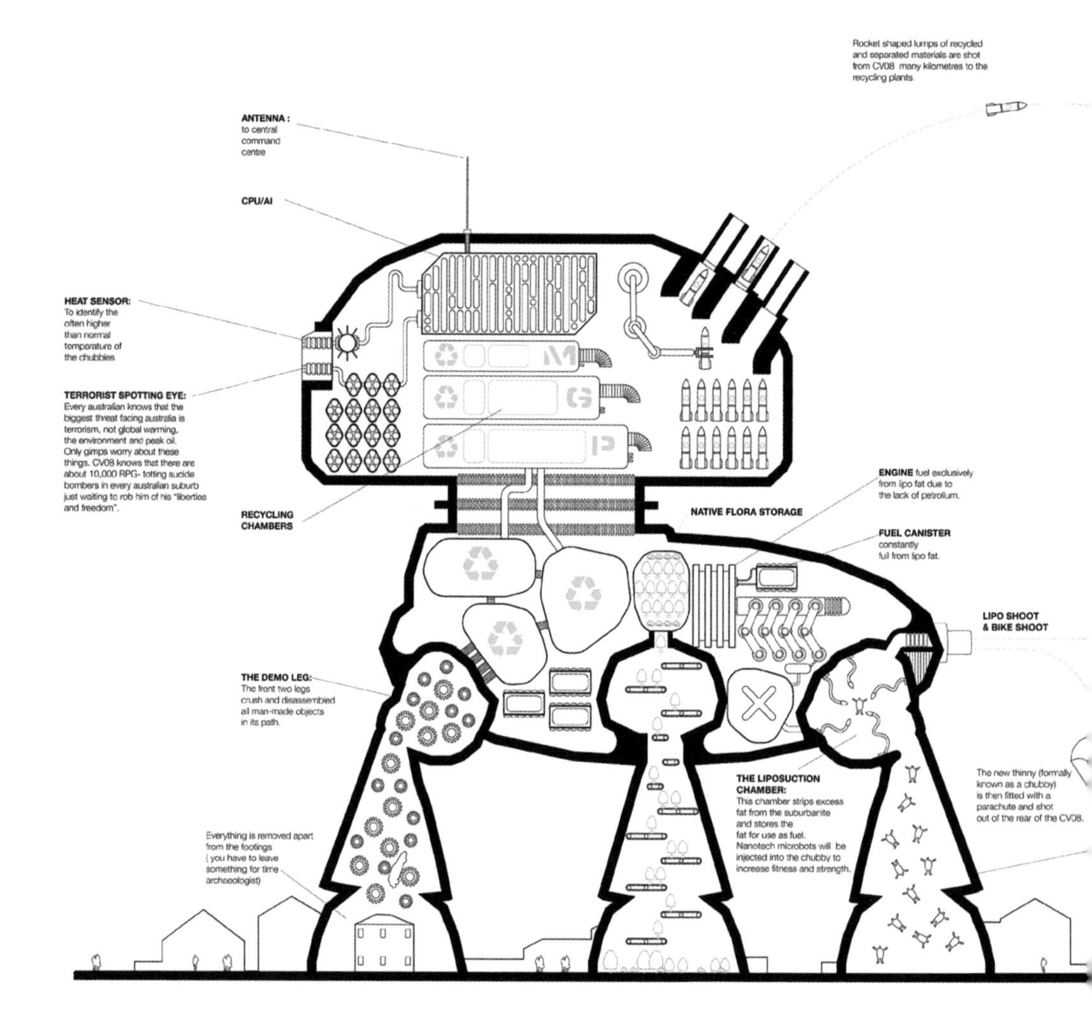

Rocket shaped lumps of recycled and separated materials are shot from CV08 many kilometres to the recycling plants.
ANTENNA : to central command centre
CPU/AI
HEAT SENSOR: To identify the often higher than normal temperature of the chubbies
TERRORIST SPOTTING EYE: Every australian knows that the biggest threat facing australia is terrorism, not global warming, the environment and peak oil. Only gimps worry about these things. CV08 knows that there are about 10,000 RPG- totting sucide bombers in every australian suburb just waiting to rob him of his "liberties and freedom".
RECYCLING CHAMBERS
ENGINE fuel exclusively from lipo fat due to the lack of petrolium.
NATIVE FLORA STORAGE
FUEL CANISTER constantly full from lipo fat.
LIPO SHOOT & BIKE SHOOT
THE DEMO LEG: The front two legs crush and disassembled all man-made objects in its path.
THE LIPOSUCTION CHAMBER: This chamber strips excess fat from the suburbanite and stores the fat for use as fuel. Nanotech microbots will be injected into the chubby to increase fitness and strength.
The new thinny (formally known as a chubby) is then fitted with a parachute and shot out of the rear of the CV08.
Everything is removed apart from the footings (you have to leave something for time archaeologist)

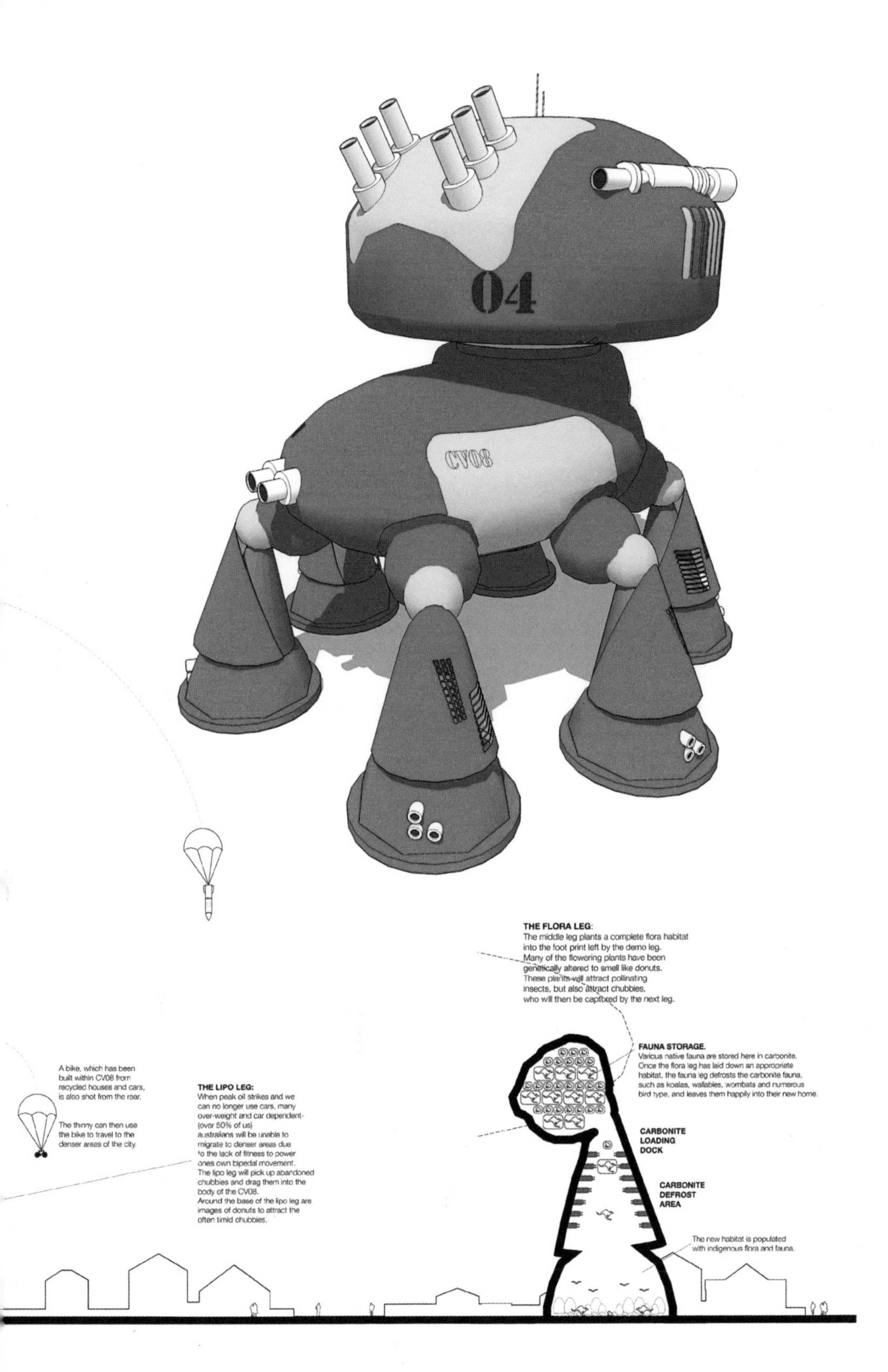
04
CV08
THE FLORA LEG:
The middle leg plants a complete flora habitat into the foot print left by the demo leg.
Many of the flowering plants have been genetically altered to smell like donuts.
These plants will attract pollinating insects, but also attract chubbies, who will then be captured by the next leg.
FAUNA STORAGE.
Various native fauna are stored here in carbonite. Once the flora leg has laid down an appropriete habitat, the fauna leg defrosts the carbonite fauna, such as koalas, wallabies, wombats and numerous bird type, and leaves them happily into their new home.
A bike, which has been built within CV08 from recycled houses and cars, is also shot from the rear.
The thinny can then use the bike to travel to the denser areas of the city.
THE LIPO LEG:
When peak oil strikes and we can no longer use cars, many over-weight and car dependent- (over 50% of us) australians will be unable to migrate to denser areas due to the lack of fitness to power ones own bipedal movement.
The lipo leg will pick up abandoned chubbies and drag them into the body of the CV08.
Around the base of the lipo leg are images of donuts to attract the often timid chubbies.
CARBONITE LOADING DOCK
CARBONITE DEFROST AREA
The new habitat is populated with indigenous flora and fauna.

Dune City: A Transgressive Biomimetics
Magnus Larsson and Alex Kaiser

Dune City is a speculative architectural project aimed at creating a network of solidified sand dunes in the desert. It advocates a radical shift away from existing construction methods towards the localized cementation of granular materials. The idea is to use this type of biocementation strategy to create a very narrow and long pan-African city capable of mitigating the shifting sands of the Sahara. Dry areas cover more than one-third of the earth's land surface; upward of a billion people live in arid or semiarid environments, where they coexist with shifting sands, sometimes struggling to get by in increasingly harsh conditions. The spatial pockets of Dune City would help retain scarce water and the mineral resources necessary to turn the scheme into a micro-environmental support structure capable of assisting the formation of the Great Green Wall for the Sahara and Sahel Initiative (GGWSSI). The final outcome would be a habitable anti-desertification structure constructed from the desert itself, a sand-stopping device generated from sand.

On 13 January 2011, *Nature* published a paper by Professor Christopher Voigt and colleagues that explained how recent advances in multicellular computing have made it possible to write software that controls the creation of genetic circuits in microbes–essentially by endowing bacteria with senses (touch, sight, smell), then programming them to perform complex, coordinated tasks based on their newly-gained understanding of the world surrounding them. Programmable biological intelligence, microbes as memory devices, biological computers frozen into buildings–all make biology the most exciting topic in architecture today.

Dune City offers one way in which such circuits could be linked to the creation of biomimetic architecture. Programming bacteria at the heart of the project with methods similar to those proposed by Voigt could add another dimension to the use of existing sand dunes as granular readymade structures by working within the material volume itself and controlling the bacteria to augment the loose sand into solid structures. This strategy can be imaginatively compared to a vast, 3D bacteria printer crawling the deserts of the world and printing new landscapes. Hopefully it will not be long before we see a biomimetic scheme such as Dune City spreading from building to building–a new kind of structure emerging from the dunescape and supporting a vast shelterbelt of trees against the encroaching desert.

Bio-cementation is used to produce a pan-African linear city that mitigates regional desertification.

Lilypads
Vincent Callebaut

Wherever the Netherlands and the United Arabic Emirates broaden their beaches in order to build short-lived polders, the Lilypad project can work with the ocean's rising waters. These floating "Ecopoli" travel the world from the equator to the poles, following currents driven by the Gulf Stream. They are truly amphibian structures, capable of supporting 50,000 inhabitants in a community of living spaces, shops, entertainment facilities, suspended gardens, interior streets, and alleyways. The purpose of the project is to nurture harmonious coexistence between humans and nature while exploring new modes of living with the sea.

Offshore, self-sufficient floating cities. Sea-steading becomes a way of augmenting existing landscapes by developing marine-based mobile communities.

Heliofield, Land Art Generator Initiative
Michael Chaveriat, Yikyu Choe, Myung Kweon Park

Throughout history, the design of the urban environment has undergone continuous reinterpretations in response to shifting technologies and cultural standards. The introduction of the automobile, the rise of industry, zoning, building code innovations, and the Information Age have all made a mark on our constructed environment. The renewable energy revolution will undoubtedly have a resounding influence on the design of public space in the coming decades, as can already be seen in the effects of the proliferation of wind turbines and solar farms in the 21st century.

Heliofield uses large, heavy feet as anchors and thin legs to elevate photovoltaic (PV) panels while delivering electricity throughout the system. Each unit can stand alone or be part of an array of thousands. The flexibility and scalability of the system lends itself to the dynamic nature of the site. In addition to meeting technological needs, the system also serves flora and fauna with a set of interchangeable habitat components that address the site's inherent ecological challenges, such as shallow soil depth and lack of trees. Its functional amenities are designed for small mammals, birds, insects, and plants, and supplement the limited habitat of the former landfill. The design of renewable energy infrastructure will inevitably adapt over time to align more closely with the needs of its users and grow more responsive to context and ecology, as can be seen in Heliofield and other LAGI design proposals. As alternative energy devices become a greater part of our lives and spread closer to where we live and work, the evolution of design archetypes based on renewable energy will begin to embrace artistic expression, both in terms of conception and implementation. In this way, cities will create culturally unique sets of iconic infrastructures that can serve to educate and inspire.

Rendering of landfill remediation system that simultaneously provides a habitat for local flora and fauna.

Ice Factory
Victor Hadjikyriacou

California's great thirst for water has transformed its landscape and allowed its cities to produce endless urban and suburban sprawl. Unchecked development combined with intermittent dry spells often increase demands on the state's already stressed system of water collection and distribution. Located at the heart of the industrial quarter of Downtown Los Angeles, "Ice Factory" is a speculative proposal to mitigate high temperatures and drought through a supply of both frozen and potable water to local residents. Much like Ulan Bator's (Mongolia) plan to cool itself with giant artificial glaciers, the project uses displaced icebergs to chill the city and slake its thirst. Excess runoff generated by the melting process is recycled through a main drainage system, transforming the neighborhood into a cold Ice Park. Directly adjacent to the project stands a small ice factory covered with a variety of thick cacti plants–a green envelope that not only absorbs heat from the city but also collects and freezes water for future use.

Giant accumulations of ice in Los Angeles slake the thirst of an expanding metropolis. A new ice economy becomes an engine of urban life.

Urbaneering Resilient Waterfront: Infrastructure as Spectacle
Terreform ONE

Urbanizing Resilient Waterfront focuses on water retention in Brooklyn, New York as well as on the effects of sea-level rise on coastal landscapes and cities. We propose the adaptive reuse of former military vessels to create a riparian buffer zone that would actively mitigate flooding in New York Harbor. The design would make use of up-cycled U.S. Naval vessels from the National Defense Reserve Fleet [NDRF] to stabilize coastal boundaries and support the growth of diverse flora and fauna. Rather than keeping water out, this reimagined waterfront would be constructed to carefully manage changing tides, storm surges, and overland flows. New York should not simply defend itself against these forces with dams and massive sea walls, but also work with the ocean's changing dynamics to improve the health of existing estuaries.

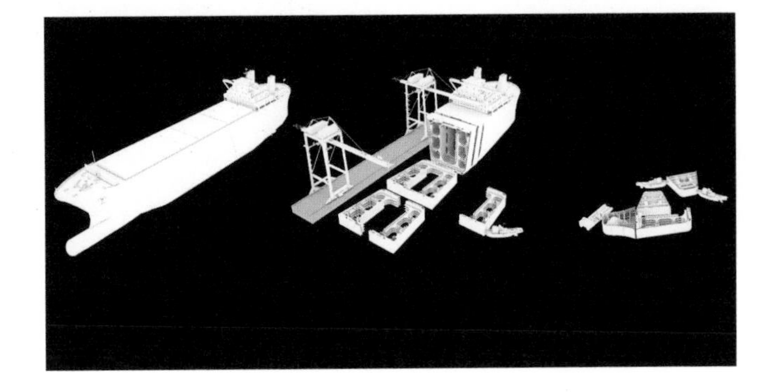

Reused military vessels for soft edges and stormwater absorption. Food, water, air, energy, waste, mobility, and shelter are radically restructured to support life in every form.

ARC Wildlife Bridge
MVVA / Michael Van Valkenburgh

The sole east-west interstate road for moving people, goods, and services through the Southern Rocky Mountain region, Colorado's I-70 corridor, is considered a significant barrier to wildlife movement. The primary goal of this competition proposal is to devise structures that ensure the safe mobility of humans and wildlife. At the core of the design concept lies the realization that this landscape is not for humans alone. Rather than allow the primarily visual, aesthetic impulse of landscape design to determine its form, we have come up with a wildlife crossing driven by the need to provide connections for a variety of animal species. Our project consists of modular, precast concrete hyperparaboloid forms that allow for easy fabrication and assembly. By combining a flexible structural solution with an adaptable approach to broad landscape management, the design offers a new way to mitigate habitat fragmentation. The flexibility and efficiency of the bridge's structural component make it extremely suitable for widespread use, while its minimally invasive construction allows it to be adapted to any location. Three-dimensional solutions are required to address the complex conflict between roads and wilderness. Our project thus untangles the conflicting demands of human and animal transportation by bridging both beneath and over the road, layering driver experience and animal preferences, and pursuing an adaptable framework for both vegetal and structural systems.

Rendering of a bridge that connects critical animal habitats while accommodating existing highway traffic.

Street view of vertical garden with reconfigurable living units.
Right: Prefab modules and robotic arms are transported to the site via light rail.

Filenes's Ecopods
J. Meejin Yoon and Eric Höweler

Taking advantage of the stalled Filene's construction site at Downtown Crossing, Eco-Pod is a proposal that will instantly stimulate the economy and ecology of Downtown Boston. Eco-Pod (Gen1) will be a temporary, vertical, algae bio-reactor and new public Commons built from custom prefabricated modules. Its pods will serve as bio-fuel sources and micro-incubators for flexible research and development programs. The voids between the pods of this open and reconfigurable structure will form a network of vertical public parks/botanical gardens that will house unique plant species–a new Uncommon for the Commons.

An on-site robotic armature (powered by algae bio-fuel) will be designed to reconfigure the modules in order to maximize algae growth conditions and accommodate evolving spatial and programmatic conditions in real time. The reconfigurable modular units will allow the structure to change in order to meet shifting programmatic and economic needs, while continuous construction at the site will broadcast a subtle semaphore of building activity and economic recovery. This is anticipatory architecture, capable of generating a new local, agile, and carbon-net positive micro-urbanism.

This proposal envisions the immediate deployment of a "crane-ready," modular temporary structure to house experimental and research-based programs. The modules can easily be disassembled and redistributed to various neighborhoods around Boston, where they can be used to infill other empty sites, test new proposals, and develop initiatives with other communities. Designed with flexibility and reconfigurability in mind, the modularity of the units anticipates future deployments at other sites. Instant architecture, designed with the idea of an afterlife(s), this is pre-cycled architecture. In our ongoing, synergistic scenario, the growth of the algae propels and is propelled by technologically enabled developments that literally and metaphorically "grow the economy."

PHONE
10 calories.
naturally
sweetened.
vitaminwater10

DS
DO NOT
ENTER

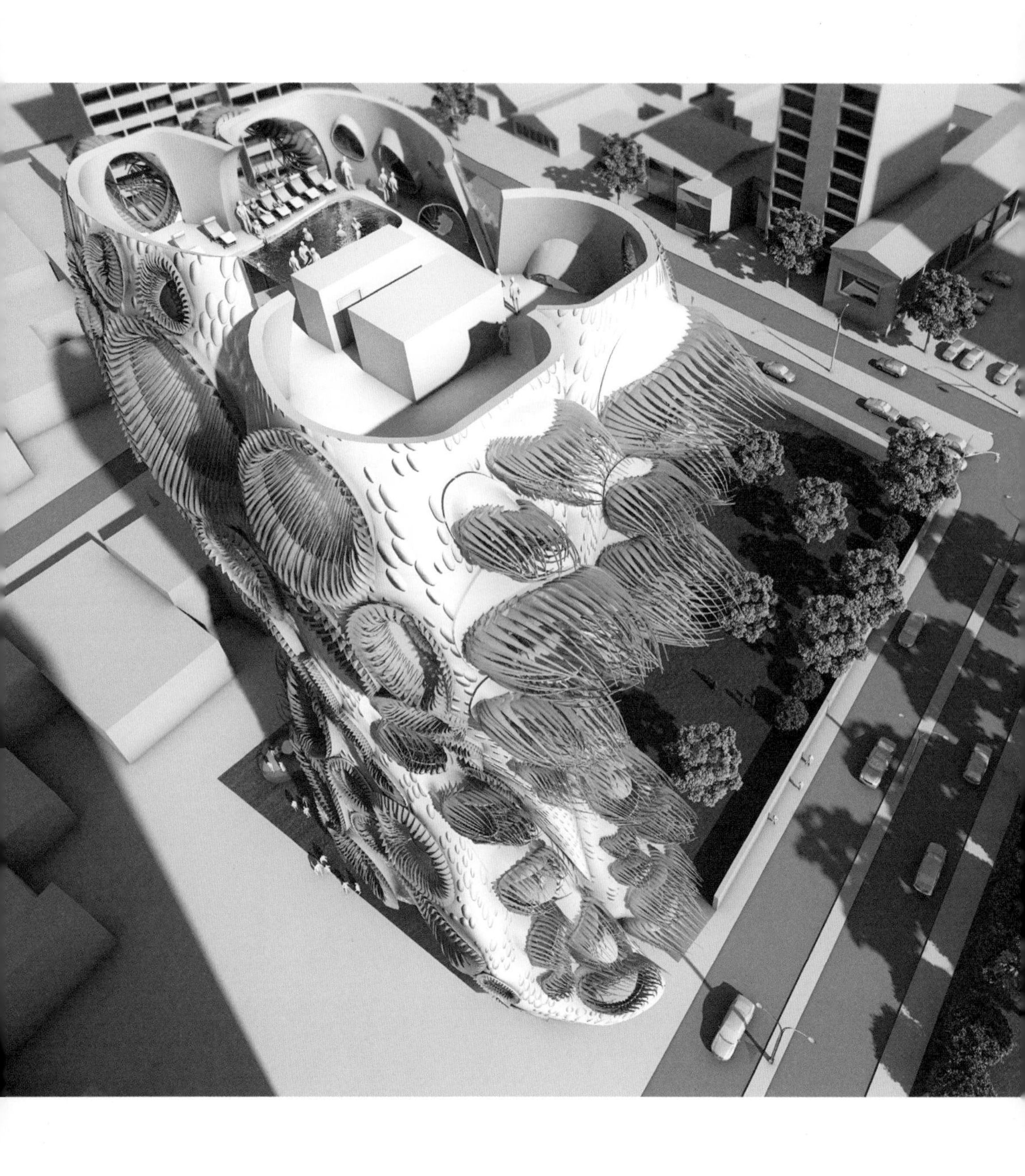

Sky Condos
Baumgartner + Uriu Architecture (B+U) / Herwig Baumgartner and Scott Uriu

Los Angeles-based B+U Architects, a design office internationally recognized for its digital techniques and use of new technologies and material resources, is pushing the boundaries of architecture and urban design with its Animated Apertures Housing Tower project in Lima, Peru. The conceptual framework for this project arose from the desire to create an architecture that exists between nature and technology, is inspired by natural patterns, movements, and colors, and results in an "interactive and intelligent building organism." According to the architects, the tower's design aesthetic embraces incongruence, disruption, and deformation rather than homogeneity and parametric smoothness, the common solution of many digital designs.

What makes Animated Apertures unique is its rethinking and redesign of windows in terms of function, components, appearance, material, and application to a 20-story residential typology. The apertures function as inhabitable spaces or thresholds between interior and exterior that respond to environmental forces such as sun and wind and exploit potential energetic exchanges between the natural and built environment. The exterior of the building is a direct result of the interior spaces and their relationships to specific points in the city, with linear extensions along window frames that create a soft, blurred building edge that is constantly in flux.

The building includes a ground-floor entry with a cafe and L-shaped living units with a north-south orientation stacked on top of each other. Each unit occupies three levels, giving it a double-height living room oriented to the park. Both living and dining areas have large foldable glass walls that can be opened to create a continuous indoor-outdoor living experience with plenty of cross ventilation. The Housing Tower also has a penthouse unit and a rooftop with a large pool and garden.

The overall structure is a cast-in-place concrete slab and core structure with most of its exterior enclosure made of cast-in-place concrete. The rough, textured concrete shell contrasts sharply against the highly articulated fiberglass composite apertures, which are translucent and illuminated by LEDs from within, giving the tower a distinctive colorful glow at night. By using advanced silicone composites that allow a gradient of material properties within a single object, these apertures are able to move without mechanical parts and mimic systems found in nature. In addition, the new window frames are coated with a thin solar film that produces significant solar energy for the building. B+U's hope is that with such special technological components, Animated Apertures will help revolutionize and redefine the built environment so that buildings grow less invasive and instead become closer to functioning as adaptable organisms.

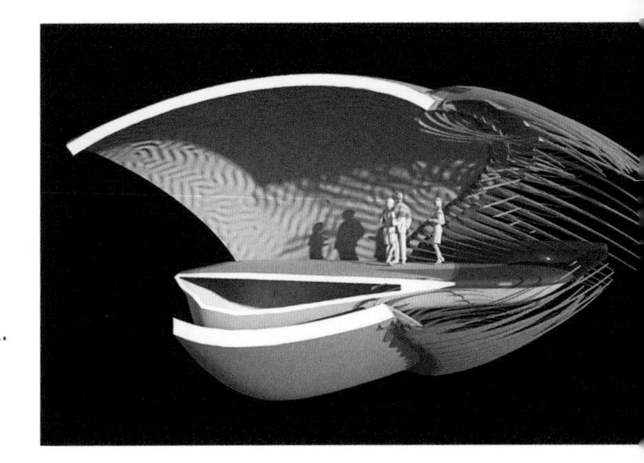

Left: Ciliated window awnings with embedded photovoltaics flex and flutter in the wind.
Above: Section through "eyelash" brise-soleil.

Halley VI: Antarctic Research Station
Hugh Broughton

This project is the first fully re-locatable research station in the world. Pushing the boundaries of design in a life-critical environment, it offers a beacon for sustainable living in polar regions, drawing attention to some of the most significant science conducted on our planet. Hugh Broughton Architects' modular design concept was developed to minimize through-life environmental impact from construction to decommissioning, with energy efficiency, reduced water usage, and an improved waste-management strategy. Halley VI's giant steel skis and hydraulically driven legs make it fully re-locatable inland if the site starts calving off in iceberg fashion, and thus helps ensure that the station achieves its minimum 20-year lifespan.

The modules are constructed of a robust steel structure and clad in highly insulated pre-glazed and painted glass, fiber-reinforced plastic (GRP) panels, forming a semi-monocoque enclosure. Water usage at the base has been drastically reduced from Halley V levels with the introduction of aerated fittings and a vacuum drainage system adapted from a marine environment, also the source of the bioreactor sewage-treatment system. Glazing is maximized for the well-being of the crew, and to reduce lighting demand during the 24-hour, day-lit summer; windows are triple-glazed with high performance glass. At the heart of the two-story central module, which houses social spaces for living, dining, and recreation, is a double-height, light-filled space clad with vertical and inclined high-performance glazing and translucent nanogel-insulated panels. After years of research and development of key technical aspects of the project, prefabrication, transport, and construction, final fit-out took place in 2011-12, and the station became fully operational in February 2013.

Left: This research station skis, floats, and travels though a shrinking landscape of melting ice. It is a fully self-sufficient modular lab dedicated to the study of global climate change. Bottom: Rendered cross section.

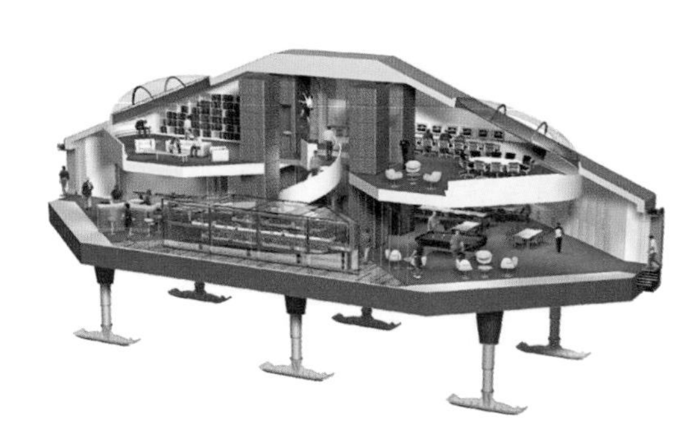

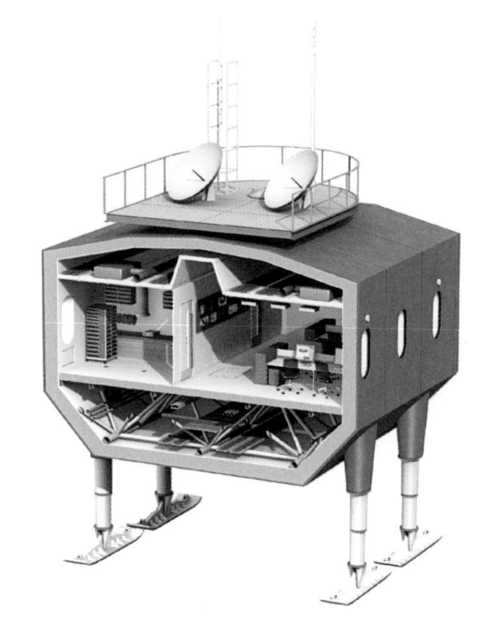

Microcosmic Aquaculture: Gelatinous Orbs
Bittertang

We imagine a future in which the vast and deep expanses of the ocean will teem with overabundant floating gelatinous reefs. Humans will be nourished both physically and aesthetically by new floating worlds that sustain large quantities of harvestable wild and captive fish. In this project, farming is viewed not as a monoculture but as an opportunity to create a new ecology in which wildlife is "raised" and its aesthetic potential enjoyed by future divers and fisherman. By encouraging the establishment of a new ecosystem, both contemporary farmers and the public can reap sustenance and aesthetic benefits from environmental stewardship.

The ocean is a vast resource that can accommodate more life if proper conditions are met. These conditions are minimal; new ecosystems can flourish around the simplest substrate. The spheres themselves serve as both reef and farm; their outer surfaces can nourish, shelter, and provide substrate for various wild animals while their interiors can be used as unmanned fish hatcheries or aquaculture pens. The advantage of this set-up is that farmed fish can be grown in a larger reef system that manages and cleans waste produced by traditional farms. Large colonies of wild fish will be attracted to the new substrate and can be harvested for the public. Once they are set loose in the wild, the orbs will literally assume a life of their own, following currents and attracting life wherever they go, perhaps even mingling with other spheres of various age and interacting with their ecosystems. Such growth can occur quite quickly in the ocean; within months of genesis, the orbs will be covered with living material and become edible, living worlds.

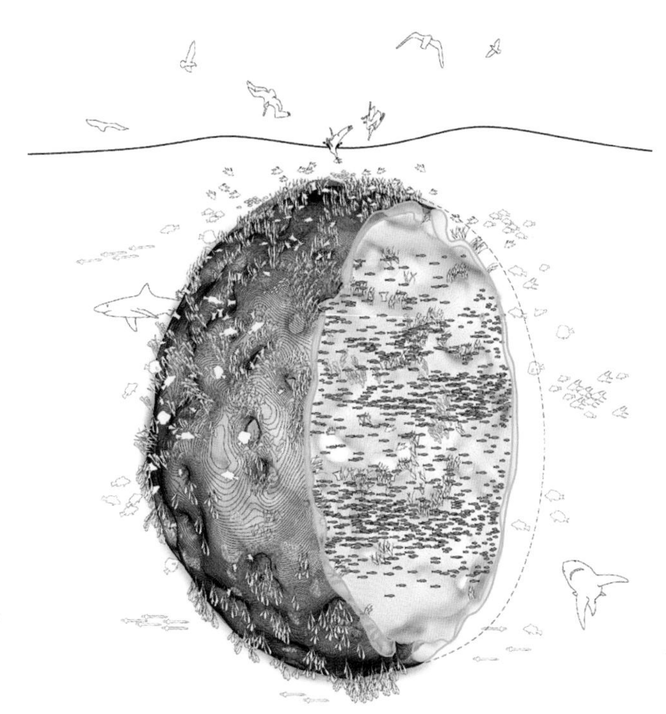

Left: A replacement for unsustainable monolithic fish-farming techniques.
Right: Outside the orb is a reef inside an aqua cultural incubator.

Amphibious Architecture
The Living / David Benjamin

Amphibious Architecture is a visual interface floating on the water's surface, a veritable looking glass into the aquatic ecosystem. This manufactured point of connection submerges ubiquitous computing into the one element that covers 90% of the Earth's inhabitable volume and that envelops New York City but remains under-explored and under-engaged.

Installed at two sites along the East and the Bronx Rivers, this project is a network of floating interactive buoys housing a range of sensors below water and an array of light-emitting diodes (LEDs) above water. The sensors monitor water quality, the presence of fish, and human interest in the river's ecosystem, while the lights respond to the sensors, creating feedback loops between humans and fish in their shared environment. Additionally, an SMS interface allows homo-citizens to text-message the fish and receive real-time information about the river, contributing towards the collective display of human interest in the aquatic environment. The aim of this is to simultaneously spark greater public interest and dialogue about our local waterways.

Distinctly moving away from the pervasive "do-not-disturb" approach to urban environmentalism, the project encourages curiosity and engagement. Treating the river water as a reflective surface to mirror our own homo-image and architecture, it establishes a two-way interface between the terrestrial and the aquatic. The project thus creates a dynamic and captivating layer of light above the surface of the river, making visible the invisible through real-time mapping of the new ecology of people, marine life, buildings, and public space.

Light rods geolocate the presence of fish in the water.

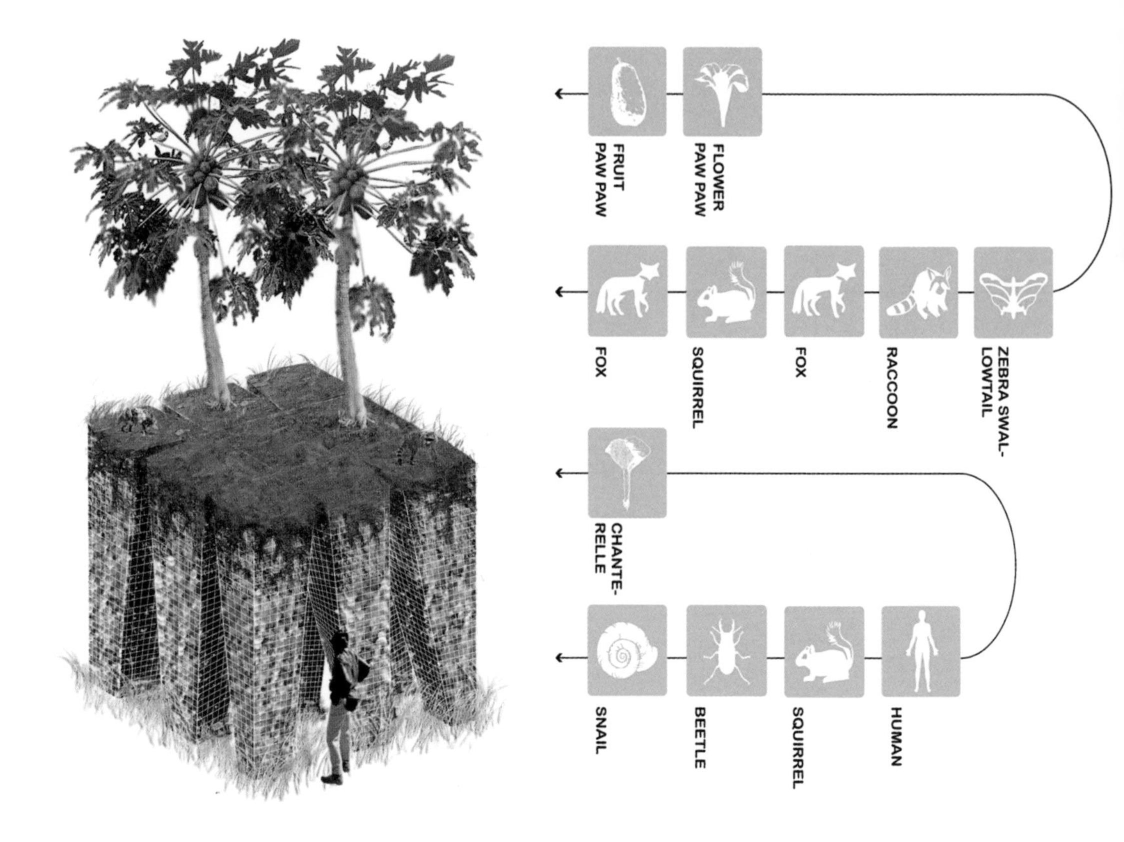

Left: A large section of earth along with its various nonhuman inhabitants displaced from the ground. In turn, this formal and material displacement serves to displace the conventions of human-nonhuman relations.
Right: Ecology diagram for human as well as nonhuman forms of inhabitation supported by the folly, the latter of which include vegetation, insects, and wildlife.

Opposite: The folly provides a space of intensification simultaneously as a "cultural object" located within the sculpture park's exhibition space and as a "natural object" both visually and ecologically linked to the tree line.

The Anthropocene Folly
Pneumastudio / Cathryn Dwyre and Chris Perry

While this proposal for an architectural folly commissioned by and situated within the sprawling sculpture park of the OMI International Arts Center in Ghent, New York, is to some extent expressive of the grand human folly that is the Anthropocene itself, it resists privileging either the human or the nonhuman. In this sense, humans and nonhumans alike, whether in the form of bird migrations, climate, or the seasonal fluctuation of plant and insect life, exist in a perpetual state of interaction, a condition no longer significant to "us" alone.

As such, the Anthropocene Folly is comprised of self-supporting gabions, filled with a matrix of local stone, and prodigiously planted with natives designed to foster biodiversity among an extended ecology of insects, birds, and small animals. Humans are able to enter the folly but in a way that is intentionally displaced from any point of assumed privilege. In this way, the gabion structure operates as a double enclosure for human as well as nonhuman inhabitation, producing variable forms of interiority and with it an intentionally ambiguous threshold between human and nonhuman space.

The folly is configured from nine columnar planters, the interiors of which are filled with gravel, soil, and vegetation. Modest interstitial spacing between each of these columns generates a second interstitial interior for human occupation. Taking the form of a series of crevice-like spaces, this second interior forces the human body to bend, duck, and slither, suggesting to human occupants that these spaces, while physically accessible, were not necessarily designed for them. Furthermore, the materiality and atmosphere of the folly's second interior confronts the occupant with a quality of "nature" that is typically kept at a more comfortable distance, a quality akin to David Gissen's concept of "subnature." The folly's second interior simulates material and atmospheric qualities characterized by dampness and lack of daylight: a dark, musty "underground" environment conducive to the proliferation of moss, slugs, and spider webs. In this way, the gabion structure is merely a loose container for gravel, soil, and roots that is, in effect, displaced from the earth itself and hosts various subterranean nonhuman objects and processes that are typically concealed in the depths of the ground. All the while, the more familiar forms of "nature"–the plants, butterflies, and birds that inhabit the top of the folly–are intentionally lifted away from the human and thus remain physically, and to some extent visually, inaccessible. As a result, the human's conventional orientation to "nature" can be understood as displaced in multiple ways. No longer safely above ground, the human inhabits the ground itself, thus occupying a simultaneous interior/exterior condition–philosophically as well as experientially–in which human-nonhuman distinctions are rendered ambiguous.

Fab Tree Hab and Plug-In Ecology
Terreform ONE

Fab Tree Hab-Living Graft Prefab Structure: Our dwelling is composed of 100% living nutrients. Here traditional anthropocentric doctrines are overturned and human life is subsumed within terrestrial environs. Home, in this sense, becomes indistinct and fits itself symbiotically into the surrounding ecosystem.

This domicile concept is intended to replace the outdated design solutions at Habitat for Humanity. We propose a method to grow homes from local native woody plants. A living structure is grafted into shape with prefabricated Computer Numeric Controlled (CNC) reusable scaffolds. The plan is to reuse the scaffolds and further enable more dwellings to be fully integrated into an ecological community.

Plug-In Ecology-Urban Farm Pod with Agronomy is a "living" cabin for individuals and urban nuclear families that will grow and provide them with their daily vegetable needs. It is an interface with the city, potentially touching on urban farming, air quality levels, DIY agronomy techniques in test tubes, algal energy production, and bioluminescent light sources, to name a few possibilities. It can be outfitted with a number of optional systems to adapt to different locations, lighting conditions, and habitation requirements. While agricultural food sources are usually invisible in cities such as New York, the pod archetype turns the food system itself into a visible artifact, a bio-informatic message system and a functional space.

The Plug-In Ecology cabin sphere prototype uses a robotic, milled rotegrity ball for the under-grid structure made of reclaimed, flat packed materials. A fully operable sub-irrigation system and shaped foam panels serve as sleeves for the potting elements and agronomy tissue culture for micropropagation. A digital monitoring platform relays information about specific plant health to the web. Our vision for future iterations of the pod is to grow structures naturally over time, within a new form of mediated arboreal culture, to integrate the biological and mechanical elements more closely, and to transform the object into one that grows and changes symbiotically. The Plug-In Ecology project sets a direction for healthy biological exchanges with urban inhabitants and contributes to the life of urban ecosystems that mediate between autonomy and community.

Above: The structure is robotically milled ply that supports soft foam pillow inserts for potted plants and a vertical irrigation system.
Opposite below and right: Village of prefabricated homes made out of trees with reusable CNC manufactured scaffolding.
Overleaf: A small sphere-shaped cabin for 1-3 people that supports a 360-degree exterior vegetable garden with optional interior grow space and artificial UV lighting.

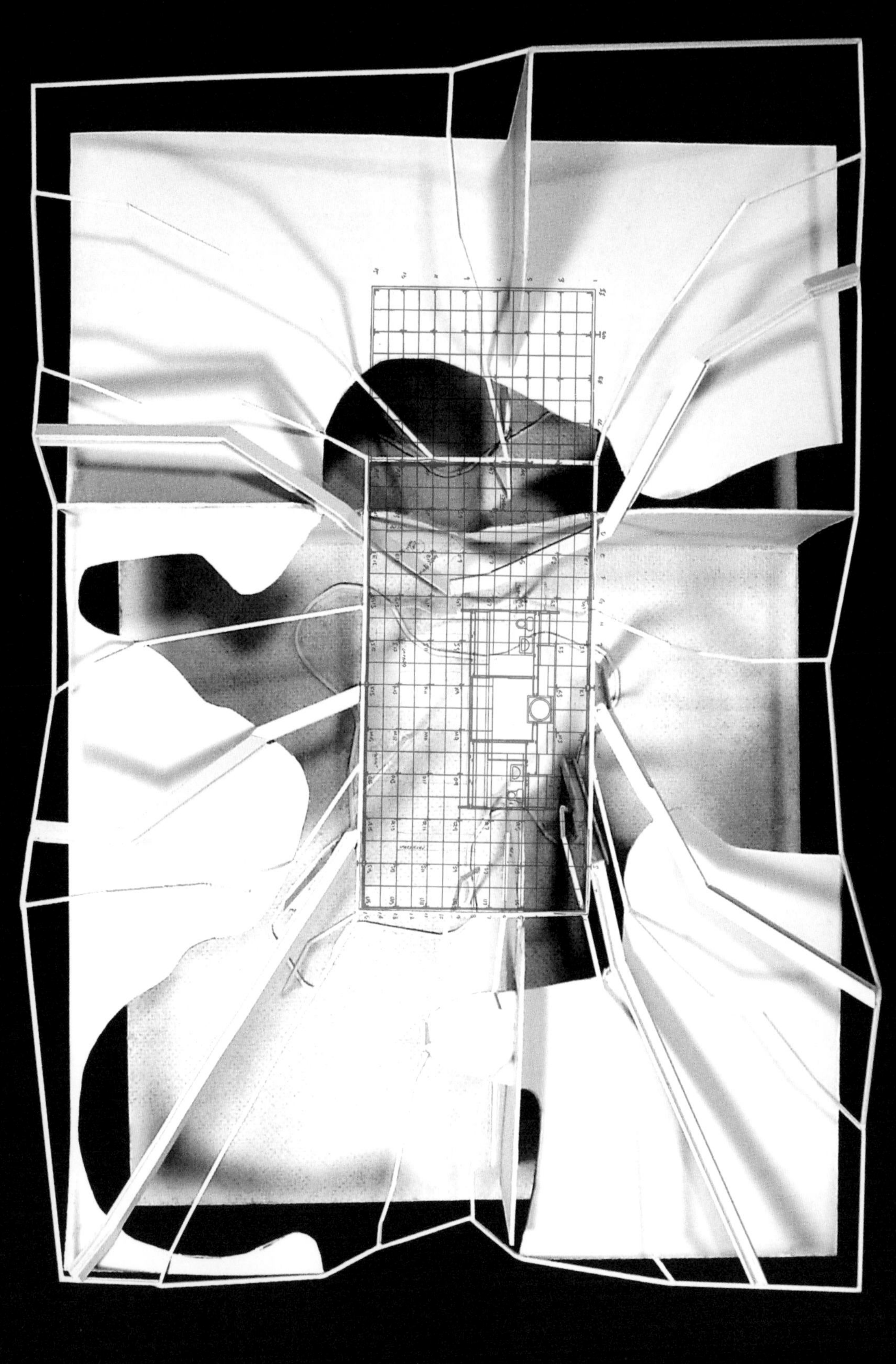

Strange Weather
Pablo Garcia

Architecture has traditionally had a direct relationship with weather: that of keeping it out or, if it is fair, accommodating it. But can weather offer any new and generative directions to architecture? To measure subtle microclimates present in all spaces, a device carrying a series of thermometers takes instant temperature readings at vertical one-foot intervals. The data is then transformed into thermograph-contour drawings of temperature variations. A second thermographic device directly translates the temperature readings into visual form. The thermometers, placed in a one-foot grid, three wide and six high, are connected to a ruled system of gauges. Discrepancies among the readings physically displace brass pistons. The resulting form is a thermally derived landscape—a thermoscape translation of fluctuating microclimates.

Weather is a vehicle through which architecture can deal with the legacy of Modernism. A century of rigid formal orthodoxy and exuberant, but naïve reliance on technology has negated thousands of years of climatic architectural lessons. We revere the spaces that Modernism invented. Today's freedom to invent is likewise a legacy of the revolution between the World Wars, but airtight steel-and-glass boxes stand as an affront to the 21st century, and need to address energy and environmental concerns.

Designed to parallel meteorological mapping, a thermographic device was transported to Mies van der Rohe's Farnsworth House in Plano, IL. Glass on all four sides and elevated from the ground, the original house is antipathetic to weather. Despite the architecture's orthodox rectilinearity, its conditions generate complex and dynamic thermal contour maps. Once the mappings are complete, mathematical algorithms lead to a thermal inversion of the house, regulating the temperature throughout it to a comfortable 72 degrees Fahrenheit. This process distorts the house, exploding it outwards to accommodate the contour shift. Through its uniformity, clarity and precision, the result thermally fulfills the promise of the original house. The copy, however, loses the form of the original, becoming a twisted and warped shell with thermally perfect comfort.

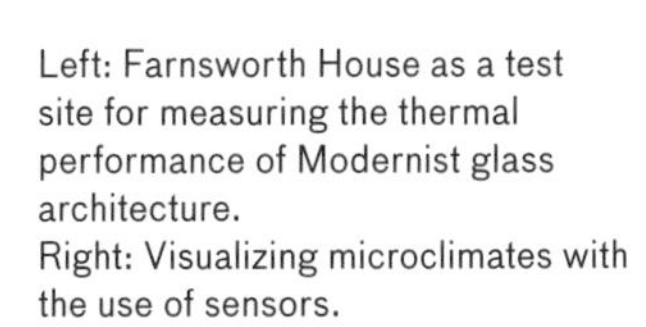

Left: Farnsworth House as a test site for measuring the thermal performance of Modernist glass architecture.
Right: Visualizing microclimates with the use of sensors.

Stripped-Down Villa
Jason Vigneri-Beane

The Stripped-Down Villa is a future niche-filler for innovative habitats in unpopulated environments such as swamps, bogs, bayous, deltas, marshlands, wetlands, and other wet-logged landscapes. It is a compact living unit that reflects the pressure on architectural equipment to co-evolve with non-normative sites in a way that is independent of property/grounding, yet highly specified to interface with natural/non-natural provisions such as airflow and water. A five-unit array of compact turbines gives it just enough lift to hover above any fluid-saturated landscape and to drift from one location to another. A dual-proboscis array allows its owner to siphon and filter water for domestic use. Air Culex is airborne, short-run mobile, and, due to its structural self-sufficiency and resource independence, a form of micro-living that is interconnected with property-independence and decentralized infrastructure.

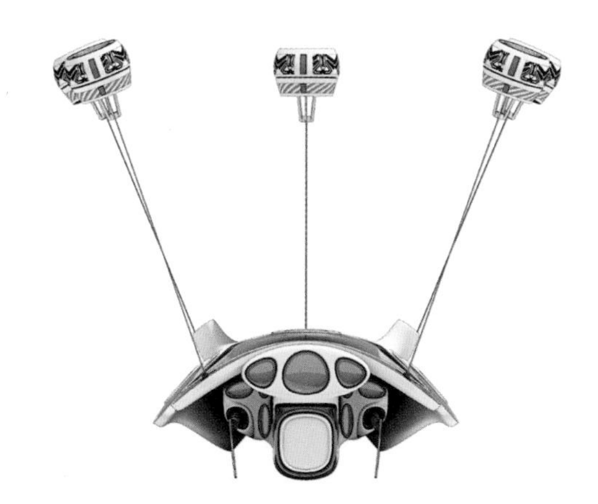

Left: A levitating, vehicular micro-estate, it has a minimal impact on the landscape.
Right: Three lift fans allow the house to achieve vertical mobility.

Ground Elemental
Doug Jackson and Mark Neveu

This house is located on a flat hilltop overlooking the vast agricultural landscape of the San Joaquin Valley in central California. It is stored beneath its site in a recessed bunker under four hinged trays that are planted to match the surrounding landscape. In order to access and occupy the house, one must activate a control box in the parking lot, which causes the grass trays to fold upward into a pitched roof. The trays are also oriented with their planted surfaces facing inward, thereby inverting the traditional relationship between interior space and exterior landscape.

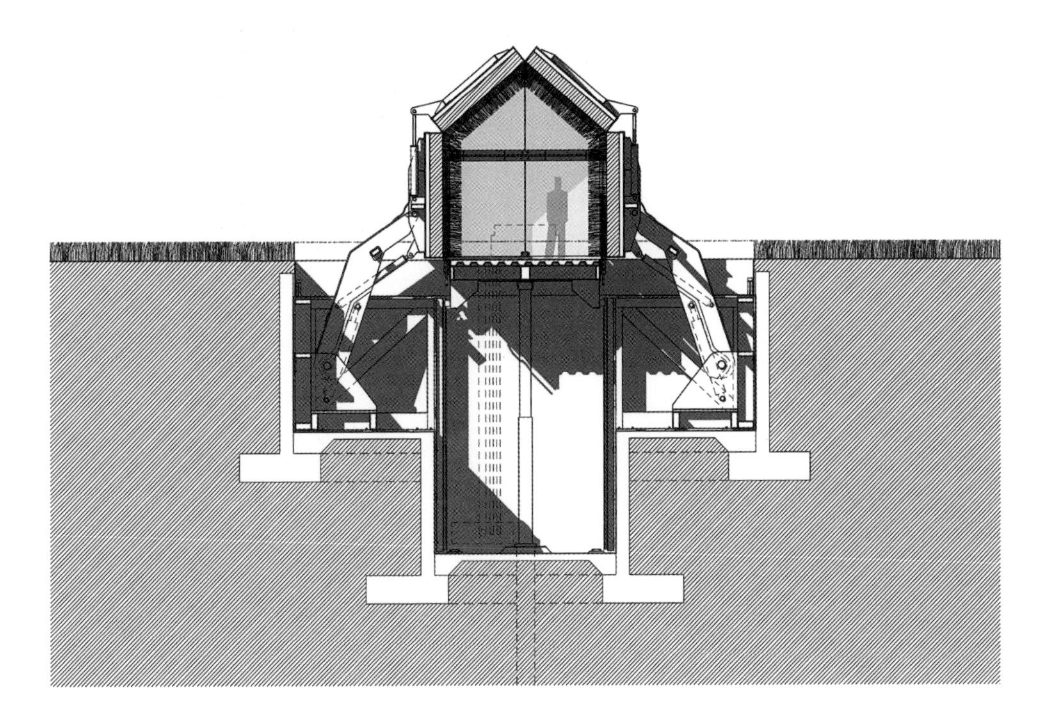

Above: Using a series of hydraulically actuated surfaces, the house is able to appear and disappear in a field of prairie grass.
Left: The building interrupts the serenity of an open landscape only when needed.

The Micro-Behavior of Multi-Agent Systems
Kokkugia / Roland Snooks

If modern architects were concerned with the assembly of large, standardized elements (steel beams, plate glass, prefabricated concrete panels, etc.), then the basic units of construction in a fibrous assemblage would have to consist of individual lines and pathways. Rather than a collection of primary, secondary, and tertiary elements cobbled together to produce a whole, composite forms emerge from non-linear variations in fiber magnitude, direction, and density. The blurring between systems–such as structure and ornament–extends to the blurring of geometric classifications. Fibrous assemblages resist being categorized as either surfaces or threads. Instead, strands bundle and weave to form skins, while surfaces delaminate and fray. This contrasts radically with the discrete articulation of structure and cladding in standardized, mass-produced architecture. With a glass-reinforced, plastic surface, there is no clear distinction between structure and skin; rather, every fiber operates structurally to produce an amorphous, mechanically redundant, and extremely strong construct.

Kokkugia's Fibrous House explores these qualities on multiple scales. The fibers of the project are bundled together to form a shell that simultaneously encloses space, carries loads, and generates ornamental effects. Bundled composites are used in a variety of applications due to their high strength-to-weight characteristics. In contrast, Kokkugia's interest in the material is based on its ability to negotiate competing design requirements within a continuous and expressive whole. Working on the level of individual fibers–especially as their intricacy and resolution dramatically increases–has significant aesthetic implications for architecture. Setting aside programmatic and contextual concerns, these multi-agent systems have been explored through abstract drawings and models. While this approach focuses more on the formal possibilities of composites, Kokkugia maintains an ongoing interest in the structural behavior of multi-agent systems. However, neither statics nor any other quantifiable science is the driver of architecture, but is merely a source of constraints that guides a given design. Likewise materials can be considered an influence on but not a principle generator of form. The ability to link geometry as well as artistic desire and use with qualities such as elasticity or stiffness enables the accommodation of both subjective intent and physical rigor.

Rendering of a shelter composed through the interweaving of fibrous strands. Instead of privileging structure, algorithmic patterns are generated for architectural effect.

Theater of Lost Species
Future Cities Lab / Jason Kelly Johnson

People simply have no history of living in a world without an abundance of other animals in the wild. We have no precedent for it. Such a world will be new to the children who come after us; indeed, it will be alien. This planet will no longer be our old, familiar home, but something completely other. And that will change the character, the aesthetics, the ideals of our descendants who will grow up on a globe that has almost in the blink of an eye been purged of its ancient evolutionary richness.

Lydia Millet, "The Child's Menagerie,"
The New York Times (September 12, 2012)

Part virtual menagerie, part memory chamber, part urban spectacle, the Theater of Lost Species, a mobile robotic device for collecting, viewing, and interacting with a collection of fantastic yet extinct sea creatures, is a place of collective celebration and mourning, a catalyst for conversation, philosophical debate, and ecological engagement. The project was inspired by a number of phenomena, such as traveling menageries, Chinese lanterns, and portable camera obscura devices from the 1800s, time capsules from the 1950-60s, and the global network that contributes to the massive Seed Bank in Svalbard, Norway.

The theater's long viewing cones focus on digital display screens that serve as portals to a seamless virtual aquarium. Inside, digital sea creatures swarm to the viewing cones, reacting to the subtle motion of spectators. In the evening, the theater glows and pulsates as the swarms slowly navigate the virtual aquarium. We began the process of conceptualizing and designing the theater after reading Lydia Millet's Op-Ed piece, "The Child's Menagerie," in the *New York Times*, determined to explore one of her central questions: "Can you feel the loss of something you never knew in the first place?"

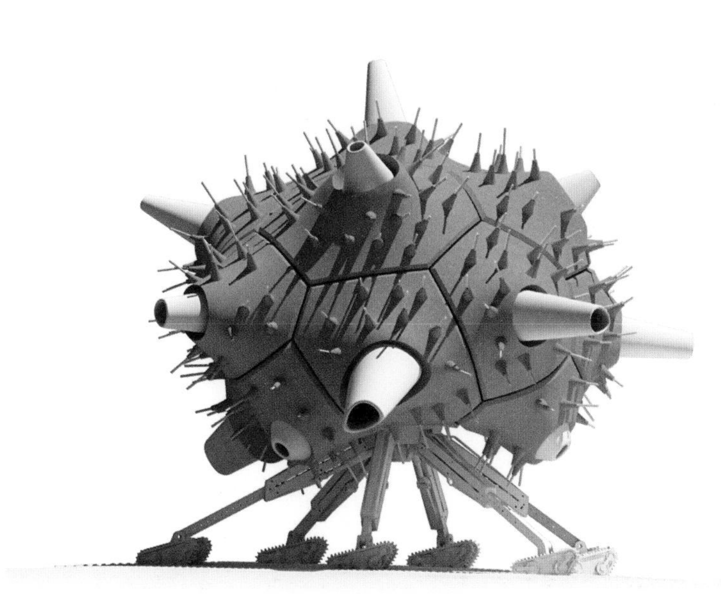

A traveling menagerie for the display of films about lost animal species.

Baubotanik: Living Plant Constructions
Ferdinand Ludwig

Trees need decades to reach maturity. But will a construction technique based on slow growth be adopted by a rapidly developing world, in which entire towns can be built in a few years? One way to tackle this question is to consider a technique called "plant addition." According to this method, young trees placed in special containers are arranged in vegetal frameworks to form a single organism. Water and nutrients are supplied to the individual plants, which are attached to an espalier-like scaffold. Strong woody structures quickly emerge as the original support system disappears. A natural example of this process can be seen in the growth patterns of strangler fig trees (*ficus elastica*). Individual plants of this species initially obtain their water and nutrients from the air. Over time, they grow epiphytically by seeking resources from terrestrial rather than non-terrestrial reserves. The vines sprout from the crown of a host and obtain water and raw materials by sending roots into the earth. The original tree serves as a temporary scaffold that is eventually consumed. When this happens the aerial roots of ficus elastica form a self-supporting framework.

A suitable joinery system is needed to realize Baubotanik structures based on plant addition. Through a variety of inosculation techniques, stems and vines intersect to form powerful, bio-mechanical bonds. In this way different joining methods can be used to encourage rapid living connections between plants. Our seven-story Baubotanik Tower was built out of young, 2-meter tall silver willows (*Salix alba*) suspended from a temporary scaffold. Once the structure grows strong enough, its initial supports are removed. With this technique a viable and self-sufficient design can be completed in a relatively short amount of time.

Living plant constructions offer new ways of creating viable green spaces for rapidly urbanizing societies. In coming decades more and more people will live in cities that do not yet exist. New urban structures will have to be built in a very short amount of time and they will not have the livable qualities of old European cities with their fully-grown parks and public spaces. As Earth's temperatures increase due to global warming, densely built-up urban centers will be subject to increasingly unbearable temperatures. Plant addition makes it possible to create tree structures in a few years, not decades. Huge green canopies that provide shade, cool the environment, and filter carbon dioxide from the air can easily be constructed. Platanenkubus is a first step in the design of an inhabitable ecosystem; vegetal structures that can grow into living cities and are an integral part of nature's life cycles.

Left: Pavilion made of bundled willows.
Right: Two separate plants grafted together to form a durable joint.

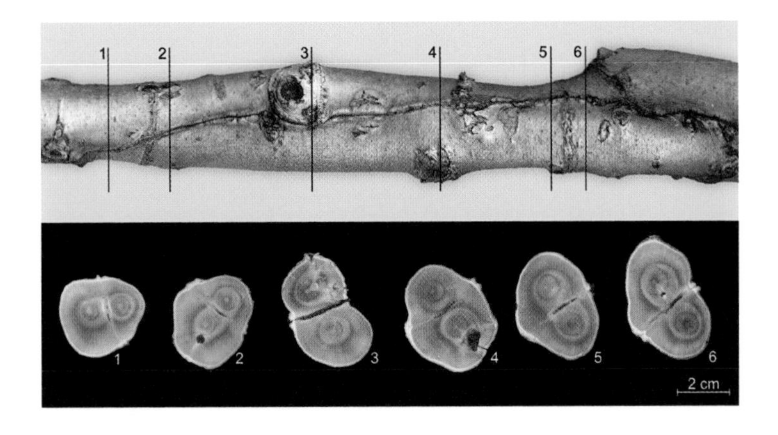

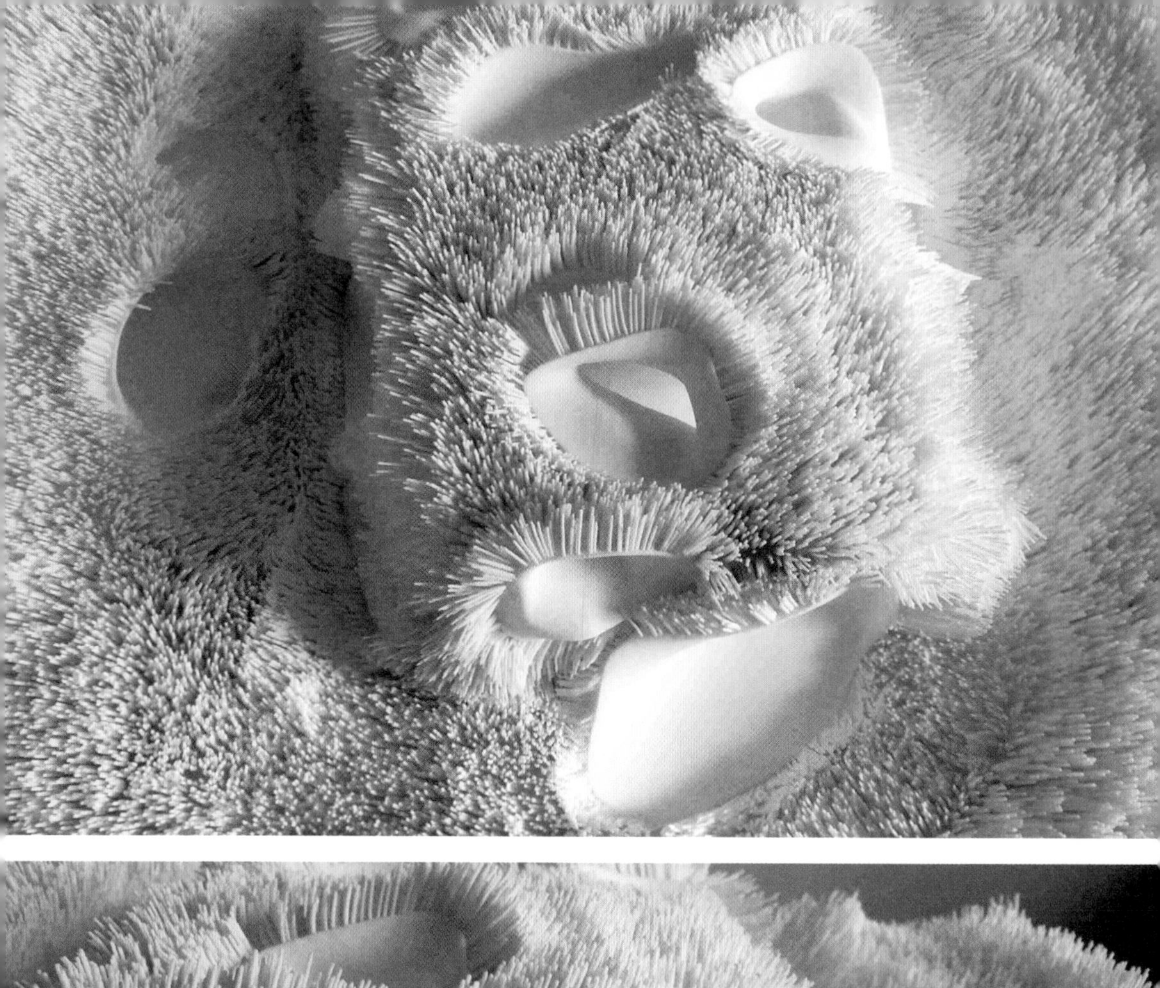

He Shot Me Down
François Roche

Located a few miles away from the politically charged border between North and South Korea, this prototypical structure uses surrounding plant life to create a viable architecture. As a multi-purpose oasis, the building includes private living spaces, dining areas, and a place for public displays. Its surrounding terrain is treated as if it were a mine field–inaccessible territory, void of human activity. Its interior spaces are shaped and maintained by insect-like robots that gather dead leaves, grass, and timber from nearby forests. These robots run on fixed tracks that stretch deep into the wilderness. The building functions much in the manner of a bunker, an isolated, self-sustaining outpost that provides active shelter amid the dangers of Korea's demilitarized zone.

Renderings of a house covered by an insect-like robot using fallen leaves and other decomposing biomass.

Head in the Clouds Pavilion
Studio KCA

The "Head in the Clouds Pavilion" located on New York's Governors Island, uses 53,780 recycled plastic bottles to create a quiet "dreamspace" for visitors. One of the most important decisions in developing the design of the pavilion was to make the plastic bottle our key building material in order to call attention to the 60,000,000 plastic bottles thrown away each day in the United States. At 40 ft. x 20 ft. x 18 in., the pavilion represents the number of bottles (53,780) thrown away in one hour in New York City alone. To collect this many bottles, we launched a recycling campaign that was supported by crowdsourced funding. We gathered used bottles from all over New York—from individuals, schools, businesses, and organizations excited by the prospect of repurposing empty containers into architecture.

Because of limited access to the island, the pavilion had to be built in components at our Brooklyn warehouse and shipped to the site by boat. One-gallon milk jugs were cleaned and organized into 3-ft., 5-ft., and 8-ft. diameter "pillows" that were used to form the outside of the cloud. Water bottles were filled with varying amounts of blue food coloring and water, and attached together into 4-ft.-wide x 25-ft.-long sheets to create the inner lining of the cloud. An egg-shaped diagrid made of rolled aluminum tubes was built in a metal shop down the street and broken down into 25-ft. lengths. Rather than rely on a high-tech fabrication technique to turn the bottles and aluminum into cladding and structure, we asked the community for volunteers interested in helping construct the pavilion for an hour or day. Because the system was repetitive but simple, no training was involved and one volunteer could teach the next one. All told, over the course of three months, 268 people were willing to put their hands (and heads) into the cloud by assisting in the fabrication of the panels, the transport of the components to the site, and the assembly of the installation on the island.

As built photograph of a small pavilion on Governor's Island, N.Y., made out of up-cycled plastic milk jugs.

Above: Taxonomy of open-source machines to build civilization 2.0. OSC Construction equipment.

Open Source Ecology
Marcin Jakubowski

Physicist Marcin Jakubowski founded the group, Open Source Ecology (OSE) as a network of farmers, engineers, and DIY enthusiasts whose main goal is the eventual manufacturing of the Global Village Construction Set (GVCS). The GVCS is an open technological platform that allows for the easy fabrication of the 50 different industrial machines that it takes to build a small civilization with modern comforts. Groups all over America are developing blueprints and building prototypes in order to pass them on to a central location called Factor e Farm. The actual devices are built and tested on the Factor e Farm in rural Missouri. The ultimate goal is to make this kind of self-sufficiency available to all. To this end, the GVCS is designed to be self-replicable. After the first set is complete, it will be used to fabricate copies of itself from raw materials for the cost of scrap metal. At that point OSE will shift to begin developing networks of interconnected self-sufficient villages and homes.

With the gift of openly shared information, OSE produces industrial products locally by using open-source design and digital fabrication. This frees people from the need to participate in the wasteful resource flows of the larger economy by letting individuals produce their own materials and components for everyday technologies. The group sees a small, independent, land-based economy as a means to transform societies, address pressing world issues, and evolve to freedom.

Taken literally, open source means that the goods and knowledge needed to reproduce the complete product are freely accessible. Additionally, ecology is the study of living interactions between organisms and their natural environment. From an anthropomorphic perspective, OSE seeks to push the vision of ecology beyond crisis mode and into ecological harmony and human productivity.

Elevator B
B/a+p, Hive City

Elevator B is an urban habitat for a colony of honeybees, which originally occupied a boarded window in an abandoned office building in Buffalo, NY. The site of the project, Silo City, consists of a group of abandoned grain elevators on the Buffalo River. Elevator B, a honeycombed steel structure designed and built of standard steel angle and tube sections, is a symbol of the site's environmental and economic regeneration. It is sheathed in perforated stainless-steel panels that are parametrically designed to protect the hive and its visitors from the wind, and allow for both solar gain in the winter and shade in the summer. The bees are housed in a hexagonal cypress box with a laminated glass bottom, through which the bees can be observed. This "beecab" provides protection and warmth for the colony. A visitor is able to enter the tower, stand below the cypress beecab, and view the bees behind glass as they build their hive. Beekeepers can access the hive to ensure the health and safety of the small insects.

Interior and exterior views of a vertical beehive located near the grain silos in Downtown Buffalo, NY.

Extrapolation Factory, Animal Superpowers
Chris Woebken

By looking towards natural systems, design can crystallize strategies that better connect us to our environment. One of my most recent projects explores how animal senses differ from those of humans. We know that animals have extraordinary abilities that sometimes allow them to feel and perceive the world better than humans can. For example, they are able to sense approaching tsunamis through low frequency vibrations that we cannot feel. Birds are able to orient their flight patterns by sensing magnetic fields. Ants, in turn, can communicate through smell, by detecting the pheromone trails of other ants. I call these sensory talents "animal super-powers." In my work I have tried to make these abilities more accessible to the ordinary person. In particular, I have used curious children to assume the characters of other creatures in "make believe games" as the main test subjects in my experiments with animal vision. The "Ant Apparatus" allows its users to feel like insects by magnifying their vision 50x through a microscopic antenna mounted on their heads. Through this apparatus they can perceive all kinds of details and tiny cracks, "see" through their extremities, and dive into hidden realms.

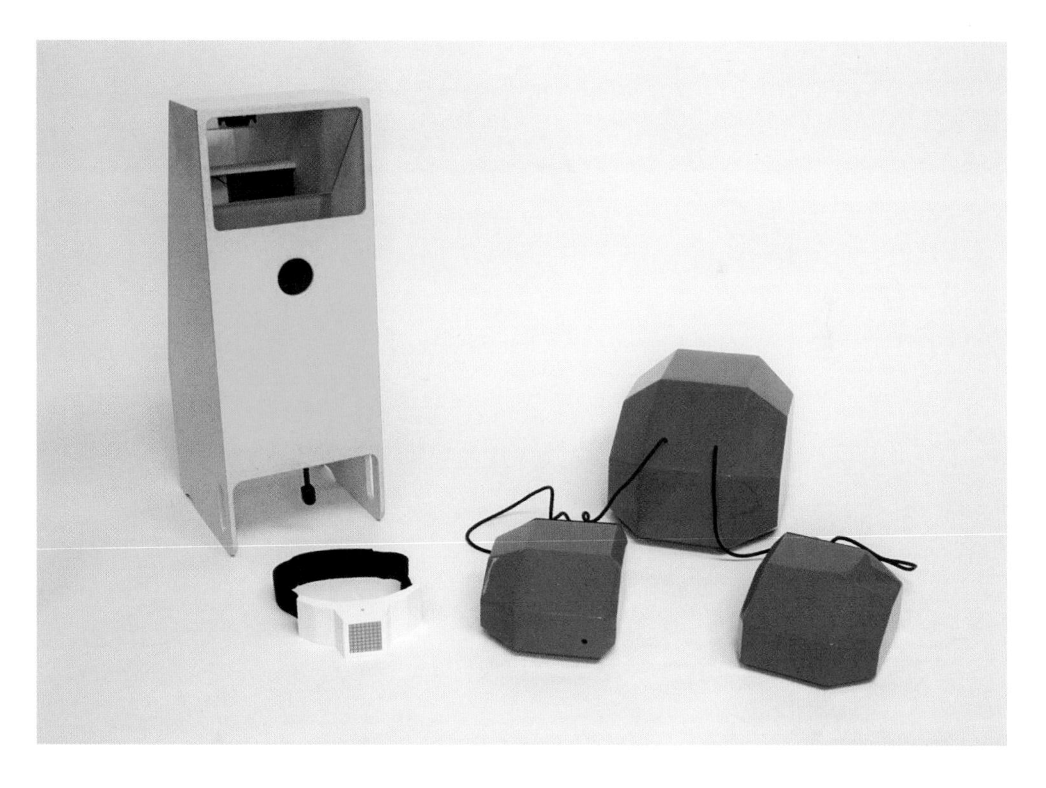

Prosthetic devices designed to give children the ability to experience the vision of ants, giraffes, and birds.

Bioreactors, Membranes, and Architecture
Zbigniew Oksiuta

Microbiologists have been building a wide range of devices for breeding life in vitro for over two centuries. From this was born a "Third Nature" as highly controlled, artificial environments began growing in isolation from their surroundings. In 1881, German biologist Robert Koch used a combination of meat extracts and gelatin to cultivate various bacteria, cells, and small plants. Today, transparent agar has become the standard medium for microbiological experiments. Agar is a polysaccharide derived from red seaweed. When placed in a container filled with nutrients, salts, and amino acids, it can support the growth of a wide variety of living creatures. The first bioreactors were simple containers used to ferment beer. These devices enabled complex chemical and biological processes to occur under controlled conditions.

After years of experimenting with different breeding-space technologies, I have developed a series of transparent, gel-like membranes that can be used as a new kind of building system. So far I have been able to cultivate living cells on the inner surfaces of large, inflatable balloons. By forming agar, starch, and cellulose inside of what are essentially three-dimensional petri dishes, I am able to create stable, semi-liquid objects on a large scale. Amorphous, living membranes can be hard or soft, moist or dry, rigid or foamy. By precisely controlling the temperature, PH, and oxygen levels in my bioreactor, I can construct multi-functional skins that manage structural loads, transmit light, and modulate the flow of air between interior and exterior space. A new kind of architectural skin can thus be produced by using what is essentially a universal construction kit that harnesses the self-organizing growth processes of nature. Architects, artists, and engineers working in the age of biotechnology need to catalyze new approaches to design that help improve the performance of existing chemical and biological processes. In other words, we need to design systems that encourage the spontaneous self-generation of novel forms and thus create conditions in which living spaces can thrive.

Architecture of biodegradable membranes. Photograph showing an inhabitable shelter made from living materials.

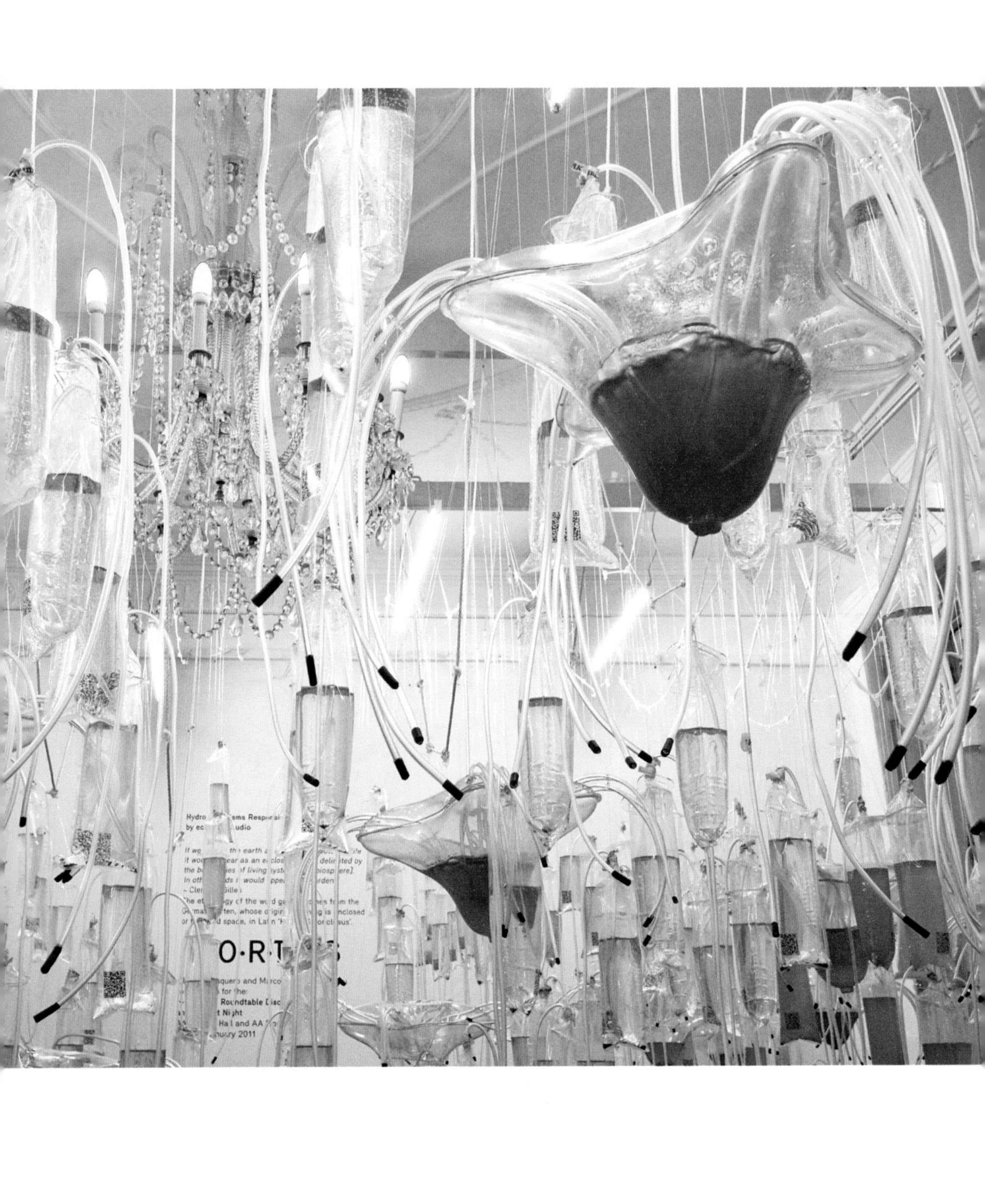

Hortus: Algae Farm
ecoLogicStudio / Marco Poletto and Claudia Pasquero

EcoLogicStudio has used the social networking website Twitter to breed a novel energy-producing infrastructure. This cyber-gardening machine establishes a link between immaterial communication protocols and the material practice of cultivating renewable bio-fuels. As these two regimes are correlated, they can support integrated patterns of consumption for a new kind of ecological architecture. We tested Hortus, our first 1:1 scale prototype, at the marine center in Shimrishamn and successively at the Architectural Association in London. It was conceived as a hanging algae garden hosting micro- and macro-organisms as well as bioluminescent bacteria supported by ambient light sensors and a custom-designed virtual interface. Flows of energy (light), matter (biomass, CO_2), and information (images, tweets, stats) were triggered during a four-week-long growing/harvesting cycle. Since algal organisms require CO_2 to flourish, visitors were invited to exhale air into the project's bioreactors. Each bioreactor had a QR code printed on its side. By scanning the code, visitors with a smartphone could access a page of information on the algae they had fostered. Tweets documenting these actions could also be accessed remotely. The project aims to challenge current discourses on sustainable design by rethinking the boundaries between global vs. local space and biological vs. virtual systems.

Algae and bioluminescent bacteria combine with virtual technologies to create a nutrient-producing interior garden.

Radiant Soil
Philip Beesley

The word "soil" might speak quietly of secure mass and compression as well as resources for framing human territory. Yet contemporary soil seethes with a myriad of seeded viscera, miniscule fragments, gathering and efflorescing, redolent with oceans chorusing of growth to come. The soil covers and retreats. Soil consumes space, erasing and consuming daily circumstances within its unspeakably silent, primal fertility. Its latent ambivalence makes it a monstrous doppelgänger of architecture. Radiant Soil forms interlinking clouds of industrial-design biomimetic components of polymer, metal, and glass, arranged in suspended filtered layers with a nearly living carbon-capture metabolism. Frond-clusters fitted with shape-memory alloy mechanisms react to viewers as they approach, flexing and setting off bursts of light that stimulate protocells and trigger chains of motion that ripple through the environment. Scent-emitting glands attract viewers and encourage interaction with the system, providing stimulus that increases air circulation and protocell formation.

A fusion of bio-materials and interactive electronics form a dense jungle-like space.
The installation consists of functioning protocols and shape-memory wire.

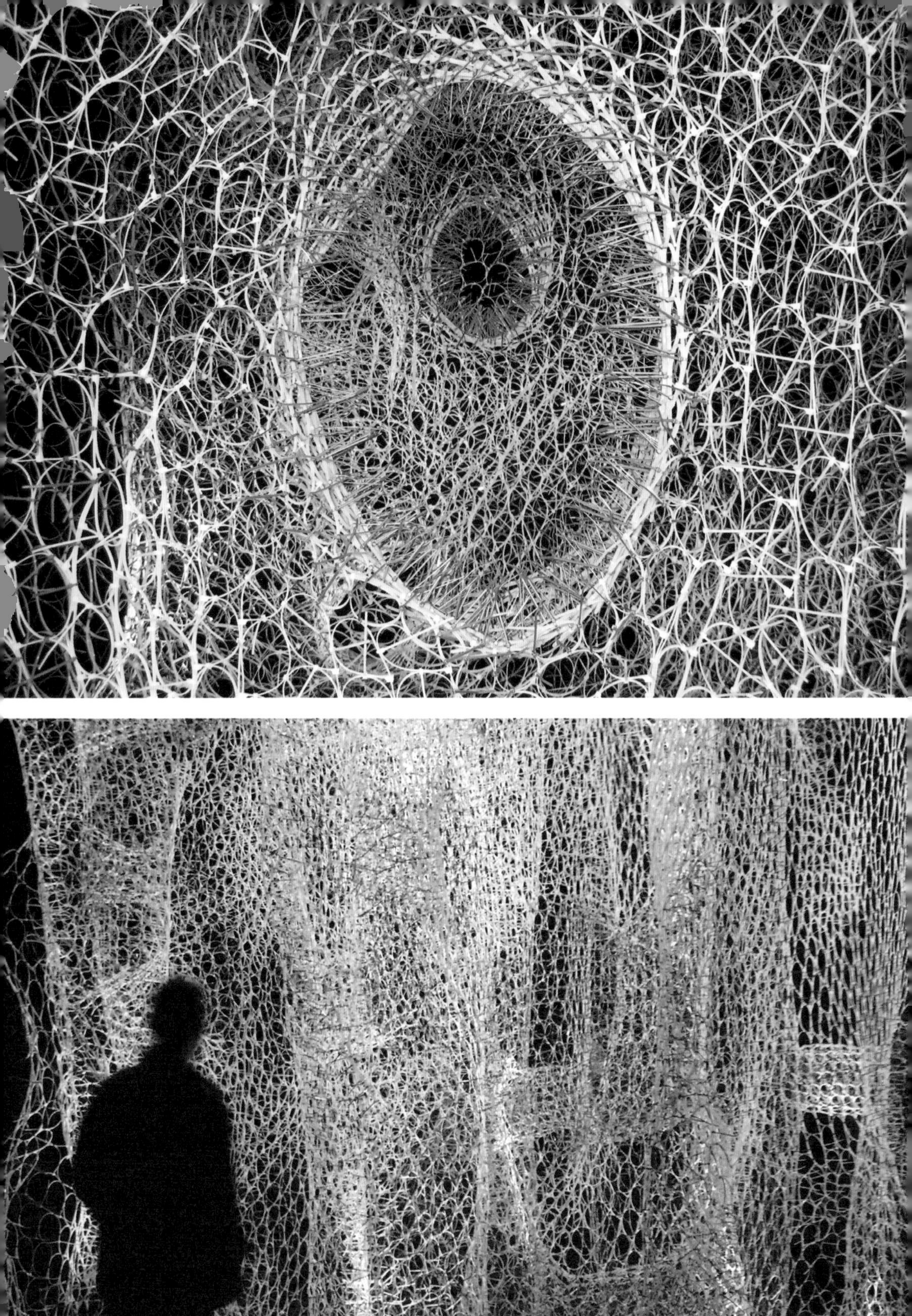

Branching Morphogenesis
Sabin+Jones LabStudio / Jenny E. Sabin

This installation materializes five slices in time that capture the force network exerted by interacting vascular cells upon their surrounding matrix scaffold. Time is manifested as five vertical, interconnected layers made from over 75,000 cable zip ties.

Branching Morphogenesis is an experimental prototype emanating from work that centers on crafting the nonlinearities of material and form across disciplines on the human scale. A primary intention is to mine the gap that exists between computational design thinking across disciplines and material manifestation. In this prototype, the concept of feedback or reciprocity is embedded on multiple scales of design exploration, both within digital tools as well as in the context of generative fabrication and material production. For example, in Branching Morphogenesis, biological reciprocity, a concept of mediation and feedback between context or the extracellular matrix (ECM) and code or DNA, informs the generative design strategy for the final installation. The ECM is a dynamic extracellular textile in which subtle changes in its architecture impact the form, function, and structure of the cell, and vice versa.

Additionally, this project incorporates long-standing traditions of shared relationships between technology, architecture, and biology, with sub-topics that include digital fabrication, textile tectonics, responsive architecture, experimental structures, and algorithmic design through scripting procedures and materials science. Techniques in parametric and associative environments are incorporated with feedback derived from material constraints as well as performance assessments. Many of our projects interrogate the physical interface between networking behavior—one biological, the other mathematical—and fabricated material assemblies in order to address novel applications of non-standard components towards the production of 3D-textured prototypes and systems in context on the human scale. The work emanating from our research, practice, and teaching, which defines a radical departure from disciplinary silos to a conceptual space where the fusion of design and science takes place, offers new formal and material expressions in architectural space and structure while also answering pressing issues surrounding ecological design.

Above: Detail showing up-cycled cable ties.
Below: Installation view.

ERO
ERO

Concrete Recycling Robot
Omer Haciomeroglu

Most demolition teams today operate manually controlled, heavy machinery that is hard to set up, operate, and maintain. Conventional demolition techniques also use massive quantities of water to prevent harmful dust from spreading through the air. After a job is done, big machines scoop up waste rebar and concrete, which is then transported off-site to remote recycling stations. This process requires huge investments in manual labor and equipment. ERO is a compact prototype robot designed to disassemble concrete structures automatically into reusable raw materials for new pre-fabricated buildings. Instead of exerting brute mechanical force to pulverize a structure, the ERO's recycled water jets and vacuum system break up cast concrete walls in situ. The robot also cleanly separates the resulting waste and transfers it to neatly sealed containers. What was previously a messy, dangerous, and time-consuming process is now significantly streamlined. A small fleet of EROs can complete a demolition job autonomously on site while consuming far fewer resources and less time.

Left: Renderings showing the safe erasure and waste management of a building being robotically demolished.
Above: Robot views.

Your Rotten Future Will Be Great
Phil Ross

In the early 90s, I began producing a series of sculptural projects by growing and manipulating fungal tissue. Such artworks can be created by infusing live fungal cells into a pulverized cellulose medium. The cellulose serves as both food and framework for growth. The aggregate solidifies in about a week thanks to fungi's natural tendency to join together smaller pieces of its tissue into a larger constituent whole. Fungi has the other exceptional ability of being able to adhere to, and possibly engulf, any other material with which it comes into contact. Once a fungal object is grown, it can be heated and dried to become a light-weight and potentially quite strong material. Like cement and plaster, fungal tissue will bind, harden, and set into a variety of solidified forms. Moreover, my ongoing research has generated a range of geometrically determined objects and engineered structures, but also some wild-looking and grotesque artifacts that resemble sea-corals, tumors, and various decomposing shapes. Initially inspired by the desire to understand how environmental conditions influence the aesthetics of life forms, my work now focuses on how to engineer and produce an entire building out of fungus-based components.

Right now it is possible to grow an enormous amount of cultured fungal tissue into a wide range of practical objects by using low-tech, low impact, well studied, and commonly practiced methods. Self-adhering tissues grown in this way can incorporate natural and artificial fibers and easily adhere to fabrics and armatures. The world needs fungus, but the world also needs many more people working to develop fungal engineering. Here in the Bay Area I will soon be manufacturing certain functional materials with techniques that I have developed over the past two decades. In my moldy lab I have begun producing locally grown objects out of materials diverted from the city's waste stream. I recommend that architects or engineers interested in working with fungal materials take a class in French cooking, perhaps with a focus on pastries. Another suggestion is to get them to experiment with edible foams, gels, and slurries, or—more importantly—simply to think about the possibilities of designing with living goo.

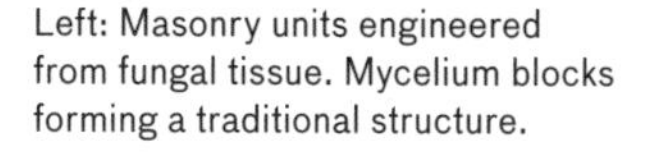

Left: Masonry units engineered from fungal tissue. Mycelium blocks forming a traditional structure.

A Call for Citizen Biotech
Terreform ONE + Genspace / Oliver Medvedik

It nearly goes without saying that in order for scientific progress to continue unabated, citizens of all nations need to be more involved in its development. As during the personal computer revolution, so now we are witnessing rapid acceleration in biotechnological change. Exponential increases in computing power based on Moore's Law are being outpaced by Carlson's Curve, which maps an even faster rate of innovation. The human genome project of the 1990s took nearly a decade to complete and cost an estimated 3 billion dollars. Nowadays, a scan of a genetic code costs about 1000 U.S. dollars with a turnaround time of 24 hours! Not only has sophisticated equipment grown cheaper and more available, but large bodies of experimental data have become increasingly accessible. These are some of the key reasons why I believe that ordinary citizens will come to play an even greater role in the production of scientific knowledge in the biotech field.

At Genspace, we have established a community laboratory where almost anyone can explore emerging tools and processes. In it, citizen scientists are able to meet, learn, and pursue novel research. Throughout the world, the individuals best equipped to tackle local problems are those with the most direct understanding of their environment. We are already familiar with one of the oldest citizen biotech initiatives: drugs discoveries from natural reserves. The development of medicines and other valuable compounds from existing flora and fauna has contributed to at least 50% of those currently used in medicine. With the advent of synthetic biology, communities will gain greater power to invent more efficient molecules that will enhance their economies and improve health. In India, the term "*jugaad*" is used to describe clever technological fixes for existing problems. The solutions discovered apply mostly to pressing problems of human survival and include the invention of improved transportation systems from locally modified tools and infrastructure. More importantly, decentralized, free-market solutions tend to be more efficient and easy to adopt. I believe that to develop low-cost, high-impact solutions in the field of biotechnology effectively, we need a collaborative, community-based, scientific culture—one perhaps built on the model of Genspace.

Above: Terreform ONE, Mycoform Surface: Multi-Curved Biomaterial. complex-shaped interlocking modular assembly with biopolymer of acetobacter, chitin, and mycelium. Below: Terreform ONE, In-Vitro Meat Habitat: The fabrication of 3D-printed, extruded pig cells to form fully preserved/non-living, victimless building skins.

Recycled Plastic Furniture
Greg Lynn

When my children were toddlers, they had lots of rotomolded plastic things. My life was surrounded by large, hollow, plastic toys—from the scale of playhouses down to rocking horses and everything in between—that we eventually brought to the secondhand store. Yet we would also grow sentimentally attached to them and hate to see them go. It was then that I began thinking that they would make great bricks, and that it would be fun to build interior walls out of these recycled, hollow plastic toys as they were lightweight and structurally sound. So that is how we started the Blobwall system, for which instead of using recycled toys, we made our own hollow plastic bricks. Afterwards, for the Venice Architectural Biennial in 2008, Aaron Betsky asked me to go back to the idea of using found toys. That is when I made the first Toy Furniture. The rotomolded toys we picked were more than 50% recycled plastic content. I really like the pop-culture materials of everyday life, but used in a way that elevates them to something that people notice and care about. Another thing I like about plastics is that they are lightweight, high-performance, and a very good substitute for metals and fired masonry. As sustainability becomes an ever greater concern, we are going to see ever more plastics.

Left: Furniture made from up-cycled toys. Digital scanning technology and 3D cutting machines were used to produce a tight connection between dissimilar parts.
Above: Fountain.

Up-Drop
Aurora Robson

Up Drop (2010) is a three-dimensional collage made from approximately 5000 up-cycled PET bottles and 300 HDPE bottle caps. This plastic debris, carefully cleaned prior to being sculpted, forms a chaotic and dense field of seemingly infinite extension. The project is a meditation on the nightmarish quantity of plastic waste that is accumulating in our oceans and on the detrimental effects that this problem poses for all life on earth. Up Drop is also about transforming something negative into something positive. Here a steady stream of garbage is transformed into a colorful and complex work of art.

Art made from discarded plastic bottles.

ANATEL: 0412-05-2618
FCC ID: RI7GE864
IC: 5131A-GE864
CE0168
Trashtrack Tag 2.0
mit senseable city lab

MIT senseable city lab:.::

Trash Track
Carlo Ratti

What if we knew exactly where our trash was going and how much energy it took to make it disappear? Would it make us think twice about buying bottled water or "disposable" razors? Trash Track relies on the development of special electronic tags that will track different types of waste on their journey through the disposal systems of New York and Seattle. The project will monitor the patterns and costs of urban disposal and create awareness of the impact of trash on our environment by tracking the final journey of our everyday objects.

Our intention is to reveal the disposal process of our everyday objects as well as to highlight potential inefficiencies in today's recycling and sanitation systems. The project could be considered the urban equivalent of nuclear medicine, in which a tracer is injected and followed through the human body. The study of the "removal chain" is becoming as important as that of the "supply chain." Trash Track aims to make the removal chain more transparent. We hope that the project will promote behavioral change and encourage people to make more sustainable decisions about what they consume and how it affects the world around them.

Trash Track will enlist volunteers in two target cities, New York and Seattle, who will allow pieces of their trash to be electronically tagged with special wireless location markers or "trash tags." Thousands of these markers, attached to a waste sample representative of the city's overall consumption, will calculate their location through triangulation and report it to a central server, where the data will be analyzed and processed in real time. The public will be able to view the migration patterns of the trash online.

Trash Track was initially inspired by the Green NYC Initiative, the goal of which is to increase the rate of waste recycling in New York to almost 100% by 2030. Currently, only about 30% of the city's waste is diverted from landfills for recycling. We think Trash Track will also point the way to a possible urban future: that of a system in which, thanks to the pervasive usage of smart tags, 100% recycling could become a reality. We have conceived a project to help people take ownership of their pollution.

Above: Self-organized complexity achieved through conservation of materials.
Below: Sensors attached to pieces of trash trace the flow of waste across America.

Cascade Formations: Low Energy—High Complexity

Rhett Russo

If the shift from arts and crafts to mass production was fueled in part by a desire to manufacture things more quickly and in greater quantities, what impacts will ecology and conservation have on production? How will our effort to design with low-embodied energies actively transform architecture and aesthetics? Certainly changes in the way we consume resources will alter the appearance and structure of what we build. Perhaps the conventional notion of "making"—usually a tightly controlled, top-down process—is no longer or at least only partly relevant today. Design strategies that actively engage the physics and chemistry of matter are becoming a more important part of architectural theory and practice. What will the future look like if our objects and spaces are actively catalyzed or allowed to grow and self-organize? What effects will careful energy management have on the process of construction?

Prior to completing my research on porcelain powders, I spent long hours experimenting with sand. I also made ceramic pieces from difficult-to-produce, digitally fabricated molds made out of toxic ingredients. The creation of shapes through the direct pouring of granular materials eliminated the need for complex tooling, CNC machines, and difficult-to-program virtual models. One would suspect that without these technologies, results would be minimal and repetitive. This turned out not to be the case. A simple, two-dimensional plate pierced with holes can channel millions of individual particles into a complex network of ridges and inverted cones. With the aid of gravity, this occurs in mere seconds and with very little effort. Grains behave like fluids, assuming the shape of their containers. These systems exhibit complex behavior at multiple scales and also form oblique slopes even on inclined planes and curved surfaces. In making the tiles described here, I carefully considered the shape, uniformity, mass, and size of each grain.

To resist water damage, granular aggregates, once formed, must be chemically or thermally bonded. Typically, post-processed ceramics are manufactured with petroleum-based resins or very hot, fuel-consuming kilns. As Ginger Dosier's Bio-Brick research has demonstrated, however, harmless bacteria can be used as alternative agents of solidification. A great deal of trial and error went into making my best tiles. In the process, I considered the filtering system, the physical characteristics of each grain, the manner in which they combined, and the initial position of the system relative to the Earth's axis of gravitation. More important to my research was finding a way to subvert a pour by circuiting its grains into shapes that they could not assume by their own power. In other words, the process cultivated complex morphologies while harnessing disequilibrium to reach calculated results with the least amount of energy.

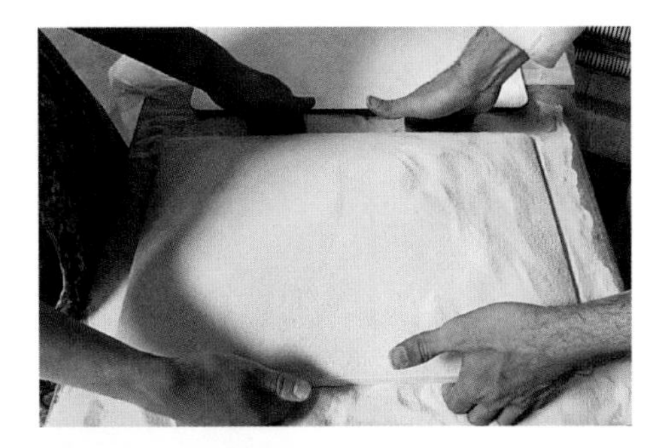

Opposite: Tableware made from a controlled process of shifting sand. Above: Self-organized complexity is achieved through the conservation of energy and materials.

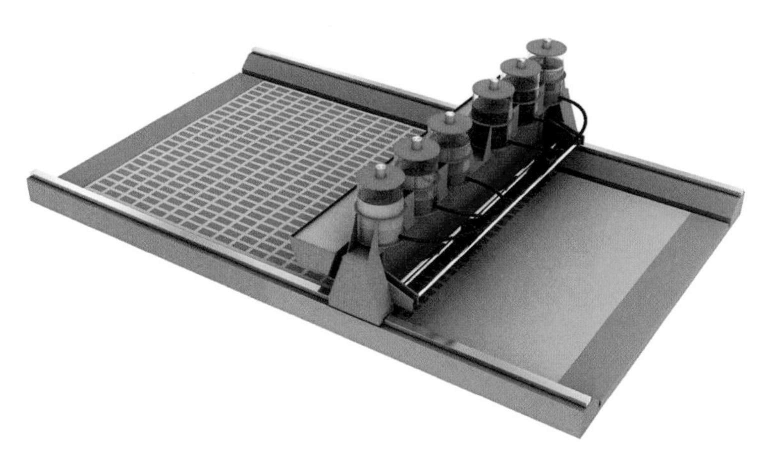

Biomanufactured Brick
bioMASON / Ginger Dosier

The built environment is constructed with a limited palette. "Modern" materials such as concrete, steel, and glass have high-embodied energies and are obtained from non-renewable reserves. Forty percent of the world's greenhouse gas pollution is linked to industrial production and the disposal of its resources. Conventional brick manufacturing uses energy-intensive processes to vitrify clay particles into hardened shapes. It is estimated that brick production alone emits over 800 million tons of CO_2 each year. The term "biotechnology" was coined in 1917 by Karl Ereky. "Biomanufacturing" can be roughly defined as a production process that uses living organisms or parts of organisms to create useful products for human consumption. Over time, nature has evolved resourceful ways to manufacture cement-like compounds with minimal energy input and waste. Simple life forms such as coral create hard mineral composites at ambient temperatures. Microorganisms are efficient metabolizers and have been employed for centuries to manufacture valuable commodities such as food and life-saving drugs. In 1978, Genentech engineered the first synthetic insulin (Humulin) from repurposed E. coli bacteria.

My research seeks a viable, low-energy replacement for traditional masonry units by employing a common microorganism to make biolithic materials. Nonpathogenic, nitrogen-fixing bacteria have the ability to produce biocementatious bricks from fused grains of sand. This process of forming hard shapes is known as microbial-induced calcite precipitation [MICP]. Bio-bricks are made by combining living cells, nitrogen, and calcium ions. Specific chemical reactions catalyze the mix to create binded aggregates with physical properties similar to those of natural sandstone. Rather than heating raw materials in a kiln, this process "grows" masonry units with extremely small amounts of energy. Current structural tests of lab-made samples exhibit compressive strengths similar to those of fired clay brick. The biomanufacturing process can be highly economical, especially if most of the ingredients are found on site. Experiments have been conducted with a variety of matrixes, including sand, soil, recycled glass, fly ash, plastics, as well as synthetic Martian and Lunar regolith. My research considers the supply chain as a whole. Employing bacteria to induce mineral precipitation is naturally one highly promising way to encourage the growth of viable and green construction materials.

1. Finished bio-masonry unit with low embodied energy.
2. Proposed 3D bio-brick printing machine.

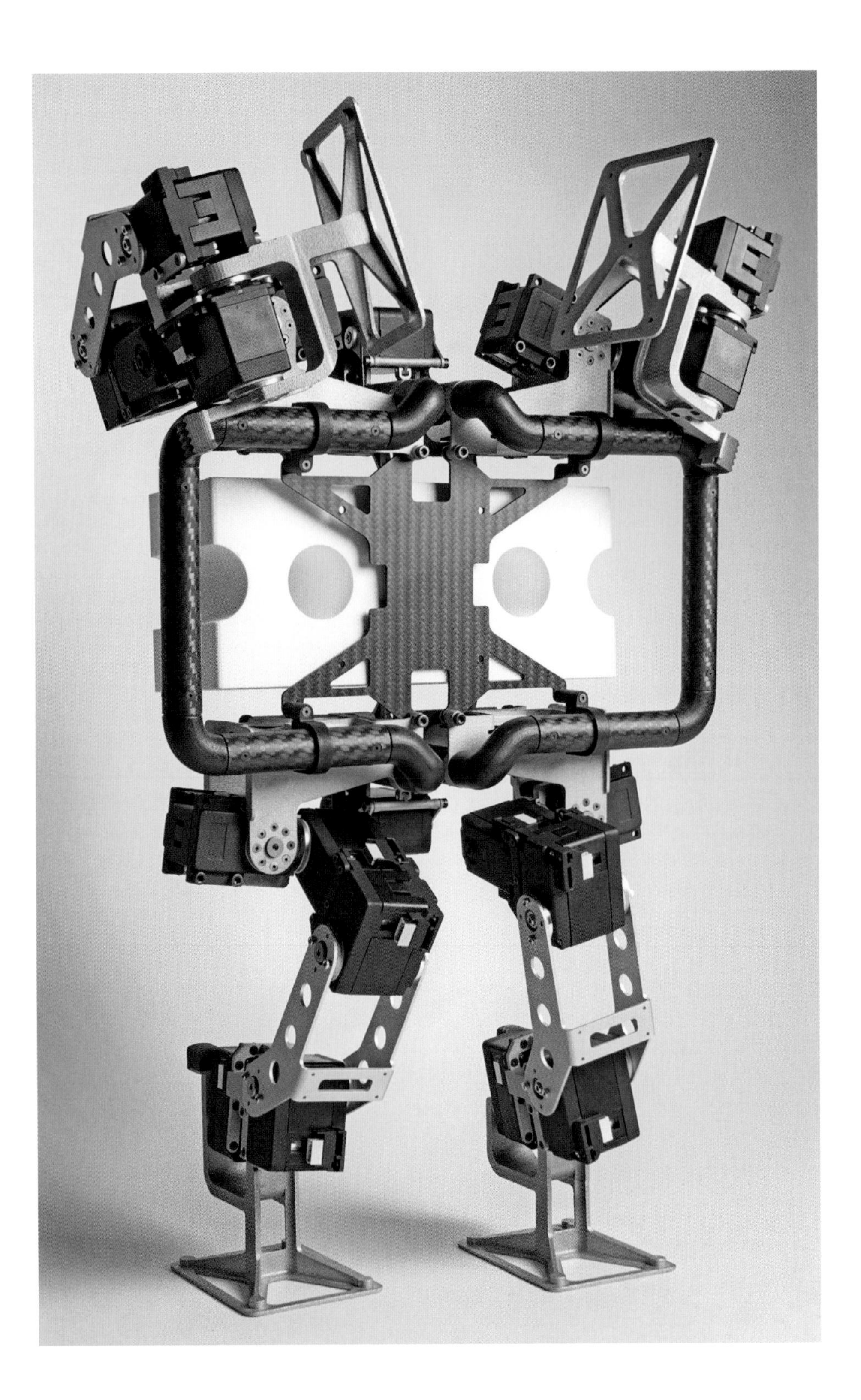

Construction Site Automation, Green Masonry, and BIM
Mike Silver

In early 2012, after the success of its driverless vehicle initiative, the Defense and Advanced Research Projects Agency (DARPA) issued a call to engineers from around the world to develop leg-based robots capable of performing a wide variety of tasks in real-world environments. The main goal of the challenge was to spur the creation of machines that could be employed on disaster sites such as the now defunct nuclear reactor in Fukushima, Japan. Inspired by the DARPA competition, our team focused on the development of fully functional, situationally aware quadrupeds and bipeds that were capable of assembling complex structures from biomanufactured bricks. Rather than pursuing new applications for factory-based articulated arms, we looked at how low-cost, BIM-networked devices fitted with sophisticated machine-vision technologies could be used to assist workers inside and outside buildings under construction.

Left: Working prototype brick-transporting robots.
Above: Information flow diagram.
Below: Machines on a job site.

Glass Works
Evan Douglis

Fascinated by the power of controlled chance and the inextricable link between geometry and matter, my current research focuses on the production of a new species of glass objects that yields critical insights into a world of exotic topological transformations. The structural netting of each blown-glass vessel is carefully calibrated to unleash exciting surface effects. In this way, my project transcends the mere representation of complexity found in bio-formalist experiments from the 1990s to crystallize real material flows in the metamorphosis from liquid to solid form. By eliminating the waste associated with intricate CNC-milled formwork, this process tends towards higher levels of complexity with fewer resources, minimal energy inputs, and modest means. Each glass object here was specially designed for a naturally lit, public stair tower of a world-renowned corporate headquarters in Abu Dhabi.

Blue Rain – Minimal wire-mesh frameworks create complex flows of molten glass.

Solar Sintering
Markus Kayser

This solar sintering experiment explores the potential of desert manufacturing by harnessing two of the world's most abundant natural resources: sunlight and sand. These simple ingredients can be used to produce intricate glass objects with a custom-built 3D printer. The machine focuses solar radiation instead of a laser beam in order to melt-bond silica into thinly stacked layers. Photovoltaic cells also convert available sunlight into electricity, which is then used to power the machine's computer and servo controls. This universal manufacturing system can sculpt almost any shape with little or no stress on the planet's eco-system. If scaled up it could even be used to make buildings. An extremely efficient fabrication system, the solar sintering process reaches beyond sustainability by producing complex and varied forms. The tight integration of technology and nature suggests the possibility of creating a new kind of industrial culture, one that is able to support human creativity through artfully conceived objects and spaces.

Left: Solar sintered bowl.
Above: Focused solar radiation is used to melt sand into precise forms.

Rewilding with Synthetic Biology
Alexandra Daisy Ginsberg

The great Sixth Extinction in the history of biology is underway, and we humans may be its cause. While conservationists struggle to protect existing "natural" species and reverse the effects of the Anthropocene (the human epoch), synthetic biologists are busy designing new organisms for the "benefit of humanity." What might the "wilds" look like in a synthetic, biological future? Designing for the Sixth Extinction investigates synthetic biology's potential impact on biodiversity and conservation. Could we tolerate "rewilding"—a conservation movement that lets nature take control—by using synthetic biology to improve on nature? Letting synthetic biodiversity loose in order to save the "nature" that we idealize would disrupt existing conventions of preservation. In this version of the future, novel companion species designed by synthetic biologists support endangered natural species and ecosystems. Financed by corporate biodiversity offset schemes, patented species are released into the wild and compensate for biodiversity lost due to widespread monoculture farming of biomass for biofuel and chemical production. For a thriving bioeconomy, the preservation of natural biodiversity is worthwhile not solely for sentimental reasons but also because it serves as a valuable DNA library for future biological designs.

Modeled on fungus, bacteria, invertebrates, and mammals, designed species are ecological machines that either fill the void left by vanished organisms or offer novel protection against more harmful invasive species, diseases, and pollution. Constructed with an expanded DNA code that produces non-biodegradable proteins, synthetic biodiversity is hardy in the face of wild predators that have not yet evolved to eat and digest its species. These operate in enclosed ecosystems, the outcome of decades of political negotiation and compromise around biosafety and release. Organisms designed to maintain or revive disappearing ecosystems demand a relaxed attitude to biological control, risk, and ownership. The taxonomic status of technologically isolated organisms that have no other purpose than to save others is also uncertain. Are they even "alive"? If nature is totally industrialized for the benefit of society—for some, the logical end of synthetic biology—will nature still exist for us to save? This project comprises a series of synthetically rewilded, biodiverse forests as well as fictional patent applications for four organisms in a closed technological ecosystem.

Synthetic biology can reshape the future of earth's plant and animal species. Engineers can design new organisms to benefit all life.

PERISTALTIC PUMP P-3

Semi-Living Victimless Utopia: Will We Ever Get There?

Oron Catts and Ionat Zurr

Growing rather than manufacturing products has been the central aim of the Tissue Culture Project (TCP) since 1996. Its work builds off recent developments in biomedical research, such as tissue engineering and regenerative medicine. Our goal is to evoke the latent, regenerative abilities of animal organs and tissue. TCP seeks to produce semi-living products for applications not considered by the medical establishment. In a series of hands-on artistic experiments, ranging from the construction and growth of symbolic to pseudo-utilitarian objects, TCP has explored the philosophical, ethical, epistemological, and practical aspects of creating living "products." For example, in its Pig Wings Project (2001) TCP developed CAD-CAM protocols for The Tissue Engineering and Organ Fabrication Laboratory at Harvard Medical School. In this project we used biodegradable scaffolds and differentiated stem cells in order to critique "Genohype," a media-based, overexaggeration of the promises of genetic manipulation. Another series of works developed for The Technologically Mediated Victimless Utopia (2000-2008) employed tissue engineering to create in-vitro meat and leather products that questioned the tendency of Western technology to obscure its victims, namely, the animals that people consume every day. These works explore post-sustainable space by presenting tangible and evocative ways of reconfiguring life through transformed raw materials developed for human purposes.

Tissue over medical grade scaffolding produces living works of art.

Below: Macro-scale tests demonstrating how different components can put themselves together with small energy inputs. Right: System for generating self-assembling forms.

Molecular Self-Assembly
Skylar Tibbits

Could buildings one day build themselves? This sounds unbelievable, but it is a very real possibility. My research with Arthur Olson of the Scripps Research Institute explores how the basic ingredients of molecular assembly could translate to self-assembly technologies at all scales. Participants at TEDGlobal each received a unique glass flask containing anywhere from four to twelve red, black, or white particles. When the glass flask was shaken randomly the independent particles found each other and self-assembled into various molecular structures. The flasks contained a custom tag that identified the type of molecular structure and the ingredients for its successful self-assembly. Programmable self-assembly has been studied extensively at the molecular level for some time now. The first large-scale applications, however, will likely take shape in extreme environments of near-zero gravity or neutral buoyancy, where the application of energy can lead to increases in interaction. Imagine using wave energy under water in order to trigger the self-assembly of multi-story structures, or dropping particles from high altitudes in order to unfold fully erected structures, or even producing modular, transformable and reconfigurable space structures!

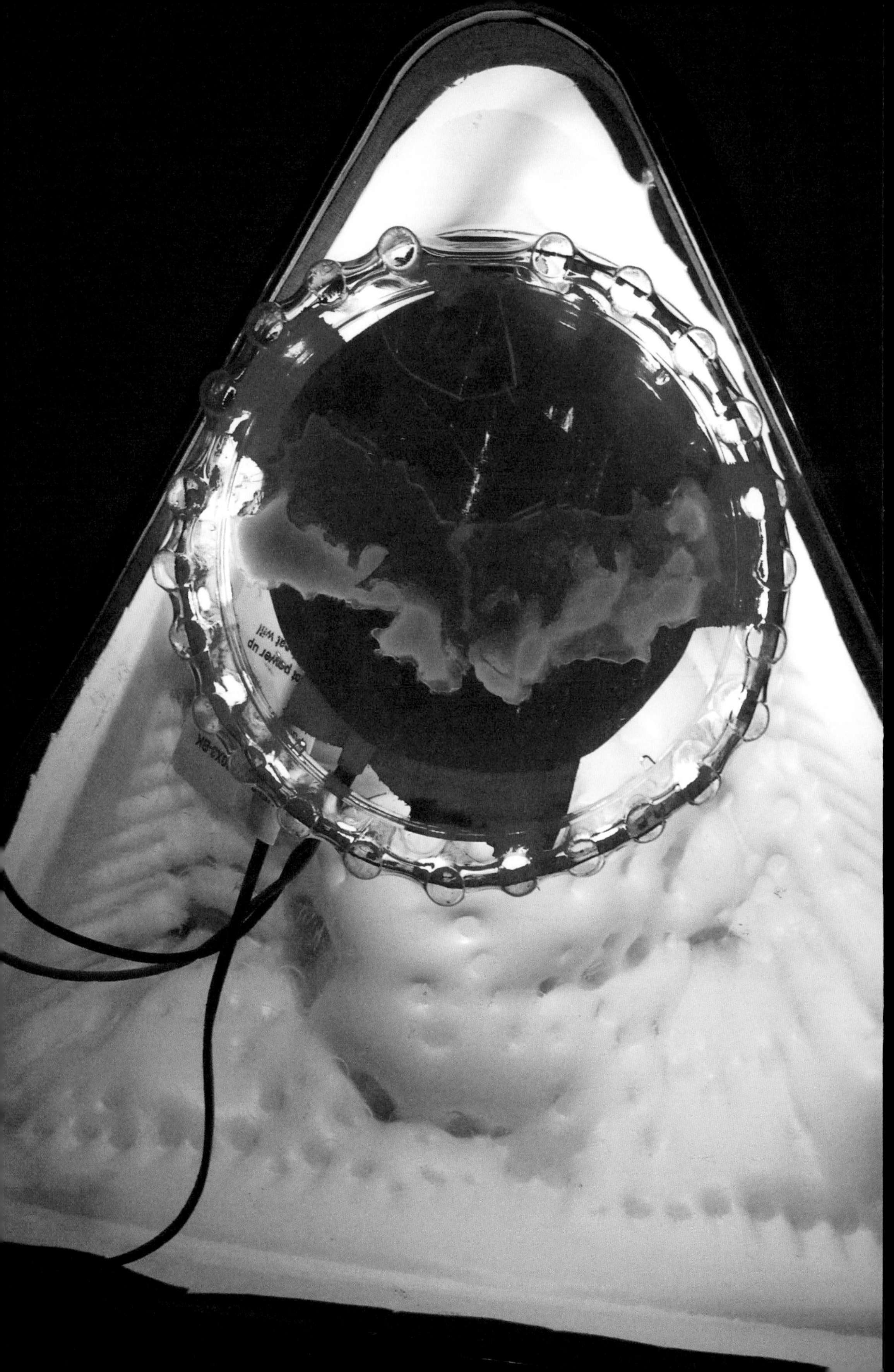

Bio City Map of 11 Billion: World Population in 2110
Terreform ONE

Bio City Map: In the next 100 years, we can expect the human population to reach 11 billion. What does this increase in growth look like? Our Bio City Map is a hybrid art and science installation that links transgenic design, cartography, urban planning, and three-dimensional parametric graphs. We have developed a world map based on the Dymaxion grid to communicate an all-encompassing view of population density in cities as estimated from probabilistic census data. The map visualizes the earth as a single, entirely urbanized system rather than as a series of unconnected settlements, municipalities, and disparate regions. If we are anticipating growth at this rate, almost everything in human society will be comprehensively stressed. Such systemic pressures will include water scarcity, food shortages, overcrowding, air-quality depletion, and traffic congestion. The public must be made aware of consequences related to uncontrolled growth. This is the first step to recognizing the universal challenge of this century. If we cannot foresee impending difficulties, potential solutions will be hard to justify.

Our Bio City Map displays population density as a parametric grid with living biosynthetic transgenic matter. These live elements focus on 25 mega-cities, genetically designed and grown inside petri dishes. Our novel approach experiments with living populations of billions of bacterial cells. Using synthetic biology, we have chosen colonies of E. coli to demonstrate exponential population growth. Population density is represented through two different forms of fluorescent transgenic E. coli under UV light. Glowing red E. coli represent future census projections, while green E. coli represent existing demographic conditions found in today's cities. Micro-stencils derived from CAD files have shaped the E. coli into specific geometries that display the current geopolitical boundaries of each municipality. Genetic modifications of benign strains of E. coli were carried out at Genspace, the world's first community-based biotech laboratory, and at Terreform ONE. We believe that most nations cannot view the effects of planetary population density through the lens of merely one city or region. The Bio City Map attempts to reveal the long-range effects of immense human growth in areas of present and speculative urban intensity.

Left: Population density expressed in E.coli bacteria.
Right: Topological forms illustrate the shift in urban population density across continents as a biological habitat for 11 billion people.

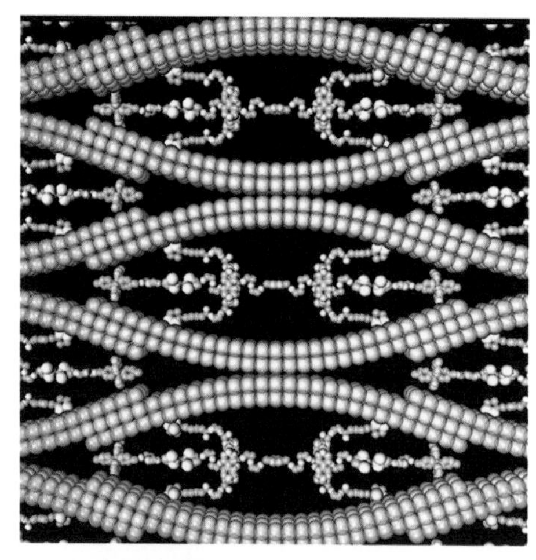

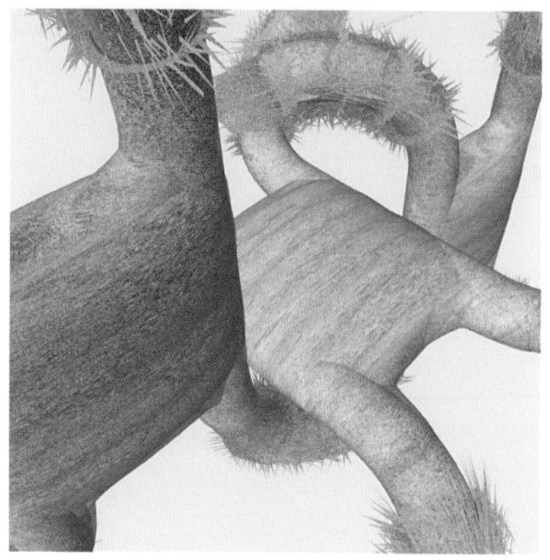

Left: Micro-scale views of nBot's controllable molecular muscles. nBot strands produce organism-like structures on a larger scale.
Below: Controllable, nano-robotic machines used to produce a fog-like urban infrastructure.

nBots: Sustaining Nano-Robotic Environments
Decker Yeadon / Martina Decker and Peter Yeadon

nBots consist of tiny nanorobotic devices designed for specific architectural applications. Made of Rotaxane molecules, nBots can move and grow when excited by visible light or electricity. These small molecular machines are built out of small rings that slide over dumbbell-shaped supports. To ensure that controlling electrical signals reach each muscle-like Rotaxane motor, nBots rely on thin graphene coatings made of carbon atoms that are uniformly arranged in a hexagonal pattern. Graphene is an extremely strong material with excellent electronic properties. An electrical charge traveling through Graphene is only 300 times slower than light, thus roughly 10-100 times faster than electricity moving through silicon.

Instead of using mechanical grippers, nBots harness intermolecular forces of attraction and repulsion to form large assemblies. Forests of carbon nano-hairs on the surface of each of their four arms generate Van der Waals forces that serve as switchable adhesives similar to the spatulas of a gecko's foot. In this way, nBots can stick to a variety of wet or dry surfaces including other nBots. As they aggregate, nBots can assume an endless variety of shapes, colors, and physical textures. Their excellent conductive properties also enable them to distribute electrical power and communicate information.

In the future, nBots might even be designed to float freely in the atmosphere and to assemble into artificial clouds that reduce solar-heat gain in cities. Other potential applications include the building of skins that instantly respond to a variety of changing environmental conditions, including seasonal temperature fluctuations. With this new kind of building technology, truly multifunctional spaces could be created to solve real-world problems such as waste management and air pollution control, or even to generate power. nBots could also be used to harvest raw materials from landfills and separate them into metals, plastics, and various organic substances. (New York City alone discards 38,000 tons of trash each day.) By disassembling and reassembling molecules one atom at a time, such nano-machines could produce a variety of atomically precise building products. Due to their minuscule size, nBots might also operate discretely and be able to process waste when and where it is generated.

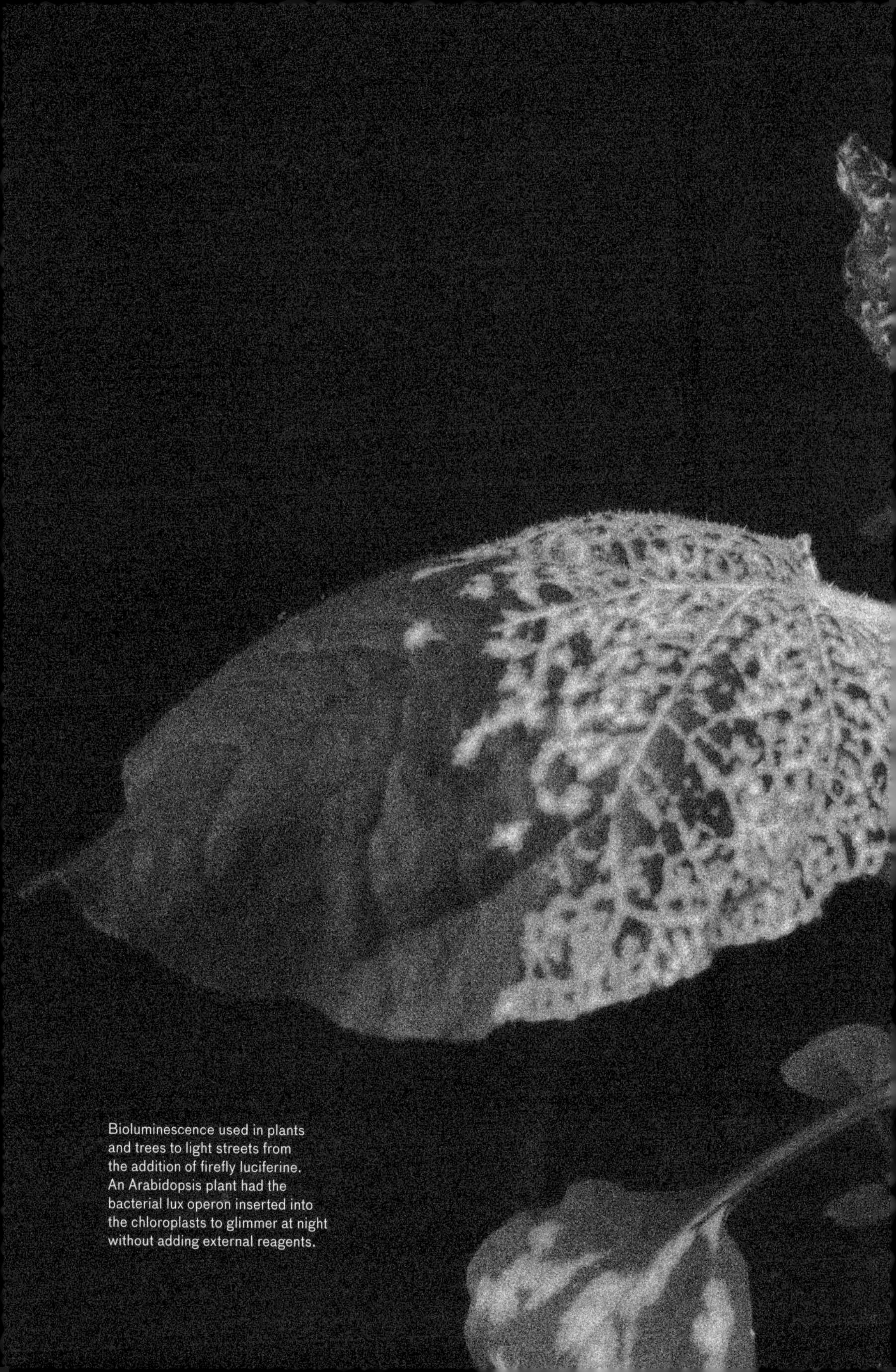

Bioluminescence used in plants and trees to light streets from the addition of firefly luciferine. An Arabidopsis plant had the bacterial lux operon inserted into the chloroplasts to glimmer at night without adding external reagents.

Essays
and Interviews

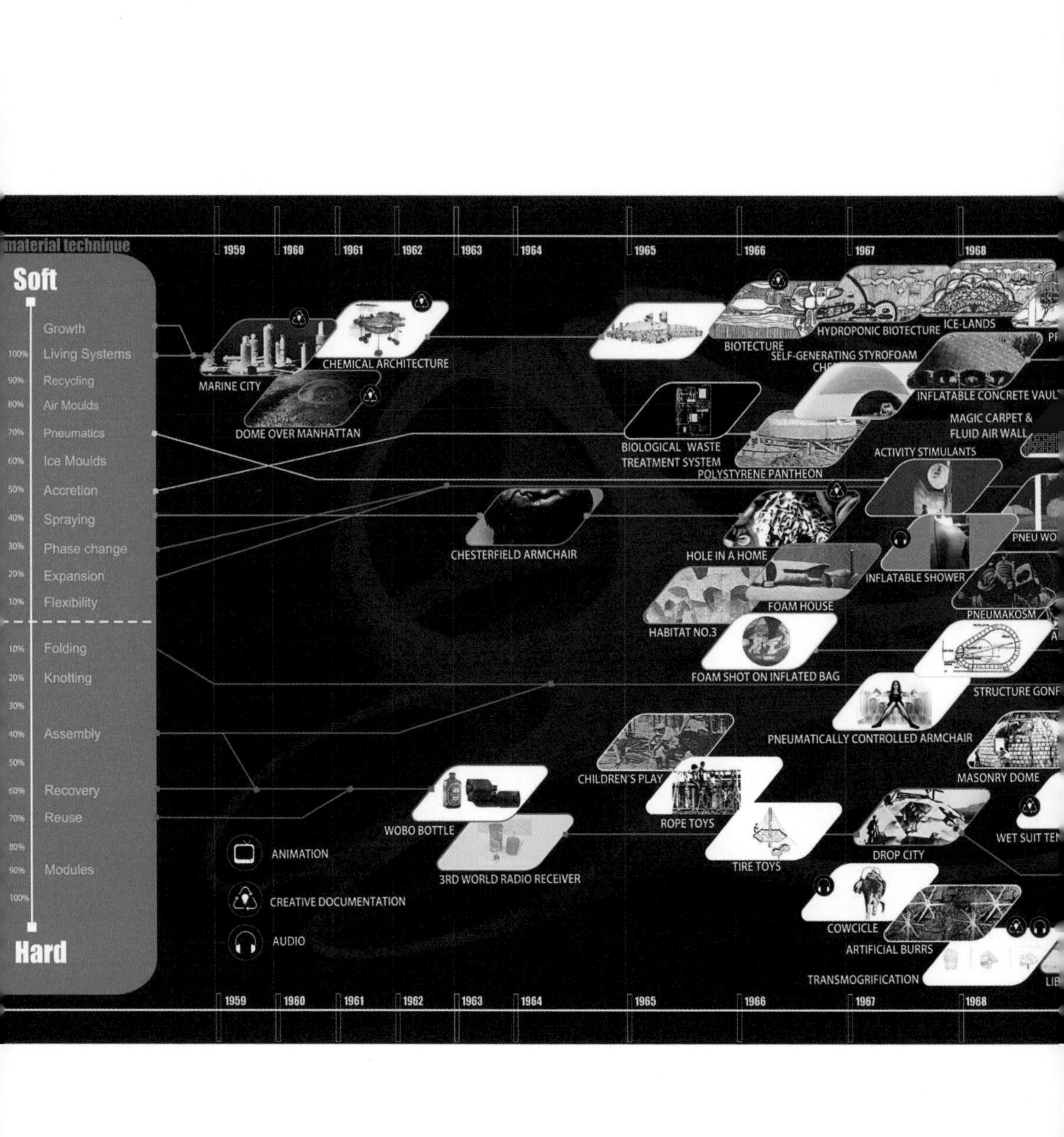
material technique
Soft
Growth
Living Systems
Recycling
Air Moulds
Pneumatics
Ice Moulds
Accretion
Spraying
Phase change
Expansion
Flexibility
Folding
Knotting
Assembly
Recovery
Reuse
Modules
Hard
100%
90%
80%
70%
60%
50%
40%
30%
20%
10%
1959
1960
1961
1962
1963
1964
1965
1966
1967
1968
MARINE CITY
CHEMICAL ARCHITECTURE
DOME OVER MANHATTAN
BIOTECTURE
HYDROPONIC BIOTECTURE
ICE-LANDS
SELF-GENERATING STYROFOAM
INFLATABLE CONCRETE VAUL
MAGIC CARPET &
FLUID AIR WALL
BIOLOGICAL WASTE
TREATMENT SYSTEM
ACTIVITY STIMULANTS
POLYSTYRENE PANTHEON
CHESTERFIELD ARMCHAIR
HOLE IN A HOME
INFLATABLE SHOWER
PNEU WO
FOAM HOUSE
HABITAT NO.3
PNEUMAKOSM
FOAM SHOT ON INFLATED BAG
STRUCTURE GONF
PNEUMATICALLY CONTROLLED ARMCHAIR
CHILDREN'S PLAY
MASONRY DOME
ROPE TOYS
WOBO BOTTLE
WET SUIT TEN
TIRE TOYS
DROP CITY
3RD WORLD RADIO RECEIVER
ANIMATION
CREATIVE DOCUMENTATION
AUDIO
COWCICLE
ARTIFICIAL BURRS
TRANSMOGRIFICATION

Lydia Kallipoliti

Ecoredux: An Archival & Design Resource for Ecological Material Experiments

EcoRedux is an online non-profit educational resource for ecological experiments in the postwar period and their potential creative reuse in contemporary design culture. The assembly of an archival database is intended to track an unexplored genealogy of material experimentation conducted by underground architectural groups, as a prehistory of a rising biotechnological imagery and a new social and planetary vision, crossbreeding different design disciplines throughout.

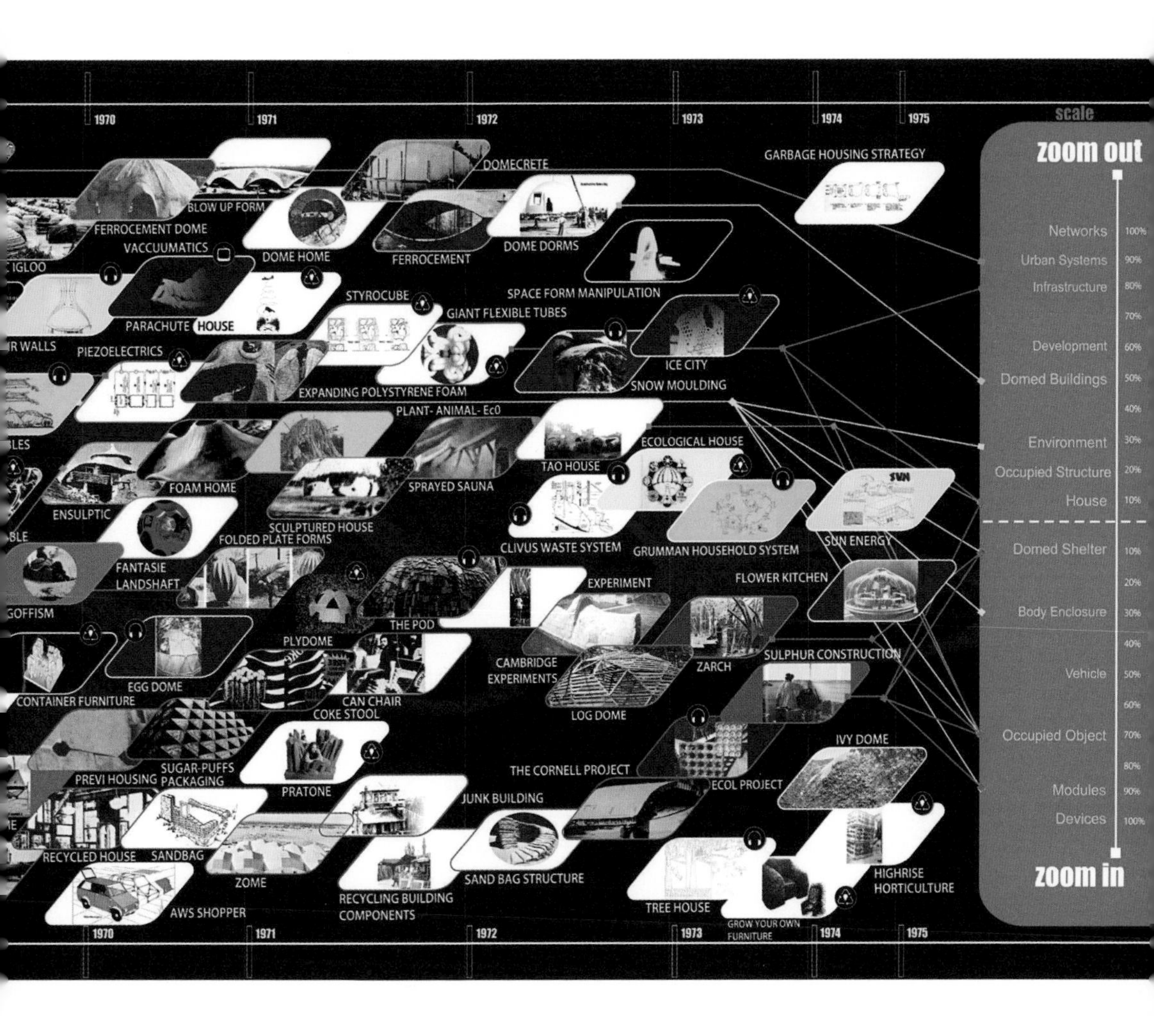

Jason Bellows

Mediterranean Be Dammed: The Story of Atlantropa

In the 1920s, the people of Europe feared the future as if it were a dark, despairing place. Aside from the loss of over five million Europeans in the Great War, the region was still plagued by the social maladies that had led to the conflict. Humans were maladjusted to the Industrial Age and the changes in labor that it had spawned. To make matters worse, both scholars and soothsayers of the day postulated that the world's fluxing economies would congeal into two economic blobs: the Americas would unify into a wealthy super-state in the West, while the East would collude into an enormous pan-Asian power. Europe would be left economically isolated, with a limited range of climates for farming and few resources at hand. Nowhere was the gloom thicker than in Germany, where the terms of the Treaty of Versailles had led to poverty and hunger for much of the population. It was in the midst of these dark times that an architect named Herman Sörgel devised a plan to preserve Europe within this daunting new worldscape.

Sörgel spent years promoting his scheme to save Europe, which entailed the construction of vast hydroelectric dams across the Mediterranean. Their massive turbines were to furnish a surplus of power, and the re-engineered sea was to turn the hostile-to-life Sahara Desert into a fertile wetland. In an era when it seemed that technology could do no wrong, a considerable segment of the German population supported Sörgel's ambitious plan.

Herman Sörgel was born on April 2nd, 1885 in Regensburg, Germany. Just after the turn of the century he began studying architecture in Munich. The first doctoral thesis that he submitted in 1908 was rejected. Five years later he turned in a fantastically similar paper. This time it was accepted and so well received that Sörgel successfully expanded it into a book. From such events he learned a valuable lesson in persistence—a lesson that served him well throughout the rest of his life. In 1914, when World War I broke out across Europe, he was working as an architect and journalist. Although his country engaged in hostilities, Sörgel professed himself a pacifist and did not participate. In the aftermath, Sörgel looked around conflict-ravaged Germany and worried about the future—not only his future, or his country's, but all of Europe's. The forecasted super-American and pan-Asian economies prompted even more fear; since the Americas spanned all the latitudes and climates, they could always farm and eradicate hunger. With its legendary abundance of resources, this super-America would not need to import anything from Europe. The possibility of a pan-Asian union presented the same problem but with a distinctly oriental lilt. Europe–small, underfed, and underpowered–would be helplessly sandwiched between these two behemoths.

Sörgel's solution lay in the very thing that was leaving so many people unemployed and destitute: technology. At the time, the pioneering footprints of the Industrial Age were still fresh, and the world was replete with a blind, loving trust in all things advanced. Electricity was the solution to every problem, and hydroelectric power was deemed cheap, exploitable, and renewable. As an ambitious architect, Sörgel was fed up with penny-ante dammed rivers. In 1927, he first published a megalomaniacally grand, but somewhat vague plan entitled "Panropa." Two years later, he unveiled a more detailed but equally egotistical version of it, which he named "Atlantropa."

Project Atlantropa proposed the construction of a dam near the narrowest point of the Straight of Gibraltar that would result in an eighteen-mile-long structure from Morocco to Spain. A second dam would halt the Bosporus, blocking off the Black Sea to the east. Although some of the Mediterranean's water comes from rivers, most flows in from the Atlantic Ocean. Pushing water through turbines would create power for all of Europe and Africa, and at the same time lower the level of the Mediterranean by more than 300 feet. 90,000 square miles of new land would surface in the area between currently beachfront properties and the relocated shoreline.

The altered sea would also dry up the waterway between Sicily and Italy, while a third dam stretching from Sicily to Tunisia would serve as a bridge to allow travelers easy access to Africa. Of course, Africa would have to be "improved" before colonization could begin. Yet another Atlantropa dam would be built across the Congo, swelling Lake Chad from its current state of "occasionally wet" to an inland sea of 135,000 square miles. The Congo lowlands would then flood the "unproductive" forests, washing away innumerable villages, species, and indigenous people.

Sörgel extolled the virtues of his mega-project in four books, thousands of publications, and countless lectures. The massive supply of electricity generated by his project was to allow nations to share a single power-grid and ease strife among them by making them interdependent. It would also–hypothetically–curb the European lust for war by providing an easy way for dense Anglo populations to move south and displace the African natives. At the time, people in Africa were generally deemed incapable of culture, purpose, or productivity, and few Europeans harbored second thoughts about rearranging the continent's natives without their consent. Sörgel and his supporters suggested that colonization would be a boon to Africa and provide the current population with water and work.

Project Atlantropa garnered a cult following, which included designers who drafted plans as well as financial supporters. As the media turned Sörgel into an engineering pop star, he founded the Atlantropa Institute to promote the project. But for all its popularity he was unable to get the project off the ground. In 1933 he took his proposal to the Nazis; if anyone had a penchant for construction on a grand scale, it would be them. After examining Sörgel's plan, the Nazis flatly refused. Aside from the fact that their main interest lay away from Africa, the pith of Atlantropa was to benefit all of Europe–something in which they had no interest.

Although the Atlantropa Institute managed to survive Europe's Second World War, it gradually lost most of its funding and public support. Never one to give up, Sörgel passionately championed the project for the rest of his life, which ended tragically in a hit-and-run automobile accident on Christmas Day, 1952. Reports indicated that Sörgel was bicycling along a road "as straight as a die" when he was struck. The driver who killed him was never found.

Though the idea itself was grand, most believe that it was utterly untenable. The construction of the Gibraltar dam would have required more concrete than the entire world's production at the time. Some critics maintained that such a change in one of the world's waterways would affect climate in unpredictable ways despite the fact that adherents argued that all of the changes–from the redirecting of the Transatlantic Flow to the alteration of the Sahara's humidity–would be for the better. Perhaps the most strongly argued point against the enormous Terraforming project was the casual conquest of Africa and its people. In 1960 the Atlantropa Institute was dissolved and its legacy left to the realm of science fiction, where it remains to this day.

Steven Cassells

Interview

M. Joachim/M. Silver: What have you learned since the Rising Currents show and in the wake of Hurricane Sandy?
Steven Cassels: What was amazing was the alignment between the early flooding maps that we generated for the Rising Currents project and what actually happened. We were therefore not surprised by the effects of Hurricane Sandy, which could actually have been much worse. Sandy caused 14 feet of flooding, but the worst-case scenarios for which we were designing were storm surges of between 18 and 24 feet, depending on the tide. We put together Rising Currents during an intense nine-week period in 2009-2010. While many design ideas have been developed since Sandy to make the city more resilient, to me the interesting thing would be to engage in far more intense engineering and analysis so that these ideas could be tested more rigorously, as, for example, by using fluid dynamic modeling to measure the specifics of storm surge hitting the coast. I don't think that kind of precision is happening right now. Ideas were floated quickly while the storm was fresh in people's minds and so that they could be included in Mayor Bloomberg's post-Sandy report. Initiatives such as "Rebuild by Design" are interesting, but real innovation comes from working hand-in-hand with a broad-based team of soil engineers, landscape architects, navigation experts, physicists, and other experts. That kind of effort doesn't happen in eight or nine weeks; it takes a year, a year and a half. But from that deep dive can come real innovation. While the Rising Currents thesis of an eco-infrastructure that works parallel to the existing infrastructure is conceptually sound–I really believe in it–there's much work to be done in areas such as water management, plantings, engineered soils, and implementation.

MJ/MS: In your opinion, what is the single most important problem facing the disciplines of architecture and ecology?
SC: The biggest challenge is to figure out how architecture and ecology can engage each other; the disciplines speak different languages. If you can't talk about things in the same way, you can't push them forward in an integrated way. A lot of current architectural thinking neglects the opportunities ecologists can offer, and vice versa. A more robust dialogue is needed. For instance, ecology is temporal in its essence. It's the study of processes unfolding over five, ten, twenty years. Of course time is super-important for architects too, but the nature of architectural representation (and therefore its development) often takes time out of the equation. In order to better marry these disciplines greater alignment in language and representation is needed.

MJ/MS: Are there specific projects you are working on now that may reflect these emerging concerns?

SC: I'm part of a wide-ranging leadership committee organizing a large-scale engineering and design competition called "Changing the Course." Sponsored by the Van Alen Institute and the Environmental Defense Fund, the competition focuses on hundreds of square miles below New Orleans in the Mississippi Delta: the "Bird's Foot." So much land has been lost in the delta over the past hundred years that the ecosystem is almost on the verge of total collapse. The situation is urgent. Nonetheless, the problem is so complex that we're giving entrants five to six months–way more time than is typical for a design competition–to create a super-robust engineering, design, and ecology framework that addresses and solves the myriad problems faced by local stakeholders: residents of local communities, the oil industry, fishermen. There are navigation problems; over thirty states are served by the Mississippi, but the river's infrastructure is aging. Coastal communities are being displaced by land loss; industries are being pushed out. Each of these issues is solvable on its own, but how can we address them all? Addressing this complex interplay calls for innovation on many levels; it is a truly complex design problem.

MJ/MS: What other architects or urban designers are you looking at? What is it about their practice that interests you?
SC: Michael Van Valkenburgh Associates are really interesting right now. They are taking on ecology, soil engineering, and large-scale urban planning in a way that's exciting and innovative. They're designing places that are getting built, like Brooklyn Bridge Park, which survived Sandy cheerily because the designers thought hard about how water engages the city. It's always a great pleasure to watch what they're doing and how they are engaging different problems.

MJ/MS: Are there any new technologies effecting how you think and work?
SC: If you can work hand-in-hand with technology, you can come up with some spectacular results. The increase in processing power allows sophisticated computer modeling that was once in the hands of scientists and dedicated consultants to become part of an integrated and iterative design process. Four years ago we worked with geo-physicists at Princeton University on a pre-Rising Currents research project sponsored by the Latrobe Prize. Called On The Water/Palisades Bay, it was led by Guy Nordenson and Associates. What would happen if you put islands at the tip of Lower Manhattan? What would be the effects of storm surge? The model was so complicated that the program kept crashing. Today, it wouldn't. As computing power increases, so does the ability to model processes not once or twice, but iteratively. If you can run these sophisticated programs again and again, they produce results that you may not have expected. Similarly, five

years ago, you'd only run a building energy model once or twice because of the complexity of information, but today you can repeat iterations that lead to surprising discoveries and innovation. The results lie at the interface of so many variables that they are not always intuitive.

MJ/MS: Are there any specialists, consultants, or disciplinary fields that you find indispensible to the way you work to achieve innovative results?
SC: We don't look to any one specific field but try to choreograph an array of different specialists. We look for the person with deep knowledge in a narrow band. Who is that soil scientist who can tell you what species will thrive in a wet city; that molecular biologist who understands toxins in run-off water; that electrical engineer who can calculate the amount of energy generated by processes that will affect your design? We look for consultants beyond the traditional realm that our discipline usually engages. To loop back to question two, part of the puzzle is knowing the terminology. You must have the right words to ask the right questions when engaging such a broad range of disciplines.

David Catling

The Terraforming of Ascension Island

For over three hundred years after its discovery in 1501, Ascension Island, which lies in the mid-Atlantic Ocean, remained arid and barren with little greenery. In the nineteenth century, people settled on this remote spot. They soon began an experiment that resulted in a luxuriant mosaic of temperate and tropical vegetation on the island's highest peak, Green Mountain, which rises some 859 meters (2817 feet) above sea level. Today, this artificial ecosystem towers above dry lowlands that serve as enduring reminders of Ascension's pre-settlement past. The man who formulated the plan to turn one of the most desolate islands in the world into a lush landscape was Sir Joseph Hooker, Charles Darwin's closest friend and the premier botanist of the Victorian era. How did he bring such a transformation about? Ascension Island is geographically isolated. Its tiny landmass, about thirteen-and-a-half kilometers long by eight kilometers wide, lies just south of the equator (7°57'S, 14°22'W), 2200 km to the east of Brazil, and 3200 km west of Angola. The island of St. Helena sits some 1200 km to the southeast.

Ascension was originally uninhabited and considered by early sailors as little more than an inhospitable heap of cinder cones. The remarks of Peter Mundy, a Cornish merchant who passed through the island in 1634, are fairly typical: "there is not so much as fresh water upon it, very bare, and nothing to be had there."[1] Eventually, mariners realized that Ascension was a nesting site for green turtles, which became a regular source of food for travelers on their way to the East Indies in the 1700s and 1800s. Today, much of the coastal landscape remains barren and covered in rubbly lava flows. Traversing volcanic fragments, or "clinker," is like walking on broken porcelain. For early visitors used to greener landscapes, Ascension's clinker, volcanic ash, and reddish hues must have evoked another planet. Indeed, Ascension's surface has been likened to Mars. Despite the surrounding ocean, most of the island is a parched desert under a relentless tropical sun.

The stark quality of Ascension results from its young geological age and sparse rainfall. The island emerged from the ocean one million years ago and represents the tip of an undersea volcano growing on a hot spot on the western flank of the mid-Atlantic ridge.[2] Some pristine, unweathered lavas suggest that volcanism may have occurred within the last 1000 years.[3] Because of the island's geological youth, few plants or animals have had time to arrive on wind or ocean currents and evolve into new species. When sailors first visited, the only obvious traces of greenery were grass and small ferns on the windward side of Green Mountain, where a little moisture had gathered. In pre-human times, the total number of plant species was probably around twenty five to thirty, of which ten were endemic: two grasses, two shrubs, and six ferns.[4] Today's verdant foliage on Green Mountain of 200-300 species is overwhelmingly artificial.[5]

The arrival of people altered the landscape in planned and unplanned ways. The Portuguese discoverers of Ascension Island introduced goats that ran wild, fed off the scant vegetation, and victualed their ships. But even greater changes came with British settlement in 1815. It was in that year that Napoleon Bonaparte was imprisoned on St. Helena after his defeat at Waterloo. Given Napoleon's previous escape from the Mediterranean island of Elba, the British thought it prudent to establish a garrison on Ascension in case his friends tried to stage another comeback. A permanent settlement meant solving the problem of a lack of drinking water and fresh vegetables.

The greening of a mountain

Although various early travelers described an island largely void of vegetation, Green Mountain was never a blank canvas. On a repeat visit in 1656, Peter Mundy noted that "the tops of the high mountains in the middle appeared somewhat green, there being a kind of rushes and spicy [spiky] grass." In a limited survey in 1698, James Cuninghame described five plant species.[6]

Fresh water was also discovered. In 1701, HMS Roebuck sank in Clarence Bay.[7] Its captain was the circumnavigator and privateer, William Dampier. According to contemporary accounts, the shipwrecked crew found a spring by following goats up Green Mountain.[8] "Dampier's Drip" was the name given erroneously to a spring on the northeast side of Green Mountain. Dampier described "continual fogs" near his spring, but he was alluding to an area facing southeast. Mist is typical in Breakneck Valley, which has a spring and a side facing southeasterly winds. Breakneck is therefore believed to be the actual location of Dampier's spring. In the nineteenth century, a concrete water catchment was built there and greenery was added.

Peter Osbeck, a Swedish clergyman who visited the island in 1752, claimed that Ascension "would be more tolerable if there were only some trees,"[9] an idea that later galvanized Hooker. Osbeck reported scrawny goats feeding on endemic Ascension Spurge and identified the same plants as Cuninghame had. Later, in 1775, Georg Forster, sailing on Captain Cook's Resolution, saw goats eating purslane, ferns, and grass on Green Mountain. Forster was the first person to suggest reshaping the landscape:[10] "I am almost persuaded that with a little trouble, Ascension might shortly be made fit for the residence of men. The introduction of furze...and other plants which thrive best in a parched soil, and are not likely to be attacked by rats or goats, would soon have the same effect as at St. Helena. The moisture attracted from the atmosphere by the high mountains...would then no longer be evaporated by the violent action of the sun, but collect into rivulets, and gradually supply the whole island...grasses would everywhere cover the surface of the ground, and annually increase the stratum of mould, till it could be planted with more useful vegetables."[11]

The British marines that arrived in 1815 established a garden on Green Mountain by planting imported plants on a plateau of cultivable soil at an altitude of about 600 meters (2000 feet). Only a thin veneer of soil sitting on lava or pumice existed above this height. However, from 1817 on, the Green Mountain Farm spread from this garden and was able to supply the island's population with fruit and vegetables.

Visiting in 1836, Darwin admired "the active industry" on Green Mountain where "the English nation would have thought of making the island of Ascension a productive spot."[12] But he also lamented that the island was "destitute of trees." At the time, the pervasive view, supported by Darwin, was that "unproductive" land in the British Empire should be transformed to support people.[13]

Not long after Darwin's visit, Joseph Hooker instigated a wholesale alteration of Green Mountain at the invitation of the British Admiralty. Hooker was well versed in Darwin's journal, having slept with the journal proofs under his pillow before his own travels.[14] After Hooker went to Ascension in 1843, he, like Darwin, was struck by its difference from St. Helena, where the governor, Alexander Beatson, had promoted reforestation. Hooker's advice to the navy involved a four-point strategy: establishing trees on Green Mountain to increase rainfall; clothing steep slopes with vegetation to protect soil; planting dry-adapted shrubs in lowlands; and introducing a wide variety of crops. From 1847 through 1850, Kew Gardens dispatched 330 plants to Ascension, "mostly trees and shrubs calculated to bear exposure to the sea-breezes and the most powerful winds, and the success of these has been beyond all expectation, affording shelter and protection where none could have been obtained before."[15] Further consignments of seeds and plants from London and the Botanical Gardens at Cape Town continued in the following decades. In fact, about 5000 trees were planted in the 1860s and 70s.[16]

The effect was striking. When Joseph Hooker visited, there was only one tree on Ascension.[17] By 1865, "there were thickets of upwards of forty kinds of trees, besides numerous shrubs and fruit-trees."[18] Many exotics, such as orange trees, however, failed in the long run, and only the fit survived, leaving a potpourri of plants from all over the world.

The extent to which the new vegetation caused an increase in rainfall cannot be quantified because we lack suitable "before and after" rainfall records. Curiously, there are anecdotal reports of greater precipitation before Hooker's scheme, when cultivation first began. As reported by Caroline Power, who visited in 1834, "in the last three years a considerable change in the climate has been perceived. For months together, I have been told by several who have been resident from 3 to 7 years, as well as by Captain Bate, not a cloud would pass over the heavens, nor a drop of water fall; but since the land on the mountain has been so much cultivated, a gradual increase of rain has taken place–seldom more than a day passes over now without a shower or mist on the mountain; and during the first ten days we were here constant little showers fell." Despite our uncertainty about long-term rainfall trends, today's vegetation above 600 meters clearly prevents direct run-off of moisture on wet days.

The modern flora of Green Mountain is divided among three zones. A dry zone below 330 meters has patches of grass, dry-adapted shrubs, and small thorny mesquite or tree tobacco (*Nicotiana*). From 330-630 meters, coverage, including grasses, prickly pears, and trees such as juniper, she-oak (*Causarina*), and acacia, becomes fuller. Above 660 meters, the zone is misty, completely vegetated, and includes areas of dense trees and bushes interspersed with some grassy slopes. The plant varieties include banana, ginger, juniper, raspberry, coffee, ferns, fig trees, Cape Yews, and Norfolk Island pines. At the summit lies Dew Pond, the only open body of fresh water on Ascension, replete with blue water lilies. Sheltered by tall bamboo, the pond is remarkably still, wet, and cool–seemingly a world away from the oppressive heat of the lowlands.

Terraforming, aesthetics, and the conservation of endemic species

"Terraformed" Green Mountain is an environmentalist's quandary. On the one hand, it has great aesthetic charm. It is also typically 7°C cooler than are the lowlands, and thus provides an escape to the countryside for tourists and residents. In 1926, A. C. H. Rice extolled its virtues: "Here lovely walks wind round the heights...How glorious is the heavenly air up here! How cool and clean after the dusty dried-up lava pandemonium below!"[19] On the other hand, the introduction of alien species has endangered endemic plants. Before people arrived, the island's ecology was in early development; the possibility of studying such a stage of evolution, however, is now lost. Tension therefore exists between remaking the landscape for people and conserving native species.

"Terraforming" once served the vital purpose of supplying fresh water and food to Ascension's population, but it does not do so any longer. Fresh water now comes from desalination plants, while the farm has ceased operations since the 1990s. Food is imported by sea or air. The current greenness of Green Mountain now serves other purposes; declared a national park in 2005, it is a recreational area and a natural habitat–in climatic terms–for conserving native plants and animals.

Hooker came to regret that he had ignored the impact on native species: "The consequences to the native vegetation of the peak will, I fear, be fatal, and especially to the rich carpet of ferns that clothed the top of the mountain when I visited it."[20] Out of the ten endemic species, three are extinct. In more recent years, non-native plants, such as a thorny Mexican mesquite, have even spread in the lowlands. Mesquite was introduced as an ornamental plant in the 1960s, but gastronomically indiscriminate feral donkeys have since spread its seeds.

The consensus amongst ecologists is to try preserving endemic species in pockets of habitat and nurseries while enjoying the aesthetics of Green Mountain. The ecologist Herbert Prins argues that Ascension is a classic example of "post-modernistic nature" being "a fact of life."[20] Prins believes that while there is a duty to prevent extinction, "the answer may be found in re-locating such threatened species." This can take the form of managed plots on Green Mountain, a means similar to conservation approaches elsewhere.[21] On the other hand, Prins argues for a balance with human interests because "aesthetic concerns...give satisfaction, spirituality or delight (and even tourist revenues) to us."[22]

Does Green Mountain mean that we can green other landscapes?

Global net deforestation has averaged 5.2 million hectares (the size of Costa Rica) per year from 2000-2010.[23] The rapid creation of a functioning ecosystem on Green Mountain provides hope that one day such negative global trends can be reversed. However, any optimism must be tempered by the knowledge that Green Mountain had some especially favorable conditions for Hooker's experiment. Ascension enjoys persistent southeasterly trade winds. Mist forms when the moisture-laden air ascends Green Mountain, then cools. Today, vegetation on the summit catches the mist and drips constantly. So, a plant system like that of Green Mountain cannot be transferred to any arid location. Hooker's principles of planting trees on highlands to increase rainfall, of using vegetation to protect soils, and of planting dry-adapted shrubs in lowlands, are general enough to apply to many places in the world, however. A famous case of the link between forests and fresh water was demonstrated in the nineteenth century by forest clearance in the Tijuca Mountains next to Rio de Janeiro, which ruined the city's watershed. The Brazilian government was forced to appropriate the land and reforest.[24] Today, Tijuca is the world's largest urban forest, a beautiful escape from Rio's hustle and bustle, and a haven for species endemic to what remains of Brazil's Atlantic Forest.

There is ecological debate about the success of the strange mixture of species that co-exists on Green Mountain. Some collections of plants may be considered transplanted assemblages that co-evolved elsewhere,[25] but other species may have bucked the standard theory that complexity emerges only through co-evolution. As an alternative to ecological fitting, some species accord with the local ecology by chance and establish a colony despite a lack of co-evolutionary history.[26]

Irrespective of disputes in biology, the success of Green Mountain's ecosystem must give some insight into transforming environments elsewhere. The positive lesson here is that further study of Green Mountain might help inform strategies to green certain deserts or other barren locations in the world. The caveat is that we must be mindful of physical constraints, such as meteorology, as well as the need to conserve endemic flora or fauna that may otherwise vanish.

Notes:

1. *The Travels of Peter Mundy, in Europe and Asia, 1608-1667,* ed. Richard Carnac Temple (London: Hakluyt Society, 1905).
2. Dennis L. Nielson and Bruce Sibbett, "Geology of Ascension Island, South Atlantic Ocean," *Geothermics* 25 (1996): 427-448.
3. J. E. Packer, *A Concise Guide to Ascension Island, South Atlantic* (Ascension Island: Ascension Island Heritage Society, 2002).
4. A. Gray, T. Pelembe, and S. Stroud, "The Conservation of the Endemic Vascular Flora of Ascension Island and Threats from Alien Species," *Oryx* 39 (2005): 449-453.
5. Philip Ashmole and Myrtle Ashmole, *St Helena and Ascension Island: A Natural History* (Oswestry, Shropshire: A. Nelson, 2000).
6. James Cuninghame, "A Catalogue of Shells, etc. Gathered at the Island of Ascension," *Phil. Transactions of the Royal Society* 21 (1699): 295-300.
7. M. McCarthy, *His Majesty's Ship Roebuck (1690-1701)* (Western Australia Maritime Museum, 2002).
8. Bruce S. Ingram, *Three Sea Journals of Stuart Times* (London: Constable and Co., 1936)
9. Peter Osbeck, *A Voyage to China and the East Indies*, vol. 2 (London: Benjamin White, 1771).
10. George Forster, *A Voyage Round the World*, vol. 2 (London: Benjamin White, 1777).
11. H. R. Brandreth and Caroline Power, "Communications on the Island of Ascension," *Journal of the Royal Geographic Society London* 5 (1835): 243-262.
12. Charles Darwin, *The Voyage of the Beagle* (London: John Murray, 1839).
13. Richard H. Drayton, *Nature's Government: Science, Imperial Britain, and the "Improvement" of the World* (New Haven: Yale University Press, 2000).
14. Joseph D. Hooker, "Reminiscences on Darwin," *Nature* 60 (1899): 187-188.
15. Eric Duffey, "The Terrestrial Ecology of Ascension Island," *Journal of Applied Ecology* 1 (1964): 219-251.
16. William Hooker, "Popular Guide to the Royal Botanic Gardens of Kew," *The Quarterly Review* 90 (1851): 34-62.
17. John C. Brown, *Forests and Moisture: Or Effects of Forests on Humidity of Climate* (Edinburgh: Oliver and Boyd, 1877).
18. Wendy Fairhurst, *Flowering Plants of Ascension Island* (Higham Press, 2004).
19. A. C. H. Rice, "A Day in HMS Ascension Island," *Spectator* 137 (1926): 273.
20. Joseph Hooker, *Indian, Moroccan and Syrian Journals,* National Archives, Royal Botanic Gardens, Kew, 1839-1911.
21. H. H. T. Prins, "Global Concepts for the Restoration of Nature Applied for Africa: Is the Restoration of the Dry and Humid African Savanna a Dream or a Possibility?" in *Ecological Restoration of African Savanna Ecosystems. Proceedings of the Third RNSCC International Seminar,* eds. T.B. Mayaka, H. De Iongh and B. Sinsin (Leiden: Leiden University. 2007), 7-19.
22. M. E. Dulloo, S. R. Kell, and Jones, "Impact and Control of Invasive Alien Species on Small Islands," *International Forestry Review* 4 (2002): 277-285.
23. Food and Agricultural Organization, *Global Forest Resources Assessment 2010* (FAO, United Nations, 2010). CDRom
24. Warren Dean, *With Broadax and Firebrand: The Destruction of the Brazilian Atlantic Forest* (Berkeley/Los Angeles: University of California Press, 1995).
25. Alan Gray, "The Parable of Green Mountain: Massaging the Message," *Journal of Biogeography* 31 (2004): 1549-1550.
26. David Wilkinson, "The Parable of Green Mountain: Ascension Island, Ecosystem Construction and Ecological Fitting," *Journal of Biogeography* 31 (2004): 1-4.

AUDC / Robert Sumrell + Kazys Varnelis

Another Green World

Sustainability is another way of looking at economics. Both disciplines focus on the way in which scarce resources are allocated. For economics, the problem is adjusting the system through which things are distributed. For sustainability, the problem is determining which things within the system can be allowed to disappear in order to make more valuable resources last.

By the 1960s, modernity had advanced across the Earth. In so doing, however, it had progressed to the point that it was clear to many that the planet's resources were in danger of being permanently contaminated and exhausted. In 1962, Rachel Carson's *Silent Spring* gave rise to widespread awareness of the toxicity of modern substances and the damage that these were doing to the environment, while in 1968, Paul Ehrlich's *Population Bomb* predicted impending mass starvation. Even if there was no clear agreement on the extent of the damage, the modern environmental movement concluded that disaster was imminent. The movement coalesced around the image of the Earth taken from outer space in 1968 by astronaut William Anders aboard Apollo 8. Intended as a record of the crowning glory of modernity's progress, the photograph was soon understood as cautionary. Seeing how small and fragile the Earth looked from a car-sized capsule drifting in space, individuals worldwide came to understand that their own plight was little different. "Spaceship Earth," as Buckminster Fuller called it, was revealed to be a small, isolated environment, vulnerable and limited.

Although futurists hoped that the planet's limits could be transcended either through vast space habitats or terraforming in outer space, cutbacks to NASA's budget and the agency's floundering after the end of the Apollo program revealed such hopes to be naïve. The 1970s were marked by the end of modernity and widespread pessimism regarding the future, best embodied perhaps in a series of science fiction movies starring Charlton Heston –*Soylent Green*, *The Planet of the Apes*, and *The Omega Man*– which depicted the world after it had fallen victim to environmental devastation. These suggested that far from delivering us a Utopian future, modern science and industry were leading us to destroy our surroundings.

Architecture had two responses. The first, more familiar but ultimately less influential, was a nihilistic postmodernism that celebrated the death of modernity by montaging classical symbols with modernist forms and leaving both ruptured. The second was a frank response to the situation, which addressed an increasingly toxic urban environment by replicating NASA's self-enclosed space capsules and creating sealed, conditioned environments that could exist anywhere. Unlike space capsules, however, these were green interiors, home to new, post-sustainable landscapes filled with living plants that made them seem more natural. Offices became refigured as office landscapes, bars became fern bars, and homes became colonized by spider plants, ferns, philodendrons, and avocado trees.

Green interiors have a long history, however, and first emerged in Early Modern Europe when plants intended for ornamentation rather than cooking or medicinal purposes began invading the home. In 1608, the year of his death, Hugh Plat published *Floraes Paradise*, an early manual on gardening that included a section on plants for the home and recommended the introduction of flowers.[1] As Platt concluded, "I hold it a most delicate and pleasing thing to have a faire gallery, great chamber or other lodging, that openeth fully upon the East or West sun, to be inwardly gardished with sweet hearbs and flowers, yea & fruit if it were possible."[2] Plants kept solely for their beauty, it was thought, brought happiness to households, creating visual relief from the emerging industrial city. As useless objects, ornamental houseplants also appealed to the aesthetic sense of the time, which dictated that only objects without utility could be fully appreciated for their formal perfection and serve as objects of the highest levels of contemplation.[3] To say that these plants were mere ornament, however, would be to miss the point; many early flowering houseplants were expressly intended to improve indoor air quality by providing scents that masked bad odors.

By the mid-seventeenth century, the rise of global trade spurred a fashion for growing citrus and other frost-fearing plants in northern climates, such as Holland, England, and France. Orangeries were developed to sustain these plants and soon became a status symbol among the upper classes, which used them to display flora that they commanded be brought to them from across the globe. Early orangeries were freestanding structures, situated in formal gardens rather than besides houses, machines for sustaining plant life rather than spaces of human habitation. Only a hundred years later did glass-enclosed spaces become integrated into homes.

As the modern metropolis matured, houseplants became ubiquitous, softening the hard lines of the architecture of the day and bringing nature into the harsh, man-made environment. Still, their beneficial qualities were far from clear. Although Joseph Priestly, the discoverer of oxygen, stated that "every individual plant is serviceable to mankind...[each] cleanses out atmosphere. In this the fragrant rose and the deadly nightshade co-operate," dissenters argued that gases given off by plants might be hazardous. Jane Loudon, a writer of early science fiction and popular horticultural texts, wrote that "in the darkness of night...leaves give out carbonic acid gas...and a superabundance of this gas produces stupor, head-aches, and a sense of suffocation in those that breathe it..." Newspaper stories blamed plants kept in the bedroom for otherwise unaccountable deaths at night.[4]

In the end, the advocates won and houseplants grew wildly popular throughout the nineteenth century. Houseplant lovers were particularly attracted to ferns, with their feminine, delicate appearance, and seemingly miraculous means of reproduction. Restrained and less flashy than the typical flowering houseplants popular at the time, they were viewed as a mark of intelligence and refinement. Although growing and transporting exotic ferns were not easy, the development of the Wardian Case or terrarium greatly enhanced their cultivation. Nathaniel Bagshaw Ward found that when enclosed in glass environments, ferns reproduced easily–something that had previously been difficult to achieve–and could live much longer. He concluded that his cases were successful because they sheltered plants from exposure to harmful, airborne pollutants produced by the factories surrounding his home in the East End of London.[5]

By this point, members of the upper and middle classes had begun adding conservatories to their homes. Smaller conservatories, attached to drawing rooms, were considered spaces for women, while larger ones, which required staff and significant expenditures for maintenance, were considered to be ideal sites for parties thrown by the wealthy. In some cases, guests were encouraged to seek their own desserts from fruit-bearing trees and the vines growing around them.[6]

Naturalizing interiors with plants helped attenuate the rising moral conflict between the increased sensuality made possible by expanded leisure time and the moral pursuit of self-moderation. Sensual but natural, plants were made by God and therefore inherently moral. Caring for plants was an act of faith and devotion, a form of communion with God and nature. In this vein, nineteenth-century designers and theorists, notably Owen Jones, John Ruskin, William Morris, and A. W. N. Pugin grounded their ethics of design in natural and vegetal forms. The most advanced interiors of the day were soon outfitted with wallpaper and fabric that bore motifs based on plants, a movement that finally lost its bearings with the jungle-like proliferation of leaves and vines of Art Nouveau.

In the years after World War I, houseplants and ferns became fatally associated with Victorian stuffiness and Art Nouveau's moral hysteria. Compounding matters, modern central heating systems made it difficult to raise many plants as it suffocated them with its dry heat. In the postwar era of restraint, private conservatories also fell victim to cost-cutting measures.[7] Between modernism, a neo-Georgian revival, and the Depression, clutter disappeared from homes; plants went with it, not returning en masse until Scandinavian and Californian modernism brought them back in vogue in the 1950s. During their exile from the home, plants were relegated largely to restaurants, bars, and cafes.[8]

Green interiors in spaces of hospitality emerged in the late nineteenth century when hotel owners sought to associate their establishments with upper-class life by serving food and drinks in glass-enclosed areas reminiscent of orangeries. The association remained, presumably enhanced by the relief that the feminine forms of potted palms and ferns provided to the heavy, masculine food of the time. Some kinds of potted palms–one of the few types of plants that do not die from central heat–have been common in eating establishments ever since, cementing the idea that a meal out is a getaway from the harsh realities of urban life.

In the 1930s, a new understanding of the relation between interior and natural landscape was created by Clifford Clinton, the developer of Clifton's Cafeteria in Los Angeles, which proclaimed itself to be the largest public cafeteria in the world.[9] Clifford's business plan centered on establishing a local chain of cafeterias that would charge low prices but attract a large clientele. By 1939, however, facing stiff competition and wishing to distinguish his establishments from cafeterias with an institutional affiliation, such as soup kitchens or the YMCA, Clinton turned to creating themed destinations.

To counteract the monotony of the large volume of seating inside his cafeterias, Clinton created interior landscapes, poaching from the tradition of green interiors, Hollywood set designs, and dioramas in museums and traveling exhibitions. He re-branded his first cafeteria as Clifton's Pacific Seas, an exotic tropical escape, and his second venue–still extant–as Clifton's Brookdale, reproducing a rustic vacation retreat built in 1922 to great acclaim by architect and landscaper Horace Cotton in the Santa Cruz mountains on a plot of land directly over a natural rock terrace and incorporating a stream running through the property as part of the interior.[10]

Clinton's cafeterias were not mere visual spectacles; they were immersive environments meant to remove individuals from the problems of the outside world. Both restaurants offered a therapeutic experience that replicated the benefits of the natural world within the abstraction of the urban environment while masking the industrial production of meals as part of a stage set. At the Pacific Seas, rain fell over thatched huts in which guests dined. At Brookdale, a waterfall cascaded down a twenty-foot rock-wall landscape constructed by Francois Scotti, while geysers routinely shot milkshakes into the air and customers filled their cups from a stream filled with lime soda. Both restaurants featured areas with religious themes and encouraged the singing of hymns and spirituals along with the waiters. A deeply religious man, Clinton saw his restaurants as both a calling and a form of missionary work. Refusing to turn anyone away, he allowed patrons to pay what they wished for the food.[11] To accomplish this, Clinton turned to modern technology, engineering food as well as the environment. By introducing Vita-Meal, a low cost, engineered soy-based meal product to the cafeteria menu expressly for those unable to pay for their meals, he hoped to use technology to end world hunger, showing that a more miraculous and bountiful idea of nature could be created than that of the natural world itself.[12] Under Clinton, the difficulties of urban life were best solved by technology that could simulate the natural world but overcome its limits.

As the Depression continued and the United States entered the Second World War, themed restaurants such as the Clifton's cafeteria chain suffered from a backlash among diners, who were growing increasingly suspicious that elaborate environments and low prices masked shortcuts in food production. Restaurant culture for the working class turned toward cleanliness and speed, as epitomized in the fast-food restaurants of the 1950s. Only "Polynesian" restaurants kept alive the idea of the theme restaurant, their lush interiors recalling the exotic locales recently visited by soldiers fighting in the Pacific theater, now refigured into family-oriented paradises filled with nubile young women and copious amounts of liquor to dull the memory of the recent war.

Restaurants for the elite kept to categories established in the late nineteenth century: hearty steak houses or French-styled cuisine. Interiors of such restaurants were either dark and clubby masculine affairs, or feminized with a "potted palm" look derived from hotel spaces and ballrooms.

After World War II and America's rise to superpower status, the country and, particularly New York–de facto center of economic and cultural power–sought to develop a fully modern culture that integrated modernism and the technological achievements of capitalism. In art, this was done through the modern but individualistic work of the Abstract Expressionists and later, but no less importantly, by the cool, corporate abstraction of Color Field Painting and Post-Painterly Abstraction. Modern architecture also played a key role in this transformation through buildings such as Lever House, Manufacturers Hanover Trust, and the United Nations Headquarters.

Still, such works of corporate modernism seemed only to underscore New York's role in business and administration. In contrast to the elegant refinement of Paris, the capital of civilization since the nineteenth century, New York seemed dirty and uncouth, congested and polluted. A new, more refined attitude toward urban life was needed to allow the city to fully take over Paris's role.

In architectural terms, Ludwig Mies van der Rohe's Seagram Building provided such a model. Clad in bronze, a carefully refined variation on a model by an immigrant European master, the Seagram established a link between modernism, taste, and luxury. Set back from the street behind a large plaza paved in pink granite, and centered on an axis with the exclusive old money enclave of McKim, Mead, and White's 1918 Racquet and Tennis Club, the Seagram aligned itself with New York's elegant past while also carving out a space of its own within the city.

From the start, however, Seagram was a model, not a showpiece. In a letter to students, Mies described his intention at Seagram as "completely opposed to the idea that a building should have an individual character..." Instead he sought "a clear structure and construction–this applies not to any one problem but to all architectural problems which I approach."[13]

But Seagram was more than a monument in the city. Its public interior space, the Four Seasons Restaurant, designed by Philip Johnson and housed on the first floor of the structure, was an innovative model for both interiors and cuisine, rethinking the role of nature in the city.[14]

The Four Seasons filled an unrented, commercial space on the ground floor of the building. It was proposed and developed by Joe Baum and Jerry Brody's Restaurant Associates, a company that had swiftly built a reputation in flamboyant haute cuisine, having had previous successes with the Newarker, located next to Newark Airport and notable for its flambé dishes, as well as the Forum of the Twelve Caesars, a Roman-themed restaurant in Rockefeller Center.[15] Thinking that a restaurant in a modern, sophisticated building might be successful, Baum and Brody convinced the Bronfman family that such an establishment would be ideal for the unprogrammed space inside the Seagram. In contrast to the firm's previous restaurants, however, the new restaurant had to enhance the character of the building instead of existing as a self-contained interior.

Following Mies's directions for the Seagram, Baum understood that the restaurant needed to aim for, as he put it, "fan-enduring style instead of contemporary fashion." However, impressed by the Japanese idea of change, he decided that it should focus on the seasons. At the Four Seasons, as he would soon call it, Baum found an affinity between the timeless change of the seasons in nature and those of city life, such as the theater and social seasons. Moreover, Baum felt that New York City's role as a transportation center would allow the restaurant to draw on a network of fresh produce, and that he could use this to emphasize the concept behind the restaurant. Anticipating Alice Waters and the slow food movement, the Four Seasons produced menus that synchronized with the seasons and intended to highlight the flavors of foods that reach their peaks within them.[16]

Like Clifton's, the Four Seasons did not merely scatter plants among diners; it was landscaped. The interior, designed by architect Philip Johnson, lighting designer Richard Kelly, interior decorator Bill Pahlman, and artist Richard Lippold, was serenely elegant and complemented by landscape architect Karl Linn's plantings. Linn was raised on a farm founded by his mother in order to train mental health professionals in "horticultural therapy." Although he had studied and practiced as a therapist, he had returned to landscape in hopes of promoting its healing power on the individual.[17]

In the Pool Room, Linn introduced trees that would be maintained and swapped at the start of each season by Everett Conklin & Co., a pioneering interior landscape firm and nursery based in New Jersey. Since the restaurant received little natural light, Linn and Dr. O. Wesley Davidson, a plant physiologist, worked with Kelly, the lighting consultant, to develop a system that would allow the trees to survive. If, along with the menu, the landscape was intended to mimic the four seasons, the lighting scheme was artificial and the lights were turned on high from sunrise until the time the restaurant opened. Temperatures were lowered by eight degrees at night to inhibit excess growth.[18]

But even as the Four Seasons and the Seagram Building rose in prominence, they could not save Manhattan. The glamorous world of urbanity was being undone by the naturalistic temptations of suburbanism. Art and elegance, which were in any event isolated and fleeting phenomena in New York, would be replaced by the casual life of the suburban backyard and country club. In financial crisis by the late 1960s, the city came undone amidst riots and rampant fires. The Four Seasons was in trouble as well, its exclusive nature out of touch with a more casual era. Cost-cutting measures led the management to stop changing the trees and other accessories with the seasons.[19] Nor was architecture immune as modernism became associated with the rigid and inflexible management practices of Fordist business.

Within a few years of completing the Four Seasons, Linn became disgusted with the use of landscape to signify wealth. Rejecting both urban and suburban elitism, he founded the Neighborhood Renewal Corps and devoted himself to helping the urban poor by turning blighted, abandoned sites into community gardens that he understood as "neighborhood commons."[20]

A new relationship for architecture, interior landscapes, and the workplace was offered by the Quickborner Team, a German group that proposed that offices should be restructured along management models based on communication and organizational theory. In their view, the Fordist office and its Modernist expression were too rigid and impeded efficient communication. Instead, they promoted cybernetic ecosystems based on extensive interviews on the flow of office communication with office staff. They called these ecosystems *bürolandschaften* or office landscapes, and actively sought to introduce plants to provide visual relief.

The advocates of office landscapes sought flat organizational structures that promoted communication among employees without fear. They advocated against windows in the office since these were highly sought and, in their view, created privilege and hierarchy, ruining the very principle of the flat organizational structure that Quickborner was trying to put into play.

Office landscapes were freely reconfigurable based on the needs of the office and thus promised constant change and the feeling that both employees and corporation were being catered to. Plants contributed an idea of freedom and individuality to the work environment, encouraging employees to see themselves working communally for a common good rather than as individuals in a hierarchical system.

But office landscape was primarily suburban. Its demands for large floor plates could be accommodated by few extant buildings and even fewer sites in densely packed cities. Seeking to build such offices and driven away by the decline of the urban environment in New York City and elsewhere, many corporations began decamping to office parks outside the city in the 1960s.

Commissioned to design the headquarters of the Ford Foundation, the largest philanthropic organization in the world, Kevin Roche/John Dinkeloo Associates set out to create a structure that, like Seagram, would not be a mere luxurious showpiece, but a model for future office buildings in the city, and one that the directors hoped would impact the quality of life inside it.[21]

Like the Quickborner Team, Roche started by interviewing Ford Foundation employees. He learned that instead of working in teams, they liked to work in isolation. Moreover, he discovered that they did not understand the work of the foundation as a whole or what their roles contributed to the company.[22] In response, Roche created a building that allowed individuals to work by themselves and congregate in a communal space, much as the residents of New York do around Central Park.

The Ford Foundation is staged around a large, enclosed interior landscape on the ground level, a reinterpretation of the idea of the commons. Nearly all employees are provided with equally sized offices and similar views of the courtyard. The building offers visual relief to the office-bound individual while allowing a view into every office from the ground floor. Thus, while employees can be isolated and have a degree of privacy that they can enhance by drawing the blinds, they also hold responsibility towards the group. The garden is open to the public as well, a gesture meant to undo the separation between employees and the city. The plants and trees are not installed to fill empty space, but are designed to ensure empty space from the start, offsetting the density of the rest of the building. However, because it initially lacked seating, the garden discouraged individuals from lingering.

At installation, the terraced atrium garden at the Ford Foundation was the world's largest indoor garden. Designed by landscape architect Dan Kiley, it included both temperate and tropical plants (including 20-ft.-tall magnolias) covering almost a third of an acre of space on the ground floor and along three upper floor terraces.[23] Like the Four Seasons, the Ford Foundation gardens were installed and maintained by Conklin & Co. Noting that "[t]here seems to be a general misconception that an indoor plant should last forever,"[24] Conklin developed techniques for improving the chances of indoor plants'survival by acclimating trees and plants meant for interior installations to lower levels of light before installation. Ten years after the installation of the gardens at the Ford Foundation, Conklin observed that "three-fourths of the magnolias are living, so are all of the camellias...The three *Cryptomeria japonica* planted in the highest light intensity in the gardens gradually died within 18 months. So did *Pachysandra teminalis*. Why? Nobody can give the scientific answers. I repeat, much research is needed."[25] Conklin later used the publicity garnered by the success of the Ford Foundation to expand his nursery business and launch a public campaign to educate designers on the specifics of interior landscaping and the concept of the office landscape, advocating the development of even larger inward-facing suburban corporate structures and climate-controlled urban environments, such as malls, hotels, and corporate centers, in order to alleviate the urban din.

Nurseries similar to Conklin's grew throughout the 1970s, feeding the revival of houseplants that seemed to proliferate everywhere. All this came to symbolize a relief from the anonymity of mass-produced life and offered an "environmental" counterpoint to the artificial atmospheres provided by modern HVAC.

Like the space capsules of the Apollo program, sealed interior gardens promised an escape from the wasteland of the city towards either a suburban world of self-contained corporate parks or an urban renaissance, in which people were ever more divorced from the urban condition. Green interiors thus served as a transition to completely sealed interior environments. The novelty of working among plants waned again in the 1980s as the introduction of personal computers and online messaging boards promised a radical new form of community that was not based on proximity, personal interactions, or shared space. Once again office life shrank to the space of a desktop, where monotony could be successfully alleviated with potted desk plants and an occasional window box. The remnants of atrium gardens and lobby plantings remind us of a time when there existed an exteriority to Modernism and a need to interact as a group–a romantic notion of pre-industrial life and a pastoral provided by some higher agency looking over us. But green interiors were more than an alibi; like our own bodies, they were always intended to fail. Their inability to sustain themselves means that we must take care of them, which provides us with a memory of our relationship to the natural world. Without a system in place to encourage propagation and free growth, all but the hardiest of plants have to be regularly replaced, either with newer versions of the same species or with artificial simulations that no longer require care. In this, they reflect our own lives as astronauts aboard Spaceship Earth, traveling the cosmos in a sealed environment as our systems slowly and inevitably fail. Locked indoors, sitting at the computer, we occupy ourselves sustaining the system while putting off the inevitable day of reckoning.

Notes:

1. Catherine Horwood, *Potted History: The Story of Plants in the Home* (London: Francis Lincoln, 2007), 11.
2. Hugh Platt, *Floraes paradise beautified and adorned with sundry sorts of delicate fruites and flovvers, by the industrious labour of H.P. Knight: with an offer of an English antidote, (being a present, easie, and pleasing remedy in violent feavers, and intermittingagues) as also of some other rare inventions, fitting the times* [London 1608], Early English Books Online, retrieved on 7/19/15 from: http://gateway.proquest.com/openurl?ctx_ver=Z39.88-2003&res_id=xri:eebo&rft_id=xri:eebo:citation:99855991, 31.
3. M. H. Abrams, *Doing Things With Texts: Essays in Criticism and Critical Theory* (New York: W. W. Norton, 1989), 135-187.
4. Horwood, *Potted History*, 104
5. Sarah Whittingham, *The Story of Pteridomania* (London: Francis Lincoln Limited, 2012).
6. John Hix, *The Glass House* (Cambridge: The MIT Press, 1974), 87
7. Hix, *Glass House*, 94.
8. Harwood, *Potted History*, 156.
9. Clinton combined his first and last names to create the Clifton's Cafeteria brand.
10. Frederick Jennings, "Unique Lodge in Santa Cruz Mountains," *The Architect and Engineer* (August 1924): 94.
11. "Life Visits Clifton's Cafeteria: Customers at the Pacific Seas in Los Angeles Get Tropical Surroundings and Music With Low Cost Meals," *Life Magazine* (November 27, 1944):102-105.
12. Clifford E. Clinton, "Subsistence feeding," Unpublished typescript, June 1 1945, published in Soyinfo Center, *History of Meals For Millions, Soy, and Freedom From Hunger* (1946-2011): Extensively Annotated Bibliography and Sourcebook, retrieved on 7/19/15 from http://www.soyinfocenter.com/pdf/141/MFM.pdf

13. Phyllis Lambert, "Mies Immersion," in *Mies in America* (New York: Harry N. Abrams, 2001), 391.
14. John F. Mariani, *The Four Seasons: A History of America's Premier Restaurant* (Edison, NJ: Smithmark, 1999), xv.
15. Gael Greene, "Restaurant Associates: Twilight of the Gods," *New York Magazine* (November 2, 1970): 43-51
16. Mariani, *The Four Seasons*, 20-28.
17. Margalit Fox, "Karl Linn, Architect of Urban Landscapes Dies at 81," *The New York Times* (February 13, 2005), retrieved on 7/19/15 from: http://www.nytimes.com/2005/02/13/arts/design/12linn.html
18. Mariani, *The Four Seasons*, 33-34.
19. Mariani, *The Four Seasons*, 85.
20. Marilyn Berlin Snell, "Down-to Earth Visionary: Karl Linn Cultivates Community in his Urban Gardens," *Sierra Magazine* (May/June 2001), retrieved on 7/19/15 from http://www.sierraclub.org/sierra/200105/profile_printable.asp.
21. Verne S. Atwater and Evelyn C. Walsh, *A Memoir of the Ford Foundation: The Early Years, 1936-1968* (New York: Vantage Press, 2012), 169, 171-172.
22. Mason Currey, "Rediscovered Masterpiece: The Ford Foundation," *Metropolis* 28/5 (December 2008), 95, and Olga Panelidou "Designing for The Workflow," in *Kevin Roche: Architecture as Environment*, ed. Eeva-Liisa Pelkonen (New Haven: Yale University Press, 2011), 103.
23. Everett Lawson Conklin, "Interior Landscaping," *Journal of Arboriculture* 4/4 (April 1978): 77.
24. Conklin, "Interior Landscaping," 77.
25. Conklin, "Interior Landscaping," 77-79, and Everett Lawson Conklin, U.S. Dept. of Agriculture, "Tips on Interior Landscaping,"in *Yearbook, United States Department of Agriculture* (1974), 232.

Natalie Jeremijenko

Interview

M. Joachim/M. Silver: Ok, we are going to get right to the interview. Let's talk about your Salamander project.
Natalie Jermanjenko: The Salamander Super Highway was set up in Socrates Sculpture Park in Queens, New York. This park was part of the Civic Action Exhibition, a show of urban plans that invited four teams to participate. So, the Salamander Super Highway facilitated safe passage for salamanders. I think it is important to understand that salamanders are a vital part of the ecosystem there and fascinating for me because I come from Australia where there are no salamanders.

MJ/MS: Is it too hot for them?
NJ: No it's too dry. Anyway, what I learned is that if you weighed the salamanders in a single ecosystem their biomass would be twice that of their mammal neighbors, including all the deer, and mice, and squirrels, and coyotes, etc. That's a huge amount of flesh!

MJ/MS: Right.
NJ: Literally, they have a monopoly on the limb-regeneration business. Existing predators like migrating birds eat their tails, which eventually grow back. This is a really important adaptation. It gives the salamanders the ability to regenerate parts of their bodies and produce a renewable food source for other creatures that don't kill them. This is nature's way of feeding other animals. It's a sustainable meat product.

MJ/MS: Like the three-hundred-twenty-thousand-dollar burger that was just reported in the news?
NJ: Yes, but instead of building a better burger in the lab you just have to harvest these tails as if you were milking cows.

MJ/MS: Do salamander tails taste good?
NJ: You mean salamander cocktails? I have actually served them to my audience and they are delicious–incredibly delicious, in fact. Anyway, I'm suggesting the possibility of setting up a sustainable business. In terms of total embodied energy, harvesting salamander tails is much more efficient than growing meat in a lab. You can show this if you factor in the cost of production, support for staff, and the environmental degradation involved in building artificial meat-making infrastructure.

MJ/MS: Well, the point of artificial flesh is to have biomass that is victimless, so no creature is hurt or abused. But if we can get meat from the salamanders willingly, if they somehow donate their tails, then that might be truly victimless.
NJ: Well, more important than that is the need to design food and food sys-

tems that actually improve environmental health while increasing biodiversity. To do anything less would be wrong. If lab-grown meat is not sustainable it becomes unethical to produce ethical meat. So, it's very much a matter of looking for concrete examples–ways in which an ecological system can support a huge amount of production. We have it right in front of us. And that is the point of the Salamander Super Highway project. It is an early attempt to protect, channel, and enhance salamander communities as a sustainable protein source.

MJ/MS: Well, all this meat consumption is probably not so good for the human digestive system. Vegetarianism or just reducing your intake of flesh is still the best way to maintain good health and save the planet at the same time. You don't even have to construct anything. It's just a lifestyle change. Still, I understand your point. It is especially relevant for those people whose compulsions still support the need to kill. So can you describe the project in more detail?
NJ: To create a Salamander Super Highway we began with small adjustments that could make the area more habitable for these valuable organisms. Basically, we set up a micro speed bump that facilitates safe passage for the salamanders. So, when a car drives over what is essentially a long tube, a little bump in the road, it reminds us that we are not alone. On the inside of this pipe is a passive infrared sensor. Every time a salamander goes through, it sends out a little tweet saying: "Hi, honey, I'm home." A moisture-capturing and temperature-maintenance system attracts the animals, creating a kind of signage that is also legible to humans. This organism-centric design process is one way we can make sense of complex ecosystems. In New Jersey, there is actually a husband-and-wife team that goes out every season, stands on the side of a freeway to fill buckets up with salamanders. The couple then carries the animals across the road so the creatures don't get run over by passing cars. That's one way to do it. Another way is to use technology. With our tweeting interface, people can receive updates that allow them to understand what is happening in real-time and give them more information on how to design even more effective transportation systems for both wildlife and humans.

MJ/MS: Didn't you have a salamander as a pet?
NJ: Yes, several salamanders, in fact.

MJ/MS: Can you talk a little about the Amphibious Architecture project you did with David Benjamin and Chris Woebken?
NJ: For the project we devised a system that did more than just tell us that something was wrong. Instead, the Amphibious Architecture installation gave us a way to find out how to redesign or improve the surrounding ecosystem. The Amphibious Architecture project consisted of a series of dissolved oxygen sensors, mounted on glowing buoys deployed in the East River. The sensors also monitored PH, water temperature, turbidity, and other parameters that are needed to maintain good water quality for fish. But even those of us who were very immersed in science asked: what does all the data collected by eco-researchers mean to the public? How do they access it? What does it mean?

MJ/MS: So the project was in the spirit of a monumental architecture... an active civic memorial?
NJ: Yes, you know the Clean Water Act produced all these great data sets for water quality. And what do we do with them? What actually comes from that data? Well, I can tell you–not much. Our project used a series of changing color lights visible from the water's edge. The lights told the story of what's happening in the water. Through the project anyone could develop a direct intuition about the health and vitality of the river.

MJ/MS: So it's ambient information you were displaying?
NJ: Yes, It's ambient information. You could make very straightforward observations: "Oh, when the lights are blue, green, there are lots of fish... and when the lights are red, there are no fish." Right? So you could actually make the correlation yourself. In the end the best indicator of water quality, of course, is the presence of life. If there are fish in the water it's healthy, it's livable, it's habitable. It's not about going to a public database and looking up information. Instead of just passively receiving data, you can respond to the site. In addition to being able to sense the presence of fish, you can actually text them, query them, ask them, "How ya doing?"

NJ/MS: Yes, another one. The Muscle Choir, can you talk a little about that project?
NJ: Yes, well, this is actually one of the more recent things I've been working on. Mussels are an integral part of human history. There are many interesting stories about how we get Omega-3 from our diets. Omega-3 fatty acids enable cortical expansion in humans. Humans have been foraging mussels in the sea for a long time. The mussel choir is actually being built on fifteen linear feet of reconstructed shoreline in Manhattan. Mussels are also filter feeders that are sensitive to toxic waste. They can live as long as eighty years, as opposed to seventeen, the average life expectancy of an oyster. They can absorb storm sewage because they are very robust creatures. So the Mussel Choir is a collaboration with David Benjamin. Right on the water's edge of Manhattan we are working with a population of mussels–blue and red mussels–and each of these creatures has a little sensor attached to it, a little vortex sensor, so we knew when it opens and closes its shells. The project employs a commercially available sensor that can measure water quality by detecting these changes.

MJ/MJ: What do they signify?
NJ: Mussels close up when the water is bad. They will also flap around in distress if things get nasty. They have all sorts of behaviors that are related to water quality. Mussels are incredibly sensitive, particularly to zinc contamination. So we have turned the data coming from these sensors into music–which is really just a strategy for repopulating the waterfront, an inexpensive way to attract listeners that can actually hear what's going on in real time. What I would like to instantiate in the Mussel Choir is not a form of artificial intelligence, as in computer-synthesized vocalizations of SIRI, but natural intelligence. Last year in Venice, when we put the mussels-listening devices into the lagoon, they were all singing together. So the idea is that we can instantiate natural intelligence, which is not a closed computational model of the world but actually an open

structure of living biological agents that understand their environment with humans as a conscious part of the process. I'm not sure if you've seen my phenology of the East River when muscles are spawning, when eels are migrating, when blue fish are coming through. Phenological clocks have become a really useful tool for me. They work by organizing a lot of bio-processes in an easy-to-understand diagram. I'm using these clocks to fingerprint local ecosystems. The perennial flowering of plants overlaps and connects with the cycles of other biological systems, so they become a kind of icon for changing interconnections in time. The clock can also be a sensitive indicator of climate destabilization, showing when things get out of sync. This is a measurement of the temporal structure of the ecosystem on which we depend. And so, being able to have this kind of representation allows us to easily understand interactions between organisms. It can also help us organize and figure out what to do. It's interesting because we have also used the clocks as a community-organizing tool centered on the migration of glass eel swarms in the East River.

MJ/MS: Really? In the East River?
NJ: Yes, I even invited the Department of Environmental Conservation (DEC) to attend a cocktail party where we distributed these wiggling little creatures in cups of salt water. Participants at the event were asked to release their catch back into the wild. I actually drove up to Maine where they have glass eel fisheries and where you can still legally catch them to sell to China as commercially consumed yanagi.

MJ/MS: You mean sushi meat.
NJ: Yes. So the fisheries remove all this biomass from the environment. I told the DEC guys we were going to release a thousand eels as a way to replenish the East River. If you set them free in fresh water in the Upper Bronx River, they become females. If you put them back in the sea they turn male. So they can choose their gender. Actually, you can choose their gender by deciding where to deposit them. At the party we actually ingested the water that the eels were swimming in and participants could choose to release them into the wild if they wanted to. It was a big choice because the DEC resisted the idea and it became a whole civil disobedience thing. The DEC said that you cannot release fish from one body of water into another but I argued that these were migratory organisms that didn't belong exclusively to a single area.

MJ/MS: They imposed unnecessary regulations then?
NJ: The East River eels, they are the same thing... I'm actually preventing them from becoming yanagi sushi. The DEC was telling people that it was illegal to release eels into the wild. I was saying, "Come on, this ecosystem could and should support thousands of eels." And so to choose between "do I put them into the water or not" was a big deal. Remember, this is not an invasive species; this is a native species. We were replenishing an ecosystem and people were able to make their own decision to do it. Almost half of them didn't.

MJ/MS: Out of fear?
NJ: Yes; out of fear and ignorance. So the clocks are an interesting way to represent natural time, and I'd like to see them as public instruments for insti-

gating debate about the environment. The clocks could actually help produce the kind of eco-literacy that we need in the information age. We are doing a software version of the phenological clocks too. It will allow people to upload their own nature photography–bumble bees, pollinating plants, etc. If you look on Instagram, it's all flowers and more flowers, and flowers again. Our software will simply enable people to share Instagramesque images that people love, but this time there will be a definite connection to an existing ecosystem. I can get really great data this way because it's already time-stamped. Which allows you to create a very accurate map.

MJ/MS: It's not weeds, it's only flowers, right?
NJ: You can take pictures of weeds as well, for example, the plants you find on the High Line in New York City. The High Line includes a lot of weeds. But these are weeds of a different sort. They have been put there to replace species that grow spontaneously without a predetermined plan. The High Line is very much in line with the normal "Parks and Recreation" attitude towards landscaping with perennials or whatever. It's an entirely cultivated space representing a view of nature that's still picturesque and controlled as opposed to nature that just "popped up" because it was able survive. The plants on the High Line are native but they are all industrially produced by commercial greenhouses in New Jersey.

MJ/MS: All the weeds on the High Line?
NJ: Yes, they are weeds on steroids. Every single organisms that was there before the High Line got built was incinerated as bio-hazardous waste except for a small patch that I saved at night after all my old samples were confiscated by authorities. So what the High Line doesn't show is a functioning ecology from which we could have learned a great deal. It's a very successful project, but it's not a self-sustaining system.

MJ/MS: It's an aesthetic.
NJ: Yes; it's a high maintenance, image-based approach to development.

MJ/MS: Are you familiar with the work of Dirt? They got second place in the competition to design the High Line. They wanted to produce a landscape that showed the succession of plant life over time. Small saplings would grow into dense forests. That would have been a great idea. The absence of shading trees on the High Line is a huge liability. On hot days you don't really want stay there to relax. There's too much sunlight.
NJ: Agh, that's so painful to hear.

MJ/MS: Dirt actually got a project at the Navy Yard to produce what they were talking about for the High Line. It will be a post-industrial landscape. I think they really had the right idea, which was to keep an existing ecosystem in place, encourage it to grow, and make a spectacle of succession, and not just plant these steroid weeds. I didn't know they were farmed at a nursery in New Jersey.
NJ: They replaced everything. It's extraordinary...go and see! What they have

planted doesn't survive the changing seasons. It's restocked planting like the stuff you find in the Ford Foundation Atrium near the U.N.

MJ/MS: And the stuff that is planted on the High Line is totally protected from humans.
NJ: You can't touch anything.

MJ/MS: Children can't play there, by the way. You can't really access nature. It exists as a kind of detached and sequestered display.
NJ: This disconnect is also the legacy of environmentalism. Don't touch; leave no trace; don't interfere. The implications of this whole idea, I think, is well illustrated by two students of mine, who came up to me one day and said, "you know, we print on both sides of the page, we don't eat meat, we ride bicycles. Wouldn't committing suicide be the best thing for us to do as good environmentalists?" The whole notion that we should reduce our carbon footprint by not existing as opposed to doing something positive is obviously sad to me.

MJ/MS: It's a better idea to focus on a good way to get rid of your body when your time is up. A TED fellow recently presented her project for a mushroom death suit.
NJ: Oh, you mean Jae Rhim Lee at MIT. Actually, she's my advisor right now.

MJ/MS: You're working with her?
NJ: Yes... she is great.

MJ/MS: Lee feeds parts of her body to fungi so that they are trained to eat her when she dies. Basically, Jae is creating a technique that allows her corpse to be efficiently absorbed back into the earth. It's a great project because the fungus also remediates the toxins that accumulate in the body over time. So nothing bad goes back into the system.
NJ: Yes, I'm also interested in taking similar small actions and aggregating them into larger actions, and doing that through the distributed intelligence of people. That kind of system, I think, is really important to see in contrast with the Hudson River dredging that took thirty years of legislative and legal rambling to get started. So now these awards are going to the big dredging companies that merely displace toxic sludge. In the end they put it somewhere in Pennsylvania, or Texas, or in a Third World country. The idea that we can deal with our environmental issues by moving them elsewhere is really destructive.

MJ/MS: Like nuclear waste.
NJ: Right, just put it somewhere else. It's displacement; it doesn't work. We should be treating the problem in situ.

MJ/MS: Does that make us environmental stewards? In other words, when Gifford Pinchot says that humans are the most intelligent creatures and should be allowed to extract trees from the forest, but only if they plant three trees for every one they take away. We are allowed to eat as many salmon as we want, as long as we provide fish ladders for them to mate.

NJ: I think the idea of stewardship suggests much more control and comprehensive knowledge then we actually have. To be a steward requires a "know-it-all attitude" as opposed to a more open experimental approach through which we learn how to figure things out with small and meaningful interventions.

MJ/MS: So you are a researcher but something of a steward, a steward recognizing your limits.
NJ: I'm an experimentalist who is really interested in my own health and in my children's health and in the environment. I know that the well-being of my children depends on the well-being of fish, right? So it's totally a form of self-interest, but it's also a feeling for what's important. This is the reason why I have framed my work around the health issue rather than stewardship or management. How something affects me directly is very different from saving the rainforests. That's nice but it's just not urgent.

MJ/MS: Right, health has a different signature.
NJ: Build anything, design anything, do anything, as long as you can demonstrably prove a benefit, a measurable benefit in the environment. Don't give me LEED protocols; don't give me all those guidelines. Let's figure out different strategies, all dedicated to producing enhanced human and environmental well-being. No one would be against that. It's common ground.

MJ/MS: What about a strategy like the one developed by John Muir, who talks about maintaining pristine environments. At some point, we absolutely need to do this because we recognize, as you just stated, that we have limited knowledge on how to manage nature effectively. Some areas should simply be left untouched. At some point in the future, we may be able to understand how to engage them comprehensively, but right now, we can't.
NJ: I think that preservation and conservation is the dominant thing I struggle against. It's the kind of idea that stops people from acting. You know, there isn't a single pristine environment in the world. In the Antarctic there are at least four hundred companies filling the landscape with organic pollutants.

MJ/MS: There is no nature that we have not affected already?
NJ: There is no "out-there" out there. It's this crisis of agency that's being delivered to us by the conservationists. We are conserving and preserving as opposed to acting in a way that is driven by the desire for positive change. Think of all the National Parks; you can't even take a twig out of them because that counts as interference. It's an absolutely horrible paradigm that cripples us.

MJ/MS: Are you against preservation? Perhaps we can rethink preservation in a radically new way. Some of the projects presented in this book, from Doug Jackson, Vincent Callebaut, and Split Studio, deploy higher and more advanced forms of comprehensive building technologies that satisfy human needs with close to zero impact on the ground. There are major companies that would go in and rape those environments for all their resources without thinking twice about the long-term effects. Preservation is a kind of stopgap measure. On some level it prevents the really dangerous people from entering these spaces, running pipelines through them, or building strip mines for copper.

NJ: I think the great illusion here is that we are protecting our natural world from the bad guys. Maybe there are no bad guys?

MJ: No bad guys? The CEO of Exxon is a good guy?
NJ: You know, if we could find systems that works–I mean, I don't think any CEO would be opposed to using techniques that improve environmental and economic health for everyone. I don't think a war mentality is of any value. I think that the predominant environmental mindset of fighting these big corporations is fundamentally flawed.

MJ/MS: Perhaps.
NJ: Well, certainly they are doing some bad things, but another way to respond to the problem is by figuring out how we can do things better. We've had thirty years of all those great, young minds going into environmental law and suing deep pockets. That's one way to tackle the problem. But I think we represent a different approach, one that attempts to figure out new, experimental ways of doing business. We can aggregate small interactions into significant effects, and everyone can feel as though they are doing something. Here, try a salamander tail. It's really delicious. There are a whole lot of foods out there to try. So, I suppose this is a newer kind of project. Food system design is really important.

MJ/MS: So what is your conclusion? Can you say something about future work? I was thinking of Russell Simmons. He was saying that he has such a unique style that people are copying him, and, in his opinion, this is the most important thing, otherwise he'd have no market, no dialogue, no polemic, no group to talk to. He'd just be a lonely weird guy doing this very eccentric rap. The point is to propagate ideas and get other interpretations and feedback. I think this bio, art, science approach you've developed is starting to blossom. So, I'm curious to find out where the future is for this kind of practice. Is it going to morph into an absolutely different thing? What are your long-term objectives?
NJ: There are a couple of concrete projects I am really interested in expanding. The Tree Office is one of them. It's simply a high-speed Internet co-working space built around a tree. We are actually experimenting with designing not for enclosure but for transparency. It's not about making boxes but about having a certain openness with great views of Manhattan. The main idea of the project is that it is owned and operated by the tree. It is a tourist attraction but it also a functional workspace with a tree that generates its own revenue. Definitely the project stands in sharp contrast to the environmental services model. Local, small-scale experiments can inform larger initiatives. And we can actually learn so much by doing things this way. We can also draw important conclusions and produce grounded, evidence-based experiments to find better ways of living.

MJ/MS: I think that's super cool.

Graham Burnett

A Mind in the Water

In the basement of the Stanford University Archives, weathered files, acquired at a considerable price (rumored to touch the hem of seven figures), represent the personal and laboratory papers of the most important dolphin scientist of the twentieth century, the controversial neurophysiologist John Cunningham Lilly–the spiritual grandfather, in effect, of both the New Age dolphin and its military alter ego. Lilly died in 2001, and though he is now widely reviled by those who study *Tursiops truncatus* professionally (working scientists have for some time tended to dismiss him as a lunatic or a charlatan), there is, in fact, no one who played a larger role in shaping modern ideas about dolphins. To the extent that Tursiops has been a hard-working Thoreauvian "beast of burden" for much of the last half century, it was John C. Lilly who put the smiling creature in harness.

So who was Lilly? His early biography offers little hint of what would be his enduring obsession with the bottlenose. Taking a degree in physics from Caltech in 1938, Lilly headed off to study medicine at the University of Pennsylvania, joining the war effort as a researcher in avionics. An early photo shows him as a rakish young scientist, smoking a corncob pipe while tinkering with a device designed to monitor the blood pressure of American flyboys–a number of whom, in those days, were actually using surfacing cetaceans for strafing practice.

After the war, motivated in large part by contact with the pioneering brain surgeon Wilder Penfield, Lilly turned his hand to neuroscience, applying the era's expanding array of solid-state electronic devices to the monitoring and mapping of the central nervous system. Eventually appointed to a research position at the National Institute of Mental Health (NIMH), Lilly spent the better part of a decade conducting invasive cortical vivisections on a variety of animals, particularly macaques. In the spy-versus-spy world of the high Cold War, this kind of work had undeniably creepy dimensions. *Manchurian Candidate* anxieties about "forced indoctrination" and pharmacological manipulation of political loyalties peaked in the 1950s, and security establishment spooks (as well as a few actual thugs) hung around the edges of the laboratories where scientists were hammering electrodes into primate brains. Lilly later claimed not to care for that sort of thing, but in his prime as a government employee, he had high-level security clearance–J. Edgar Hoover knew him by name–and was actively involved in research on brainwashing (or "reprogramming" as it was then called among the cognoscenti), sleep deprivation, and "operant control" of animals with wires implanted in the "pain centers" of their gray matter. Lilly's papers from this period include a black-and-white photograph of two brain-wired monkeys at coitus, ostensibly being driven by remote electrical stimulation. It may have been some sort of inside joke around the lab. Maybe not.

It was about this time that Lilly learned from a European colleague, an oceanographer with military contracts to study the physiology of deep-diving, that small-toothed whales had surprisingly large brains–proportionately speaking, nearly as large as those of human beings, but in absolute terms, bigger. Intrigued, Lilly got wind of an outfit in Florida–Marine Studios, which at the time was a cross between a public aquarium and an underwater soundstage for shooting swamp-thing-oriented B-movies–that had figured out how to keep the bottlenose in captivity. By 1955 Lilly had found his way down to St. Augustine in the company of a number of other researchers in order to hammer electrodes into Tursiops brains and see what happened.

This may sound flippant, but the basic modus operandi in the early days of neurophysiology was: stick electrode into brain; apply charge; observe animal; move electrode; repeat. The correlation of spasms, jerks, and eye-rolling with the position of the electrode eventually amounted to a cortical map. It was an ugly business, but the youthful Lilly was not a sentimental character. He wanted to get inside heads, and if possible, get his hands on the steering wheel of consciousness. This can be surmised from the title of a shocking unpublished paper that he prepared in these years, "Special Considerations of Modified Human Agents as Reconnaissance and Intelligence Devices," in which he proudly noted that "a technique for covert and relatively safe implantation of electrodes into the human brain has been devised"–a little hardware that would ultimately provide "push-button control of the totality of motivation and of consciousness."

For the most part, the dolphins, which–unlike people–do not continue breathing when anaesthetized, had the good fortune to die with merciful dispatch. But before succumbing, one of them made a set of wheezing phonations that Lilly interpreted as an effort to mimic the voices of the laboratory personnel. This was his eureka moment, which he would later equate with the Copernican Revolution. For Lilly, and for those who became his champions, that fateful day at Marine Studios would forever stand as the epiphany of a fundamental discovery: human beings were not at the center of the animal universe. After knocking firmly on countless mammalian brains, the energetic brain doctor had finally got a reply; John C. Lilly had heard a voice.

To appreciate the rings of significance that widened from this laboratory scene, it is critical to understand that no one in the 1950s thought of whales and dolphins as "musical," "intelligent," or–of all things–"spiritually enlightened." At that time, large whales were generally regarded as huge kegs of fat (useful for making soap), meat (good to feed to chickens), and fertilizer (best thing to do with what was left after the fat and meat were removed). Smaller dolphins and porpoises were mostly just a nuisance to fishermen, though the bottlenose was sometimes hunted for the fine oil in its jaw ducts, which was considered a superior lubricant for precision timepieces.

This context helps explain the furor that attended Lilly's presentation of a paper that made a set of dramatic claims for the intelligence and linguistic abilities of Tursiops truncatus at the 1958 annual meeting of the American Psychiatric Association in San Francisco. Despite his small and entirely anecdotal evidence, newspapers on both coasts picked up the fascinating story ("Talking fish! What will they think of next?"). By autumn of that year Lilly was writing grants for a major initiative to study cetacean communication and cognition. In a matter of months, he quit his job at NIMH, separated from his wife of two decades, and moved to the Caribbean. Initially using some of his own funds but soon outfitted with a string of prestigious federal research awards (National Science Foundation, Office of Naval Research, Department of Defense, even NASA), Lilly founded his own nonprofit scientific establishment, the Communications Research Institute, or CRI. He built a dedicated dolphin laboratory, complete with holding tanks and state-of-the-art bio-acoustical equipment, on Nazareth Bay at the eastern end of St. Thomas in the U.S. Virgin Islands.

Why was Lilly so amazingly successful at promoting his unlikely program of research on the bottlenose? He managed to cash in upward of half a million dollars per year in grants at his peak–big money in those days. And for what? Dolphin communication? Rolling over in the spent foam of a receding wave and looking out across the heaving blue, it occurred to me that part of the answer lies right here: in the ocean and its changing meanings.

It took a very long time for Anglo-Europeans to approach the sea with anything but anxiety and disgust. The beach as a locus of health and pleasure is a firmly nineteenth-century invention (before that it was a convenient place in which to throw garbage). Our crystalline vision of refreshing, turquoise waters teeming with beautiful fish would have had little currency before the mid-twentieth century–right about the time when Lilly turned to the bottlenose. Only then did the widening availability of inexpensive swim goggles and modestly safe diving equipment open leisured access to underwater vistas. Previously, the sea floor fell away in the imagination as murky and abysmal–unaccommodating, hostile, black.

The 1950s and 1960s saw the emergence of a new and widespread cultural preoccupation with the undersea world, a burst of interest on which Lilly drew and capitalized, and to which he ultimately contributed. It was in a file that he had labeled somewhat ominously, "Solitude," that I found Lilly's dog-eared paperback copy of *The Silent World*, the popular oceanic vade-mecum authored by the psychopomp of SCUBA, Jacques Cousteau, and popularized in the U.S. in the late '50s in connection with a successful motion picture of the same name. Significantly, Lilly had marked with care a number of passages, all of which dealt with the kinetic and tactile experience of being submerged, weightless, isolated, and sensitized by a descent into the aquatic realm.

Lilly was no diver, however. His deep fascination with these feelings hails from a very different arena: his long-standing research into that menacing corner of the human sciences known as sensory deprivation. While still working for the government at NIMH, Lilly and several collaborators developed a new technique for testing the psychological stability of human beings under sustained isolation and reduced sensory input: the flotation tank. Warm water, circulating silently through a perfectly dark chamber, buoyed a naked experimental subject over whose whole head was fitted a latex mask attached to life-support and monitoring devices. Money for this sort of research hailed, of course, from the military, which was mostly curious in how pilots and submariners (and potentially astronauts) would fare during long spells of lonely tedium. When it turned out that many subjects rapidly came unhinged in this sort of disorienting environment, unforeseen possibilities emerged; the technology could be used in personality assessment, and perhaps also in personality adjustment. Lilly himself–fearless about self-experimentation, and already beginning to conceive of himself as a cosmonaut of consciousness–spent many hours encased in his own tanks, exploring what happened when a mind in the water was left to its own devices. The results were trippy (this was, after all, the Lilly that would later inspire the sci-fi thriller *Altered States*), but he was convinced that the mentally sophisticated and strong–those with what he would eventually call "wet courage"–could thrive under these conditions. One had to transcend the terror because a kind of enlightenment lay on the other side.

Suspended in warm water, in perfect darkness, Lilly became, one might say, a brain in a vat. And he liked it–liked it enough that he took a flotation tank with him to his new St. Thomas dolphin laboratory, where it soon became an important tool in his increasingly eccentric pursuit of cetacean intelligence. His own lengthening spells in weightless submersion led him to ponder with mounting awe the sort of mammalian brain that would evolve to dwell in the deep sea. It would be, he decided, a mind like his own, only more so: fearless, deep, and self-sufficient–an expansive intelligence in contemplation of itself. Moving to the Caribbean, Lilly for the most part left the electrodes behind, and embarked on a new way of getting inside the heads of his experimental animals; rather than cracking them open like nuts and rewiring them like doorbells, he cogitated his way in, commensurating his intelligence to theirs, becoming, through strenuous exercises of sympathetic convergence, his own instrument. More and more he wanted to "think like a dolphin." Thus a nasty piece of Cold War psy-ops technology was launched on a new career path: as the head-trip, hot-tub of psychedelia. Before long, Lilly, floating in the dark, was piping the feed from the hydrophones in the dolphin tanks to his own stereo headphones and trying to imagine what it would be like to "see" with sound. That was pretty far out.

On grant applications, however, the central research project of Lilly's Caribbean dolphin institute was more straightforward: "communication." At the most basic level, this meant studying the phonations of Tursiops truncatus in an effort to understand whether they could communicate with each other, and, by extension, whether we could communicate with them. Like any savvy fundraiser, Lilly sold his idea of intelligent and communicative dolphins to different people in different ways, and he started with those he knew best; his earliest and most important backers were in the military.

By 1961, the Navy had developed its own research program on dolphin communications and intelligence. Two years later, a formal Navy facility for marine mammal study and training was opened at the Naval Missile Center at Point Mugu, a little north of Los Angeles. Lilly, however, who was spending more and more time in his flotation tank trying to commune with his experimental animals, soon became persona non grata at this facility, despite having had a hand in its creation. The buzz-headed types had noticed that Lilly was getting a little, well, weird.

But the Navy was never Lilly's only paymaster. Persuaded that he had glimpsed a genuine dolphin "intelligence" in the late 1950s, Lilly also succeeded in selling the idea that his dolphin laboratory could provide a model system for "breaking through" to a nonhuman mind to the nation's nascent space administration. In the era of Sputnik this meant actual extraterrestrials. This may sound crazy today, but these issues lay on the cutting edge of national concern in those times. If we met little green men (or, more likely, started receiving radio signals from deep space that seemed to carry nonstochastic levels of information), what would we do? Lilly promised that dolphins offered a chance to rehearse, and he positioned CRI as a visionary organization conducting fundamental work in exobiology. In fact, by 1962 Lilly was even presiding as the "Grand Dolphin" over a kind of semi-serious secret society of prominent astrophysicists, radio astronomers, atmospheric chemists, and computer engineers, who called themselves "The Order of the Dolphin," wore small, engraved Tursiops insignia (a bit like a tie clip), and exchanged messages in binary code to test each others' readiness for extraterrestrial contact. One of these visionary "Dolphins" was a brilliant young Harvard astrophysicist named Carl Sagan, who in these years made his way down to St. Thomas several times to meet Lilly's dolphins and muse about alternate forms of life in the cosmos.

The Navy definitely had no need for dolphin psychoanalysts, nor did NASA. But around the end of 1964, Lilly–whose second marriage was in free fall, and whose much-hyped research was generating nugatory publishable results–needed all the help he could get. More than ever he needed to listen to the dolphins; he needed to hear them. Lilly's final effort to hear what the dolphins were saying involved the use of lysergic acid diethylamide, otherwise known as LSD.

Now this may seem to us, perhaps, paradigmatic of the mid-'60s moment, and in this sense, inevitably, a little comic. But such a reaction trades considerably on hindsight. After all, Lilly's use of pharmaceutical-grade LSD-25 on his experimental subjects was entirely consistent with the trajectory of his borrowings from the Cold War sciences of mind and behavior.

In fact, if the project was communication–if the inhibitions and blind spots of the experimenter were no less a hindrance than the resistance of the subject, if the aim, in the end, was nothing less than the commensuration of minds–then perhaps it was the scientist who needed the LSD even more than the dolphin? Or better yet, both scientist and dolphin could take it together, and then, for the first time they might be able to come to an understanding–floating in the blue water, listening to the strange sounds echoing through their heads. Together they were drifting over a cultural watershed. Lilly and his dolphins had tuned in and turned on.

And soon enough, they dropped out. Or, more likely, were kicked out. By the end of 1965, still short of peer-reviewed publications, and with rumors of his increasingly idiosyncratic experimental practices swirling among his professional colleagues (including several who had been folded into the Navy's rapidly expanding marine mammal project), Lilly faced devastating evaluations from a visiting board of grant examiners—an assessment of his work that effectively torpedoed his research program and shuttered the Nazareth Bay laboratory. Incensed, Lilly fell back to Miami, writing furious letters to old allies and accusing Navy scientists of staging a military coup in Tursiops research.

Perhaps they had, but the damage was done. In the thick of a second divorce, all his grants revoked or terminated, his fancy computer repossessed by the Feds, a defiant and unrepentant Lilly very publicly released his research animals into the open water whence they had come. Claiming flamboyantly that these brilliant and otherworldly animals had finally succeeded in "reprogramming" him, John Lilly—the star neurophysiologist now turned pied piper of delphinid spiritual awakening—set out for the West Coast, became a regular at Esalen, took to wearing futuristic jumpsuits, and increasingly promoted Zen Buddhism and the mind-expanding virtues of a variety of psychopharmaceuticals. Meanwhile, a number of Lilly's erstwhile dolphin-researcher colleagues were doing their part to help the Navy win Southeast Asia.

This strange rupture effectively established the curious double legacy of the modern bottlenose; the flower children all learned that Tursiops truncatus was an erotically liberated, spiritually profound pacifist, intent on saving humans from their materialistic, violent, and repressive lives, while over on the other side of Point Loma, a coterie of (equally) Lilly-inspired marine mammal biologists busily worked to teach these creatures how to recognize and neutralize enemy combatants.

A caricatured view of the 1960s depicts doves and hawks facing off on opposite sides of the barricades: daisies on this side, gun barrels on that. It is easy to think of the dolphin story as similarly drawn up in ranks; the Navy's weaponized dolphins belonged to the hawks while the stained-glass dolphin decals on VW microbuses swam with the freaks and the hippies. But what Lilly's several lives show, what the bottlenose story shows, indeed, what a host of deeper researches into the history of Cold War military technology, computing, sexual identity, music, and the drug culture all show, is that the two sides that later came to blows—the Cold War and the counterculture—were initially quite intimate, were born, in fact, as Siamese twins.

And they continued to play footsie even as they were pried apart. For instance, the Navy's failure to win life-support contracts for the American space race (the Air Force prevailed) left the blue-water forces in the military on the sideline of the era's flashiest techno-scientific research initiative. Fighting back, the Navy spent much of the 1960s touting the sea as Earth's forgotten "deep space," perversely overlooked in the country's preoccupation with the remote and irrelevant heavens. Thus SEALAB and the Man in the Sea programs were conceived to parallel space-station work and manned interplanetary travel.

With the oceans intensively reimagined in these years as our as-yet-unexplored "inner space," Navy propaganda and research could not but reinforce the notion that dolphins were a kind of neighboring extraterrestrial, awaiting contact. In fact, one of the first undertakings of the new Navy Marine Mammal Program was to train dolphins to work in the open sea as messengers to underwater SEALAB stations. They even made a thirty-minute propaganda film–narrated by Glenn Ford and entitled *The Dolphins that Joined the Navy*–that depicted Navy researchers testing a perfectly fantastic "Human-Dolphin Translator," an audio-frequency converter capable of shifting the acoustic profile of human commands up into the sweet-spot of delphinid hearing. And the Navy scientists ultimately decided to try speaking to them in Hawaiian on the grounds that this language seemed likely to be closest to their own. The big blue, it turned out, really did have its own little green men, but they were big and gray and always smiling.

The shattered remains of the Communications Research Institute are set on a stony promontory, and over these ruins hangs a twisted, overgrown sea grape tree. A scaffold-like wing of the building juts out over the rocky basin; it once held the dolphin "elevator," in which the animals rose to enter the flooded rooms of the lab. In the incandescent endgame, Lilly imagined such a device configured so as to be operated by the animals, permitting them to come and go as they wished. The skeleton of this superstructure gives the dolphin pool the shadowy solemnity of a hidden grotto. A loose doorjamb swings pendular in the breeze before the encroaching vegetation. A storm-crumpled beach chair is embedded in the straggling limbs of a bougainvillea, itself nearly swallowed by its strangling vines.

Like the cavernous halls of the Natural History Museum, this too is a good place to contemplate the essential nature of the bottlenose. Or, perhaps even better, this is a good place to dismiss the very idea of such an essence. Ruins have always been helpful in this way, since they are so candid about the passage of time, so articulate about the inevitability of change. There are, in the end, no fixed definitions, only histories; no essences, only genealogies. Over time, and through the workings of an improbable series of personalities, technologies, and cultural preoccupations, the dolphins became, as the anthropologists like to say, "good to think"–an animal through which we came to see ourselves in new and disorienting ways.

As Thoreauvian beasts of burden, the dolphins have certainly done their share of heavy lifting. What they've been thinking along the way remains very hard to say, however.

Jessica Green

The Indoor Microbial Forest

We can see the skyline, sometimes even the trees and mountains in the distance. Nature is close, but we feel disconnected from it, hermetically sealed inside a glass and steel tower. We and about a quadrillion other creatures, including some very small ones.

The indoor environment is a rainforest teeming with diverse life forms invisible to the naked eye. During the time we spend indoors, we are submerged in an ocean of air that holds hundreds of thousands of individual microbial cells. Even greater densities of microbes, including bacteria, archaea, viruses, and fungi, inhabit the surfaces surrounding us. The walls, windows, carpets, and furniture are packed with microbes intensely competing, cooperating, and communicating with one another.

This indoor ecosystem is our primary habitat; we will spend 90% of our life there. Rather than embracing this ecosystem, we wage war on it. Architects and engineers do their best to keep microbes outside of buildings using elaborate, energy-intensive mechanical ventilation and filtration systems. Microbes that infiltrate buildings are subject to relentless cleaning and disinfecting regimes.

Why this microbial genocide? We are afraid, and justifiably so. There are microbes lurking in our surroundings that can make us miserably sick, or worse, kill us. But the majority of microbes are benign or good for our health. By waging war on all microbes in our homes, offices, schools and hospitals, we kill the "good" along with the "bad." There are numerous reasons–anecdotal as well as scientific–to believe that our ignorance and fear of microbes is making our buildings–and us–unhealthy.

Winston Churchill said that "We shape our buildings, then they shape us." It is universally accepted that buildings exert considerable influence on human health, learning, and productivity. Yet despite thousands of studies attempting to connect attributes of the indoor environment (day lighting, ventilation, temperature, moisture, odors, and sound) to our well being, we continue to live in an era in which buildings make us sick. It is shocking that in the twenty-first century we have yet to tackle "sick building syndrome," a condition in which occupants are plagued by a large number of adverse health effects, including headaches, dry cough, itchy skin, nausea, and fatigue. The World Health Organization published a report stating that up to 30% of new and remodeled buildings worldwide are linked to symptoms of sick building syndrome. More disturbing is the fact that entering some modern buildings can be deadly. In America, hospital-acquired infections kill at least 2,000 people per week–as many lives as taken by AIDS, breast cancer, and auto accidents combined.

What are we doing wrong? We are ignoring microbial science. More specifically, we are failing to integrate modern microbial science with contemporary building engineering.

In recent years, microbial science has advanced at an extraordinary pace due in part to the DNA sequencing revolution. Armed with new technologies, microbiologists have been intensively studying the collection of microbes living in and on our bodies. It is becoming increasingly clear that our health relies on microbes in multiple ways. Good microbes help protect us from pathogens, harvest energy from our food, and regulate our immune system. Mounting evidence suggests that they may even influence our mood and levels of stress, anxiety, and depression.

If we need an army of good microbes to stay healthy, it is sensible to care for microbes in our bodies and in our surrounding environment. But we do not. As detailed in Jessica Sachs's *Good Germs, Bad Germs*, there is growing consensus in the scientific community that the modern practice of microbial genocide through the widespread use of antibiotics and obsessive sterilization has invoked major health crises in the developed world. These crises include antibiotic resistance and the unprecedented modern epidemic of allergies, auto-immune disorders, and other inflammatory diseases.

The relationship between building design, indoor microbiota, and human health has been recognized for centuries. A prominent example is the work of Florence Nightingale, who over 150 years ago wrote that open windows were the hallmark of a healthy hospital ward. Underappreciated is the fact that buildings are a major reservoir not only for pathogens, but also for beneficial microbes that can colonize the human body.

Over the past sixty years there have been two major changes in building design that are likely to have affected the balance of good and bad microbes indoors. Both are coupled with the advent and widespread use of heating, cooling, and air-conditioning (HVAC) systems.

One of them has been the growing disconnect between the outdoor and indoor environment. Many buildings with HVAC systems do not have operable windows; for outdoor air to reach indoor spaces, it commonly needs to pass through a filter. We would intuitively expect the process of sealing and filtering the indoor environment off from the outdoors to result in lower diversity. Furthermore, we might expect the composition of microbes indoors to be more "human-like" than those outdoors. Humans are significant dispersal vectors; by directly shedding and re-suspending microbes from surfaces, humans contribute an estimated 37 million bacteria to indoor air every hour.

Scientists at the Biology and Built Environment (BioBE) Center recently published data suggesting that these intuitions are well founded. They conducted an experiment in a hospital, sampling airborne microbes in two types of patient rooms: those with mechanically ventilated air (business as usual), and those in which air from the HVAC system was diverted and windows were pried open. The mechanically ventilated rooms had a lower diversity of microbes than did window-ventilated rooms, suggesting that the HVAC system was successfully keeping the outdoors "out." The mechanically ventilated rooms also had a larger number of human-associated microbes and microbes with DNA sequences closely related to known pathogens than did the window-ventilated rooms. These findings suggest that the HVAC system was successfully keeping human and building-associated microbes "in."

The second major change in building design lies in greater control over and a more static indoor environment. HVAC systems have replaced operable windows. Fluorescent lighting has replaced daylight. Human indoor comfort has been redefined. Industry standards have moved towards a narrow band of acceptable indoor temperature and humidity, meaning that we can wear a sweater when it is over 100 degrees outside or shorts when it is minus 20. There is good reason to believe that by shifting from a dynamic to a static indoor environment, we are selecting unwanted indoor microbiota. Decades of research on plants and animals have shown that the homogenization of the physical environment, particularly in urban spaces, promotes the growth of weedy and invasive species that are detrimental to our health and out-compete native ones. Through a process dubbed "biological homogenization," we risk the establishment of such microbes in buildings.

Rethinking our relationship with microbes could influence our approach to the design and operation of buildings. Current practices invest extraordinary resources to maintain perceived standards of comfort and protection from microbial life. Future designs will capitalize on the health benefits of the small creatures surrounding us indoors. All quadrillion of them.

Anna Dyson

Beyond Sustainability: Identity Formation and Built Ecologies

Given the persistent ambiguity of the term "sustainability," it is perhaps surprising that the word has provoked such profound and general antagonism to its own endurance, particularly from the most socially negotiated spheres of activity, such as architecture, for example. In line with the fragmentation of knowledge production and exchange, shaped by more than a century of ever entrenched specialization, the semantics of sustainability invariably complies with whatever value structure has developed within different fields of discourse. Thus we might expect that the term would be malleable enough to co-opt and adapt to the predominant forces at play. However, it seems to encounter the greatest dissonance when associated with value frameworks that are the least adaptable, that is, unsustainable. Current socioeconomic frameworks for producing architecture effectively reveal the increasing irrelevance of their own entrenched priorities when the discipline's various governing bodies coalesce in order to legislate reward systems for "sustainable" practices. Within a thoroughly embedded practice such as architecture, any decision made in isolation from a complex array of considerations inevitably invalidates itself as integral to the activity. Not only will it be rejected for its piecemeal and prescriptive directives, but it often proves to be ineffective in the very performance parameters that it is dictating.[1] Thus the absurd degree of categorical accounting of independently considered features of various point systems is gradually losing legitimacy even within the established parties responsible for upholding them. It is difficult to escape the question of what is being sustained with these practices. Does the status quo of building practices become even more intransigent (sustained) because a system has been established for measuring diminishing harmful environmental impacts? The exercise of grafting the definition of sustainability from other practices onto architecture reveals much about the significance of our trajectory towards creating the myth of permanence within our cultural production, and within that everlasting myth, the extent to which we have been driven to crave the illusion of constant change and thus the resistance to any perceived determinism in the performance metrics of our cultural products.

From a much wider social standpoint, the history of discourse on sustainability has broadly referred to human-centric ecological systems, from the earliest cultures to contemporary civilizations, and has traced the variable successes and crises of different societies that have led either to persistence ("sustainability") or decline. The key moment with respect to urban and architectural production was the discovery that fire could be used to produce foods, tools, and built environments. This irrevocably altered the composition of plant and animal communities and our relationship to them, so that debates on the "maintenance of natural systems" that infuses so much of the discourse is inherently antagonistic. In ecology, the term sustainability typically refers to the means through which biological systems remain diverse and productive over time. Yet if we place ourselves back at the center of these biological systems, it becomes obvious that we have evolved over comparatively long periods to coexist transitorily and opportunistically with relation to extremely dynamic conditions that were shaped by the bioclimatic flows of the ecologies within which we have lived. It was only roughly 10,000 years ago that we "fixed" those flows internally through agrarian and later urban settlements, in which occupants had to rely for the first time on their environment and the creation of a "structure of permanence."[2] Much of the discourse today regarding "on-site net-zero energy consumption" and the like is discounting the fundamental conundrum of its own premise, namely, that we are attempting to harness and "fix" fluctuating, diffuse bioclimatic energy flows to power a predetermined energetic and technological framework that has evolved only through the underpinning of concentrated fire-burning energy processes. Notably, these processes only occur within non-human-centric ecological systems as large-scale cleansing procedures.

If the received term "Built Environment," which broadly encompasses the sphere that includes architecture, transitions towards the term "Built Ecologies," then we are immediately required to consider that our built environment actually comprises a plethora of life forms that we have not conventionally associated with our definitions and identification of the human. The timing is excellent for such a transition because in addition to our obvious need to understand and respond to the catastrophic relationships that we have created, our tools for observing and visualizing our world is provoking a critical transition in how we understand the boundaries of our own beings–how we project ourselves into the world and how we, in turn, are integral to a far more deeply imbedded continuum than previously imagined. Metagenomic studies are revealing that we coexist in such rich microbial communities with plants, animals, and other humans that we are most accurately viewed as consortia.[3] These microbial cells far outnumber the human cells in and around our bodies; they are critical for all aspects of our immune systems and metabolisms, and are informed by and constituted of ecological processes many, many miles away from where we are located.[4]

When we transition from "Built Environment" to "Built Ecologies," the fallacy of our previous boundary conditions and identities of both our own bodies and their relationship to space becomes particularly acute in the way that we have attempted to insulate ourselves from biological energy flows. This overriding value of insulation and separation infuses most cognitive and technological manifestations of modern building systems–from building envelopes to mechanical environmental controls systems in all their forms. With built ecologies, we ultimately acknowledge that we are shaping energy flow as well as flora and fauna, and that any type of cognitive or social boundary condition that we might insert into the context serves only pragmatic or executive ends and has potentially little bearing on the phenomenon of interest, if we are looking to coexist with bioclimatic energy flows. In this way, a building envelope transitions from attempting to "separate" towards behaving as a "transfer" or medium through which energy flows.

The transition towards cultivating bioclimatic energy flows in the urban context clearly encompasses the cultivation of biodiversity within our cities and particularly inside our buildings, where many spend upwards of 95% of their time. It is projected that by 2050 over two-thirds of the world's population will reside in urban environments that will have limited contact with green space or biodiverse natural systems.[5] After many years of hypotheses as to why "developed" economies have seen disproportionate rises in certain health disorders, large-scale epidemiological studies have finally interrelated precipitously decreasing biodiversity to another global megatrend, namely, the critically rapid rise in chronic inflammatory diseases among urban populations.[6,7,8,9] Emerging at the same time are large data sets demonstrating that architectural and environmental control-system design critically informs the diversity and structure of the built environment's microbiome, and that the biodiversity of mechanically ventilated interiors are significantly less diverse than those of urban airstreams outside and contain certain taxa that do not exist outdoors.[10,11] Furthermore, recent data acquired from patients in neonatal hospital units has correlated the microbiome of the built environment with the microbiome of the human gut, thereby underscoring the critical need for understanding the interdependent relationship between the microbiome of the built environment and human health and wellbeing.

Contemporary HVAC systems have thus been proven to be essentially "antibiotic." By removing the biodiverse character that is essential to maintaining healthy air, they have created environments for potentially dangerous levels of pathogenic activity indoors, particularly for fragile and immune-compromised populations. Data on possibly catastrophic public health effects on declining immunity among global urban populations is emerging.[7,10,11] In addition, "fresh air" entering buildings is currently mandated by building codes as "exterior air intake," with heating and cooling comprising the majority of HVAC energy-consumption profiles across the nation. However, in emerging conditions around the globe, urban air is highly compromised with carcinogenic compounds, which, in certain cases, existing mechanical ventilation systems do not adequately remove regardless of the cost of filtration. [8, 9, 10]

Notes:

1. Emerging LEED lawsuits and disputes are a testament to the ineffectiveness of an individual point system that is associated with disparate add-on technologies for determining and/or measuring overall building performance behaviors.
2. Clarke, "The Structure of Permanence: The Relevance of Self-Subsistence Communities for World Ecosystem Management," in *Subsistence and Survival: Rural Ecology in the Pacific*, eds. T. Bayliss-Smith and R. Feachem (London: Academic Press, 1977), 363–384.
3. Fang Sungsoon and Ronald M. Evans, "Microbiology: Wealth Management in the Gut," *Nature* 500 (August 29, 2013): 538-539.
4. Peter J. Turnbaugh, et al., "An Obesity-Associated Gut Microbiome with Increased Capacity for Energy Harvest," *Nature* 444 (December 28, 2006): 1027-1031
5. United Nations, *World Urbanization Prospects: The 2007 Revision* (New York: The United Nations, 2008).
6. Ilkka Hanski et al, "Environmental Biodiversity, Human Microbiota and Allergy are Interrelated," *Proceedings of the National Academy of Sciences USA* 109 (2012): 8334-8339.
7. J. F. Bach, "The effect of infections on susceptibility to autoimmune and allergic diseases," *New England Journal of Medicine* 347 (2002): 911–920.
8. G.A.W. Rook, "99th Dahlem Conference on Infection, Inflammation and Chronic Inflammatory Disorders: Darwinian Medicine and the "Hygiene" or "Old Friends" Hypothesis," *Clinical & Experimental Immunology* 160 (2010): 70–79.
9. D. Graham-Rowe, "When Allergies Go West," *Nature* 479 (2011): S2–S4.
10. Steven W Kembel, et al., "Architectural Design Influences the Diversity and Structure of the Built Environment Microbiome," *International Society for Microbial Ecology* 6 (2012): 1469-1479.
11. J. F. Meadow, et al. (2013) Indoor airborne bacterial communities are influenced by ventilation, occupancy, and outdoor air source.
12. World Health Organization, International Agency for Research on Cancer (2013).
13. H. Guo, et al., "Risk Assessment of Exposure to Volatile Organic Compounds in Different Indoor Environments," *Environmental Research* 94 (2004): 57–66.
14. Shun-Cheng Lee, et al., "Inter-Comparison of Air Pollutant Concentrations in Different Indoor Environments in Hong Kong," *Atmospheric Environment* 36 (2002): 1929–1940.

Nina Tandon

Biology is Fabrication: Energy, Food, and the Third Industrial Revolution

Imagine a world in which creatures from outer space harvest our food, broken bridges repair themselves, and plumbing systems adapt to our needs. Every part of this future civilization seems to "know" what to do: power plants are hooked up to "smart grids," structures self-assemble, and everything "talks" to everything else. In many ways, we already live in this world. Our bodies are exquisite ecosystems that have solved many problems: bacteria live in our gut, helping us digest food; mitochondria convert energy at a rate that is 10,000 times more efficient than that of the sun; osteoblast and osteoclast cells break down and repair our bones every day; and our heart and vasculature adapt to changing oxygen demands and stress.

The first Industrial Revolution was about the mechanization of manual processes, the second about mass-customization. As we find ourselves facing the problems of deteriorating infrastructure, globalizing job markets, aging populations, food, water, and energy shortages, we are now in desperate need of a third revolution, one in which factories and products will begin producing themselves. This new era will be characterized by increasing efficiency, flexibility, and adaptability–a "smart" manufacturing revolution that will be more life-like and less industrial. And so it seems appropriate for us to look to nature for inspiration, to rethink the future beyond sustainability, and to look to biology as the potential technological partner.

Digital manufacturing processes such as 3-D printing, user-friendly robotics, and collaborative manufacturing services are showing us the beginnings of such a change, making it more economical to produce objects in smaller numbers, with greater flexibility to respond to local demand, and with a much lower input of energy and labor. However, if these digital manufacturing processes were combined with new biotechnologies such as cell printing, bioreactors, gene transfection, and BioMEMS, we could open up a new world, one which would seem like science fiction to us now. In this not-so-distant future, tobacco leaves and eels may combine to form electric power plants, and viruses may be reengineered to construct batteries. This ability to adapt biological processes to civilized ends, a process called biofabrication, will significantly transform the twenty-first century.

Biofabrication

Cells are Nature's building blocks. Today we have only begun to harness their power. In fact, it has been little over a hundred years since biologist Ross Harrison grew his first tissue samples in a lab. While it is possible to argue that we have been harnessing yeast to make beer and bread for millennia, it has only been in the past several decades that we have directly employed cells in the biomanufacturing of drugs and other useful molecules.

Biofabrication technologies will change the way in which we design and produce everyday objects. Consider the traditional processes of textile manufacturing. Designer Suzanne Lee, for example, has developed prototypes for seam-free "clothing" by using fiber-secreting cells that are molded into shape without the need for traditional stitching.

Biofabrication technology could also eliminate the need to slaughter animals for meat and leather. Vital human organ could be replaced by cultivating live cells or through new tissue engineering techniques. In our lab, for example, we use scaffolds and bioreactors to create living three-dimensional structures that can serve as replacements for human body parts or as platforms for testing new drugs. In order to grow these samples, we provide the necessary ingredients of life, including growth factors and biomaterials that allow microorganisms to assemble themselves. In a sense we treat them like the "real" engineers. This is the essence of biofabrication: the creation of tightly controlled environments that use regulated chemical and mechanical cues to "coax" cells into producing useful forms.

Finally, we may envision the development of biological systems that generate hitherto unknown products, such as living lasers, or protein factories made for the construction of nanoscale materials. If we begin to cooperate with biology and create new technologies, we may also be able to meet the demand for ever-shrinking electronic devices. 300-nm viral rods have been redesigned to deposit inorganic oxides, and mutants with altered amino acids have the ability to generate metal nanoparticles and nickel wires.

The emerging field of biotechnology is poised to set new standards of productivity across all disciplines. As we look ahead and face the challenge of feeding a hungry world, reducing the environmental impact of manufacturing, and perhaps even finding new sources of energy, let us not forget about the living systems we are destroying each day on this lonely planet. Let us make room for biology so that our third industrial revolution is not our last.

Anil Netravali

Green Composites

Fiber-reinforced plastics are used for a variety of structural applications due to their high strength-to-weight characteristics. (Carbon fiber is stronger than steel and 10 times as light.) Initially developed for the aerospace industry, these high performance materials are now being used to make automotive parts, circuit boards, and even sporting goods. While composites have excellent mechanical properties, they suffer from two serious problems. First, they are made from polymers or resins such as epoxies, polyimides, and polyurethanes, which are reinforced with fibers such as graphite, aramids, and glass. Most of these ingredients are derived from petroleum, a non-renewable resource. By some estimates, current reserves are expected to last only 50-60 more years. We are consuming oil at 100,000 times the rate our earth can produce it. (Roughly one million barrels per day are used for making composites.) Second, most of these fibers and resins are not bio-degradable.[1] Composites are made from two dissimilar materials that are difficult to reshape and recycle. This is particularly true for thermoset resins such as epoxies. A small fraction of these materials are incinerated to obtain energy in the form of heat. However, like most other plastics (over 94%) they end up in landfills at the end of their life-cycle.[2] In 2003, 27 million metric tons of plastic waste were discarded. In the anaerobic conditions of a landfill composites may not degrade for several decades or even centuries. In addition, the incineration process creates toxic gases that require expensive scrubbers to mitigate pollution. Finally, these methods are expected to get more expensive as pollution laws around the world become stricter and the number of available landfills decreases.

The rush is now on to apply composites to a wide range of civil engineering and architectural projects. Although it has been a slow process, designers, architects, and engineers increasingly prefer fiber-reinforced composites for structural applications. Stronger and lighter products consume fewer resources, require less energy for their production, and are easier to transport. Some buildings already use composites in place of conventional steel rebars, which makes them far more resistant to earthquakes. Current technology allows for the construction of all-composite bridges that can be installed in a very short time. Such applications are bound to increase, making their demolition and disposal more problematic. To face these challenges, many governments have established new laws to encourage the use of recycled and/or bio-based "green" plastics.[3] Undoubtedly, environment-friendly, fully biodegradable materials will play a major role in the future.

"Greener" composites

Renewable, plant-based binding agents and "cellulosic" reinforcing fibers are now being used to make composites "greener." Inexpensive plant-based materials obtained from agricultural waste are fueling the development of cheap, non-toxic alternatives. Commonly sold engineered wood products such as medium density fiber board (MDF) contain formaldehyde, a probable carcinogen. Since pseudo-green composites combine non-degradable resins with degradable fibers, at the end of their life they cannot be returned to the earth as nutrients or upcycled as raw material for new industrially produced products. In other words, they get downcycled.

Longer plant-based fibers such as abaca, bamboo, banana, flax, henquen, hemp, jute, kenaf, pineapple, ramie, sisal, etc., have excellent mechanical properties and are being adopted as low cost alternatives to common reinforcements such as glass. These fibers, obtained from plant stems and leaves, are annually renewable, unlike wood, which takes 20-25 years to grow. As a result, the supply of biofibers is virtually endless. While these materials may not be as strong or stiff as graphite and Kevlar® when employed in advanced composites, on a "per-weight" basis, flax, jute, bamboo, and hemp have a higher modulus of stiffness than does E-glass. The hollow tubular (cellular) structure of cellulosic fibers also provides better insulation against noise and heat in applications such as automotive door/ceiling panels. Such fibers may easily be used in housing construction to replace particle board, plywood, and MDF.

Today, material scientists and engineers have been able to create inexpensive "green" composites made from natural fibers and biodegradable soy-based resins. While the technology needed to make economically viable products is still in its early stages of development, some companies have been able to market them on a small scale. These composites are environment-friendly and fully degradable. At the end of their life cycle they can easily be disposed of or composted with no harm to the environment. Green composites can be used to make mass-produced consumer goods with short life cycles of 1-2 years, but they can also be employed in long term, architectural applications as replacement for plywood, particle boards, MDF, or even gypsum wall boards. Furthermore, the properties of these composites can be engineered to fit specific structural and aesthetic requirements. Prefabricated buildings that are green, inexpensive, and non-toxic can be constructed from lightweight panels, which can be assembled very quickly on site.

We even have the ability to build complex composite structures using multi-axis CNC fiber placement machines. Precise fiber layouts can form ultra-lightweight tubular structures using a computer-automated taping head. In addition, in-situ infrared curing can be employed during fabrication in order to eliminate the time and energy consumed by autoclave post-processing techniques. This process also allows for the incorporation of wireless sensors, piezoelectric transducers, fiber optics, and micro-actuators that detect damage, monitor structural integrity, and obtain advanced warning in case of catastrophic failures. Now within reach are buildings made of advanced materials that are both green and smart.

Notes:

1. E. S. Stevens, *Green Plastics: An Introduction to the New Science of Biodegradable Plastics* (Princeton: Princeton University Press, 2002).
2. A. N. Netravali and Shitij Chabba, "Composites Get Greener," *Materials Today* 6/4 (April, 2003): 22-29.
3. M. M. Nir, et al., "Update on Plastics and the Environment: Progress and Trends", *Plastics Engineering* 49/3 (March 1993): 75.

Alex Felson, Jacob Dugopolski

Re-Wilding the Suburbs: Housing Taxonomy

We will inevitably continue to develop and build houses, but can we develop new practices that will improve the social, economic, and ecological function of these communities? As human activity continues to degrade biological systems, sites that involve human agency, such as suburbs and infrastructure, could be coordinated to balance development with site-specific active and adaptable ecological manipulations and long-term management practices.

Through The Museum of Modern Art and the Buell Center's exhibition, "Foreclosed: Rehousing the American Dream," such ecological drivers were integrated into Andrew Zago's team proposal for Rialto, California, which re-envisioned poorly situated dense housing developments as frameworks in which active and adaptive ecological strategies could be integrated into construction and lot divisions through "misregistration" in order to promote ecosystem restoration, wildlife management, and waste reuse.

The ultimate goal is to shift the paradigm of exurban sites from one that disregards the surrounding environment to one that turns creates a positive relationship between suburb and ecology and takes into account material flow, construction activity, and potential for the human management of ecosystems over time.

Pleistocene Rewilding

Large predators are often instrumental in maintaining the structure, resilience, and diversity of ecosystems through "top-down" ecological (trophic) interactions. They, in turn, require resources such as nesting and foraging areas, water and large areas of protected landscape and connectivity that ensure long-term viability.

The suburb offers a potential site for testing re-wilding through the use of the zoological park as a suburban amenity. In the proposal for Rialto, California this included the development of a principal wildlife corridor to the National Forest and the annexation of a larger adjacent area as part of a re-wilding experimental zone. Here large carnivores could be introduced and assessed for survival and reproduction through enhanced ecosystems and engaged management.

In a collaborative endeavor the government would finance habitat links to the suburb while development would incorporate topological joints with intensified habitat zones and productive ecosystems, generating jobs, public amenities, and regional habitat resources. This partnership would spur a new suburban model based on the promotion of–rather than disregard for–ecosystem services.

Notes:

1. David Foreman, *Rewilding North America: A Vision for Conservation in The 21st Century* (Washington, D.C.: Island Press, 2004).
2. Michael E. Soulé and Gary Lease: *Reinventing Nature?: Responses To Postmodern Deconstruction* (Washington D.C.: Island Press, 1995).
3. C. Josh Donlan, et al., "Pleistocene Rewilding: An Optimistic Agenda for Twenty-First Century Conservation," *The American Naturalist* 168/5 (November 2006).

Mitchell Joachim

Ten Archetypes of Nature in Design

What we mean when we use the word "nature" critically affects design culture. Since nature has many different interpretations, the following lexicon is not intended to be an exhaustive exploration of the word's etymology or usage by designers. Instead, I offer ten archetypical perspectives of nature that can help designers and non-designers alike clarify the different, sometimes overlapping, sometimes conflicting ways in which we understand the fundamental relationships between humans and our environment.

"Nature" is...

1st) **Primordial**: Nature means earth in its elemental state, before humans. Within this archetype, the natural state is often that of genesis or beginning, such as an early (pre-human) biogeological epoch, for a type of organism, or, for a specific organism, an early developmental stage.
Examples: Pangaea, and Precambrian to Mesozoic epochs.[1]

2nd) **Eden**: Nature is an idyllic paradise where all beings live in harmony, including early humans. Every human, animal, and plant thrives in tranquil equivalence. Notions of the noble savage, uncorrupted by civilization, characterize this period.
Examples: Biblical "Garden of Paradise" (Genesis), Arcadia, Animism, and Mother Nature.[2]

3rd) **Wilderness**: Nature exists in mostly inhospitable, dynamic environments where indigenous species thrive and humanity lives on the edge of catastrophe. Adverse conditions such as storms, periodic floods, extreme temperatures, difficult terrain, poisonous vegetation, and aggressive predators dominate the landscape. Though cruel, the wilderness is also a pristine environment in which human influence is negligible.
Examples: Papua New Guinea, Grand Canyon, Kalahari Desert, Congo, Everglades, Marianas Trench, and Amazonia.[3]

4th) **Agrarian**: Humanity has established enduring methods for self-sufficiency, advanced control of crop plants and domesticated animals, and bounteous provisions leading to food surpluses and population growth. Nature in this case is an instrument for cultivation and nutrient resource management. It is continually productized and hybridized in direct service of humanity.
Examples: Early Mesopotamia, Ancient Egypt, Machu Picchu, and Jeffersonian planning.[4]

5th) **Garden**: Nature is controlled for aesthetic purposes. The beauty found in nature is transformed and aestheticized into a pleasurable cultural spectacle.

Humanity uses nature as a prop to generate feelings of the sublime, the leisurely, and the pastoral, as well as conviviality and spirituality.
Examples: Versailles, Ryoan-ji, Keukenhof, Garden of Earthly Delights, and the Hanging Gardens of Babylon.[5]

6th) **Industrial**: The overuse of biocides, artificial chemicals, manufactured toxins, and disinfectants to control organisms that are deemed detrimental to human productivity threaten nature. Also, the indirect yet intentional pollution of the biosphere through constant resource extraction, unmitigated mechanized growth, waste creation, and sprawling development destabilizes our ability to find and recognize nature as such. Within this archetype, we can periodically lean on earlier meanings of nature (that is, we can greenwash our activities) without seriously threatening the industrial. This phase of nature is synonymous with the Anthropocene and/or Capitalocene.
Examples: Great Pacific Garbage Patch, Chernobyl, Bhopal Disaster, and Love Canal.[6]

7th) **Preservation/Conservation**: Preservation seeks to protect nature from human consumption, for example, by creating wildlife sanctuaries. Inversely, conservation regulates the use of nature in order to benefit humanity. Conservationists seek to foster a cyclic economy through the vigilant replenishment of biotic resources. Conservationists believe that natural resources can be sustained if they are cultivated, exploited, distributed, and re-cultivated under the careful stewardship of humanity.
Examples: Yellowstone, Galapagos, Great Barrier Reef, and Gaia Hypothesis.[7]

8th) **Socio-ecological**: Nature is regenerated through social and biophysical schemes such as adaptive reuse, climate resilience, upcycling, ecosystem integrity and stress absorption, highly advanced sustainability, restorative infrastructure, continual evolution, and post-industrial thinking. These complex ecological feedback mechanisms achieve positive-gain characteristics or abundance attributes in relationship to design. In this variant, goals are set to go beyond zero-impact models and produce designs that manifest a plentitude of additional benefits towards ecosystem health.
Examples: Kalundborg, Masdar, Curitiba, Freiburg, Singapore, Portland, and Arcology.[8]

9th) **Biosynthetic**: Nature is the product of the design and manufacture of novel biological components, devices, and systems. In addition, technology allows us to reengineer existing, natural biophysical structures for programmatic human use. Geoengineering is an extreme version of designing with nature, within this archetype.

Examples: Terraforming, tissue engineering, artificial bones, 3D-printed organs, ocean fertilization, algae-coated buildings, stratospheric aerosols, and afforestation.[9]

10th) **Extraterrestrial**: Finally, we must include an alien nature that is not within the current superorganism of this planet.
Examples: Mars, orbital satellites, and asteroid impacts.

As we can see from this list, choosing methods for designing with nonhuman living things entails taking into account more than one perspective on what "nature" is and how humans should protect, reify, alter, or exploit it.

It's important to note that the most current archetypes presented here–numbers 8, 9, and 10–are major departures from the everyday meaning of "nature."

As designers, instead of engaging in a practice that we might call "designing with nature," perhaps we should seriously consider biosynthetic design together with its more expansive variation, socio-ecological design. Because nature is not one agreed-upon thing, we must combine explanatory frameworks from scientific and cultural disciplines in order to successfully design with it. [10]

Notes:
1. Robert M. Hazen, *The Story of Earth: The First 4.5 Billion Years, from Stardust to Living Planet* (Penguin Books, 2013).
2. Umberto Eco, *The Book of Legendary Lands* (Rizzoli Ex Libris, 2013).
3. Jared M. Diamond, *Guns, Germs, and Steel: The Fates of Human Societies* (W.W. Norton & Company, 1999).
4. Max Weber, *The Agrarian Sociology Of Ancient Civilizations* (Verso World History Series, 2013).
5. Geoffrey Alan Jellicoe and Susan Jellicoe, *The Landscape of Man: Shaping the Environment from Prehistory to the Present Day* (Thames and Hudson, 1995).
6. Niall Kirkwood, ed., *Manufactured Sites: Rethinking the Post-Industrial Landscape* (Taylor & Francis, 2001).
7. Buell Laurence, *The Environmental Imagination* (Harvard University Press, 1995).
8. William McDonough and Michael Braungart, *Cradle to Cradle: Remaking the Way We Make Things* (North Point Press, 2002).
9. Mitchell Joachim and Nina Tandon, *Super Cells: Building with Biology* (TED Books, 2014).
10. Timothy Morton, *Ecology without Nature: Rethinking Environmental Aesthetics*. (Cambridge: Harvard University Press, 2009).

Ioanna Theocharopoulou

Ekiosis: A Guide to Adaptive Behavior[1]

Any idea of "sustainability" or even "post-sustainability" needs to draw attention to the vital interrelation and interdependency of all forms of life–not only between humans and animals and plants, but also between humans and other humans. To navigate the future and survive the challenges of global climate change, we need an enriched vocabulary that will help us imagine and articulate a set of adaptive behaviors, including a closer and kinder relationship to other living beings. Design can serve as a powerful tool here.

The problematic of our relationship to other living beings and nature was raised in the nineteenth century, during the Industrial Revolution, which caused major transformations in landscape and human lifestyles. Ralph Waldo Emerson, among others, foresaw that "progress" had negative sides, that it was leading to an increasingly distorted view of nature, and would eventually turn man into "a broken giant." As he noted in a remarkable passage in his 1841 essay "Nature:"

> *A man is a bundle of relations, a knot of roots, whose flower and fruitage is the world. His faculties refer to natures out of him and predict the world he is to inhabit, as the fins of the fish foreshow that water exists, or the wings of an eagle in the egg presuppose air. He cannot live without a world.*[2]

Before sustainability can help us plan the future of our cities, we need to expand on the potential meanings, capabilities, and implications and sheer complexity of the term. The most pressing question today is not simply how to design in a technologically savvy, energy-saving way, but whether–or how–design may help restore man's "bundle of relations" to other living beings and the planet. Developing a vocabulary for discussing sustainability could broaden the discourse both within the design professions and beyond.

Ecology and Ekiosis

Introduced by Ernst Haeckel in the nineteenth century, the term "ecology" derives from the Greek "*oikos*", meaning "home," and "*logos*," meaning "order," "logic," "speech."[3] *Ekiosis*, too, stems from oikos, and has to do with the process of familiarity, a broadening of our sense of home. Consider this description of ekiosis by Hierocles, a Greek Stoic philosopher of the early second century CE:

> *Each one of us is, as it were, entirely encompassed by many circles, some smaller, others larger...The first and closest circle is the one which a person has drawn as though around a center, his own mind. This circle encloses*

the body and anything taken for the sake of the body. For it is virtually the smallest circle, and almost touches the center itself. Next, the second one further removed from the center but enclosing the first circle; this contains parents, siblings, wife, and children. The third one has in it uncles and aunts, grandparents, nephews, nieces, and cousins. The next circle includes the other relatives, and this is followed by the circle of local residents, then the circle of fellow tribesmen, next that of fellow citizens, and then in the same way the circle of people from neighboring towns, and then the circle of fellow-countrymen. The outermost and largest circle, which encompasses all the rest, is that of the whole human race...it is the task of a well-tempered man, in his proper treatment of each group, to draw the circles together somehow towards the center, and to keep zealously transferring those from the enclosing circles into the enclosed ones.[4]

This relatively forgotten term has been discussed more recently in a fascinating way by the psychiatrist Adam Philips and the historian Barbara Taylor in their book *On Kindness*, where they note that "in a well-ordered personality," the Stoics deemed ekiosis, "whether directed at strangers or intimates...a pleasurable virtue." Stoics were ascetics and "the pleasures they endorsed were not appetitive or sensual but 'soul states' that enhanced the goodness of the individual by bringing him into harmony with the oneness of nature."[5]

Ekiosis raises the question of how to think of the world as "us." It can help us understand the concept of "community," which has been viewed skeptically by many in the architectural profession–especially in recent decades–in new and interesting ways. In trying to expand the meanings and implications of this term, we may also look to anthropology, for it is exactly this idea of the self as one among many and of the world as "us" that characterizes many traditional societies.

In a slender manifesto-like book published in 2008, anthropologist Marshal Sahlins, points to insights from worldwide ethnographic studies that reveal that in opposition to competitive self-interest, there is "an alternative conception of order and being: a kinship community." Ethnographic reports speak of "the transpersonal self" (Native Americans), of the self as "a locus of shared social relations or shared biographies" (Caroline Islands), or of persons as "the plural and composite site of the relationships that produced them" (New Guinea Highlands). Clearly the self in these societies is not synonymous with the bounded, unitary, and autonomous individual as we know him–and him in particular. Rather, it is the locus of multiple other selves with whom he or she is joined in mutual relations. For the same reason, "any person's self is more or less widely distributed among others."[6]

Kin relationships, Sahlins explains, have to do with "an internal condition" in which others become predicates of one's own existence and vice versa.[7] Philips and Taylor, too, note that ekiosis is linked to "kinship." Furthermore, "kindness" and "kinship," which they define as "a sympathetic expansiveness linking self to other," have the same root. Psychoanalysis, they explain, includes the compelling story "of how and why we can so strongly defend ourselves against too much involvement, too much feeling for both the pleasures and the sufferings of people other than ourselves."[8]

Sahlins calls this "collective survival enterprise" culture, noting that "culture is older than *Homo sapiens*, many times older, and culture was a fundamental condition of the species' biological development. Evidence of culture in the human line goes back about three million years; whereas the current human form is but a few hundred thousand years old."[9] If the idea of an avaricious human nature does in fact originate in the "particularly Western metaphysics" of a rigid opposition between "nature" and "culture" (as suggested by Hobbes and so many others), how do we re-invent a twenty-first-century mode of being that is less (self) destructive?

For Sahlins, trying to see "nature" and "culture" as less oppositional and more porous, as they were perceived in Ancient Greece, would be a good start.[10] According to Philips and Taylor, we need to embrace kindness–not the sentimental, nostalgic, overly romanticized view of kindness as self-sacrifice, charity or moral self-righteousness but rather that of Stoic ekiosis, a kind of opening up to others, which "in Rousseau's terms, 'enlarges' us and so gratifies our profoundly social natures." Modern psychoanalysis has much to say about our fear of kindness since one of its goals is to understand what brings people together, what pulls them apart, and why they are so frightened of each other. Philips and Taylor point out that this conversation began with Rousseau, then continued with Dickens, not to mention Darwin and Freud. But by now "we are all Hobbesians;" we have become phobic of kindness, which we take as a sign of weakness.[11] Indeed, kindness has all but become taboo. But does it need to remain that way?

Synergy and cooperation or cooperative synergies

Without much new theoretical speculation, some of the most interesting and innovative design practices have steadily and increasingly taken up the challenge of looking for ways to incorporate socially engaged work into their practices. In architecture, there has been a noticeable shift away from self-aggrandizing, unsustainable, and excessive projects, such as those of the 1990s (think Dubai), to a renewed and genuine interest in the other 90%, as exemplified by the projects in Design Like You Give a Damn 1 and 2 (2006 and 2012), Design for the Other 90% (2007), Design With the Other 90%: Cities (2011), and by new departments devoted to Social Innovation.[12]

This turn towards a more social form of behavior and away from "individuality" and "self-sufficiency" is not unique to design, but is part of a broader cultural transformation taking place in the developed world, which is being discussed by scientists in a broad range of disciplines from neuroscience and psychology to sociology and behavioral economics. An example of such is the work of Michael Tomasello, a developmental psychologist and co-director of the Max Planck Institute for Evolutionary Anthropology in Leipzig, who studies the transmission of culture among children. Claiming that "what makes us human is not simply a giant brain and its outsized cognitive capacity, but the ability to participate in social interactions of a unique nature,"[13] Tomasello argues that as children grow, they become "equipped to participate in this cooperative groupthink through a special kind of cultural intelligence, comprising species-unique social-cognitive skills and motivations for collaborations, communication, social learning, and other forms of shared intentionality."[14] According to Tomasello, children possess a kind of social rationality rooted in a "he is me" attitude of identification with others, and a conception of the self as one among many, especially in group activities with shared intentions.[15] In other words, cooperation and ekiosis seem to overlap at a young age. But what happens later?

Tomasello also works on identifying the unique cognitive and cultural processes that distinguish humans from their closest primate relatives, the great apes, especially chimpanzees. His recent book, *Why We Co-operate* (2008), argues that humans "are adapted for acting and thinking cooperatively in cultural groups. Indeed all of humans' most impressive cognitive achievements, "from complex technologies to linguistic and mathematical symbols to intricate social institutions–are the products not of individuals acting alone, but of individuals interacting."[16]

Others, such as biologist Peter Corning, Director of The Institute for the Study of Complex Systems in Washington D.C., study the concept of cooperative synergies in order to understand how "complex, coordinated activity over sustained periods, leverages the power of physical tools, cultural discoveries, and social organization." Corning's research points to the biological importance of cooperation "from the symbiotic origins of mitochondria and chloroplasts to symbiotic microorganisms in the digestive systems of ruminants and humans, to social insects, to the evolutionary leap from tree-dwelling primates to savanna-dwelling humans, cooperative synergies at the level of the cell, organism, species, and ecology have been central, not peripheral to the evolution of life."[17] He also claims that "the evolution of human cultural traits such as social complexity, language, social foraging, the use of fire and cultural transmission of tool use and implement creation, settled agriculture, the invention of technologies and symbolic communication of means for inventing technologies, were both driven by synergies [or cooperations] and necessitated new social arrangements that led to new synergies."[18]

In the design disciplines, the terms "synergy" and "synergetic behavior" are familiar from the writings of Buckminster Fuller (1895-1983). In his *Operating Manual for Spaceship Earth* (1963), Fuller noted that "synergy is the only word in our language that means behavior of whole systems unpredicted by the separately observed behaviors of any of the system's separate parts or any subassembly of the system's parts [...] Universe is synergetic. Life is synergetic."[19] An eccentric inventor and self-proclaimed "futurist," Fuller probably understood the continuity of "culture" and "nature" better than did most of his contemporaries. Today scientists know for a fact that cooperative synergies are central, not peripheral, to the evolution of life on a biological level.

How can these terms and the concepts behind them become part of our everyday vocabulary? Can we use our knowledge of design to facilitate greater cooperative groupthink? How can we design cooperative synergies to get along better and improve our daily lives? Can we imagine a future in which design is less about making more or better things, buildings, cities and more about helping shift human behavior to encourage greater synergetic cooperation?

Synergetic design and cities

In view of these discoveries and questions, we need to revise the current definition of ecological design–"incorporating intelligence about how nature works... into the way we think, design, build, and live"–to include a more pronounced social component[20] and express sympathetic extension to others. Perhaps it is no accident that concepts such as sociability and cooperation are starting to play an increasingly important role as the world grows more urban. There is no better place than a city for advancing this "cooperative groupthink" and the refinement and progress of "cultural intelligence." "Civility" and "civilization" began in cities and need cities in order to survive and flourish.

These days we can look to cities for successful attempts at more socially engaging projects. Can the same terms be used to articulate the goals of relatively stable, well-established cities and those of rapidly growing ones? For wealthier cities such as those of the Global North, synergetic design may be directed primarily at resilience to climate change and to learning to do more with less so as to maintain a high standard of living with fewer resources. But for newer megacities with rapidly growing populations, especially of the poor, the challenges are broader, more pressing, and evident in every aspect of urban life: housing, jobs, energy, transportation, clean air and water, sanitation, food, safety, and education. It is here that sustainability with a pronounced social component engages in the tensions between urban growth, waste, and vulnerability.

It is precisely in the impoverished and distressed cities of the Global South that some dramatically successful examples of a new synergetic design imagination have arisen: Latin American favelas, South African townships, Nairobi's Kiberra, and Mumbai's Dharavi. The ongoing explosive growth of these nonlegal, informal cities requires a different set of tools from those used in state plans and capitalist property development. They demand the active participation of inhabitants and in the best scenario, a knowing collaboration between them and authorities.

The initiatives of activist municipal governments by radically innovative urban leaders in cities such as Curitiba or Bogotà demonstrate the achievements made possible by a political imagination placed at the service of urban populations, in which the enfranchisement of the poor is addressed directly through environmental action. Jaime Lerner's initiative for developing a rapid bus service in Curitba and distributing bus tickets to the urban poor in exchange for their collecting garbage in the favelas is a classic example of synergetic politics. Contemporary interest in Dharavi not merely as a "slum," but as a vast recycling workshop and a vibrant social and economic entity makes it better capable of resisting proposals for politically and financially motivated "clearance" or "renewal."

Other extraordinary projects include "Incremental Housing," a program initiated by Alejandro Aravena and the Elemental Group in Chile and more recently Mexico, which allows inhabitants to construct their own homes and thus invest in activities that they can do well by themselves.

The 10-by-10 Sandbag House designed by Luyanda Mpahlwa for Design Indaba, a South African advocacy organization, to improve informal settlement in Freedom Park, South Africa, involves using structural timber frames for tensile strength, and sandbags with chicken wire for reinforcing walls, which are then covered with plaster and timber cladding.

The Bangladeshi architect Mohammed Rezwan's "Floating Community Lifeboats" are designed to withstand monsoons and floods in low-lying areas.

These lifeboats, which already serve 90,000 families, provide low-cost portable solar electricity, and can be adapted for use as schools, medical clinics, and libraries. The community cooker designed by architects James Howard Archer and Mumo Musuva for Kibera, Kenya, and serving that community since the early 1990s, consists of a large, inexpensive and innovative oil and water combustion machine. Its users pay to cook on it by sorting trash and other refuse, which further benefits the community. The "Platform of Hope" in Korail, outside Dhaka, was designed by architect Khondaker Hasibul Kabir, who lived with a local family and collaborated with them over a period of three years to build this outdoor bamboo platform that serves as a much needed, clean, safe, and impervious-to-flooding public space for the Korail community.[21]

All these projects were initiated by individuals who invested their time and talents to help those in greater need, worked directly with locals, and collaborated across sectors and disciplines with limited resources to find solutions for some of the most urgent problems facing the urban poor. Biologists claim that "we are preprogrammed to reach out," and that "biology constitutes our greatest hope."[22] Today we are called to create or conceive of a new twenty-first-century city–a global polis that must mirror the ways in which we need to act towards nature, the environment, and our planet. Synergetic design can instigate a new kind of balance, new ways of living together. A twenty-first-century definition of synergetic or post-sustainable design should help us not only design better buildings and cities, but also understand something about humanity, the qualities of being human, and how to preserve those qualities for the future.

Notes:

1. Stoicism was a school of philosophy founded in Athens by Zeno of Citium in the early 3rd century BC.
2. Ralph Waldo Emerson, *Nature* (London/New York: Penguin Books, 1985), 80.
3. Ernst Haeckel (1834-1919), an eminent German naturalist, biologist, physician, philosopher and artist, described and named thousands of new species, and also popularized Charles Darwin's work in Germany. He coined the term "ecology" in his book *Generelle Morphologie* (1866).
4. As quoted by the Roman Stobaeus (4.671-673)
5 Adam Philips and Barbara Taylor, *On Kindness,* (New York: Farrar, Straus & Giroux, 2009),18. I am using "ekiosis" rather than "oikiosis" to emphasize the parallels with our better known "ecology". Both are equally correct transliterations from Ancient Greek.
6. Marshal Sahlins, *The Western Illusion of Human Nature* (Chicago: University of Chicago Press, 2008), 48. On p. 44 Sahlins notes that: "[there are] some remarkable recommendations of kinship community and subjectivity on the part of the ancients. Plato and Augustine both formulated a broad system of Hawaiian-type kinship as the mode of society most appropriate for mankind: Augustine asserting that this conception of humanity as family was the original, divinely-ordained social order; Plato, that it was the ideal civil society among the enlightened classes of his utopian Republic." On p. 45, he writes: "For Aristotle, kinsmen are the same entity in different subjects; children are their parents' other selves; and brothers, cousins and other relatives are people who belong to one another, if in varying degrees."
7. Sahlins, *Western Illusion*, 49
8. Philips and Taylor, *On Kindness,* 66.
9. Sahlins, *Western Illusion*, 104.
10. Sahlins claims that culture is human nature, and that we can only understand nature through our culture/s.
11. Philips and Taylor, *On Kindness,* 7.
12. Stanford's d-lab, MIT's d-lab, Parsons the New School's DESIS lab, Columbia's Slum-lab, etc.
13. Carol S. Dwek writing about the work of Michael Tomasello, in *Why We Cooperate* (Cambridge MA/London: MIT Press, 2009), 127.
14. Michael Tomasello, *Why We Cooperate*, x- xvi.

15. Tomasello cites philosopher Thomas Nagel in *The Possibility of Altruism* to make this point. Tomasello, *Why We Cooperate,* 40-41.
16. Michael Tomasello, *Why We Cooperate*, xv.
17. "Corning brings together the latest findings from the behavioral and biological sciences to help us understand how to move beyond the Madoffs and Enrons in our midst in order to lay the foundation for a new social contract–a Biosocial Contract built on a deep understanding of human nature and a commitment to fairness. He then proposes a sweeping set of economic and political reforms based on three principles of fairness–equality, equity, and reciprocity–that together could transform our society and our world." Retrieved on 7/20/15 from (http://www.cooperationcommons.com/taxonomy/term/25)
18. Corning, as in note above.
19. *Operating Manual for Spaceship Earth* (New York: Simon & Schuster, 1970), 71 and 73.
20. David Orr, "Designing Minds," in *Earth in Mind: On Education, Environment and the Human Prospect* (Washington D.C./Covelo CA: Island Press, 1994), 104-111. The full paragraph is of course more illuminating but still lacks the social component: ""Ecological design competence means maximizing resource and energy efficiency, taking advantage of the free services of nature, recycling wastes, making ecologically smarter things, and educating ecologically smarter people. It means incorporating intelligence about how nature works... into the way we think, design, build, and live. Design applies to the making of nearly everything that directly or indirectly requires energy and materials or governs their use, including farms, houses, communities, neighborhoods, cities, transportation systems, technologies, economies, and energy policies. When human artifacts and systems are well designed, they are in harmony with the larger patterns in which they are embedded. When poorly designed, they undermine those larger patterns, creating pollution, higher costs, and social stress in the name of a spurious and short-run economizing. Bad design is not simply an engineering problem, although better engineering would often help. Its roots go deeper".
21. The projects mentioned here are drawn primarily from the beautifully curated exhibition and the catalogue *Design With the Other 90%: Cities* [ed. by Cynthia Smith (New York: The Cooper-Hewitt Smithsonian Institution, 2011).
22. Frans de Waal, "The Age of Empathy: Nature's Lessons for a Kinder Society," *The New York Times* (November 30 2009), retrieved on 7/20/15 from: http://www.nytimes.com/2009/12/01/science/01human.html?_r=1&pagewanted=all

Biographies

Dr. Michelle D. Addington, Hines Professor of Sustainable Architectural Design at Yale University School of Architecture, holds a joint appointment with the Yale School of Forestry and Environmental Studies. She has co-authored the book entitled *Smart Materials and Technologies for the Architecture and Design Professions* (Routledge, 2004).

Dr. Rachel Armstrong, Professor of Experimental Architecture at Newcastle University School of Architecture and a Senior TED Fellow, embodies and promotes new transferrable ways of thinking "outside the box," which she discusses in *Living Architecture: How Synthetic Biology Can Remake Our Cities and Reshape Our Lives* (TED Books, 2012), while also encouraging others to develop innovative environmental solutions.

Herwig Baumgartner and Scott Uriu, architects and founders of B+U, a Los Angeles-based firm that pursues a visionary aesthetic encompassing all fields of design, experiment with concepts and techniques drawn from science, computation, and especially music, in which both have early training. They teach at the Southern California Institute of Architecture (SCIARC), and, in the case of Uriu, also at the University of Southern California.

Philip Beesley, architect, digital media artist, and Professor in the School of Architecture at the University of Waterloo as well as director of the University's Integrated Group for Visualization, Design and Manufacturing, is the founder and director of PBAI, Toronto, an interdisciplinary design firm that combines public buildings with exhibition design, stage, and lighting projects, and incorporates industrial design, digital prototyping, and mechatronics engineering into its practice.

Jason Bellows, a writer with an intense interest in fiction, sci-fi, and fantasy, is a self-proclaimed Renaissance Man, who likes to read constantly, keep up with the sciences, maintain an open mind, and do his best "to bring about his personal ideas on utopia through the means available to him: writing and sarcasm."

David Benjamin is an architect and co-founder of The Living, a research firm that brings new technology to life in the built environment and integrates design innovation, sustainability, and the public realm. He is also Assistant Professor at Columbia University's School of Architecture, Planning and Preservation (GSAAP) and Director of its Living Architecture Lab.

Dr. D. Graham Burnett is a historian of science, writer, Professor at Princeton University and editor of *Cabinet Magazine*. His interests include the history of natural history and the sciences of the earth and the sea, including cartography, navigation, oceanography, and ecology/environmentalism, from the seventeenth through the twentieth centuries. A recipient of many awards and fellowships, he is currently working on connections between the sciences and the visual arts.

Vincent Callebaut is an archibiotect and leader in innovative green design, whose work is deeply interested in positive visions of eco-lifestyles inspired by biomimicry. A recipient of many awards for his futuristic, eco-responsible designs inspired by naturally occurring forms, he has been the subject of a monograph published in 2013 by Hachette in its "Masters of Architecture" series.

Dr. David Catling holds a joint appointment in Astrobiology and the Department of Earth and Space Sciences at the University of Washington (UW), Seattle. His research falls under the broad umbrellas of geobiology and astrobiology, a new branch of science concerned with the origin and evolution of life on Earth as well as the possible variety of life beyond Earth, which he introduces to the general public in *Astrobiology: A Very Short Introduction* (OUP, 2013).

Oron Catts, artist, researcher, and curator, is co-founder of SymbioticA, an artistic research center housed in the School of

Anatomy, Physiology, and Human Biology at the University of Western Australia. Often working in collaboration with other artists and scientists, Catts has developed a body of work that speaks about the need for new cultural articulation of evolving concepts of life. His ideas and projects reach beyond the confines of art and are often cited as inspiration for diverse areas such as new materials, textiles, design, architecture, ethics, fiction, and food.

Giacomo Costa is an Italian artist who uses digital technology to generate futuristic cityscapes inspired by science fiction that aim to capture the depersonalization of the contemporary city. He exhibits internationally and represented Italy at the 53rd Venice Biennale (2009). His work has appeared in *Digital Photo*, *Ru*, *Evolo*, *Frame*, and *C-Photo Magazine,* among others and is featured in *The Chronicles of Time* (Damiani, 2009).

Martina Decker, architect and Assistant Professor at the College of Architecture and Design at NJIT, focuses on how new materials with novel properties might generate solutions to various contemporary challenges in sustainability and health and safety. Decker has worked on a wide range of award-winning projects that represent a penchant for interdisciplinary work, including art installations, consumer products, and buildings.

Ginger Dosier is an architect with additional experience and training in material science and microbiologically-based materials, who works in new material development for the AEC [Architecture Engineering and Construction] sector with an environmental focus. She is the founder of bioMASON, a unique biotechnology start-up manufacturing company that employs natural microorganisms and chemical processes to manufacture biological cement-based masonry building materials that can be manufactured on site in ambient temperatures with local materials and without the use of fuel.

Evan Douglis is the Dean of the School of Architecture at Rensselaer Polytechnic Institute and the principal of Evan Douglis Studio LLC, an architecture and interdisciplinary design firm that does cutting-edge research in computer-aided digital design and fabrication technology and applies it to a range of diverse gallery installations, product designs, commercial and residential projects, urban redevelopment schemes, and prefabricated modular building components. Douglis has received many awards for his innovative approach to design, and his works and writings have been widely published.

Jacob Dugopolski is Senior Architect and Urban Designer at WXY Studio in New York City. Upon graduating from Yale in 2011, he received a Parsons Memorial Medal for demonstrating promise in city planning. In 2012, Dugopolski's work was included in Zago Architecture's contribution to MoMA's exhibition, "Foreclosed: Rehousing the American Dream."

Anna Dyson teaches design, technology, and theory at the School of Architecture at Rensselaer, and is the director of its Center for Architecture, Science, and Ecology (CASE). She holds multiple international patents for building systems inventions and is currently directing interdisciplinary research to develop new systems for on-site energy generation. She has worked as a design architect and product designer and has had her work exhibited in the MoMA Young Architects Series.

Dr. Alex Felson is an urban ecologist, landscape architect, and Professor in the School of Forestry and Environmental Studies and School of Architecture at Yale University as well as founder of its Urban Ecology and Design Lab. His research and work is directed towards seeking new ways of constructing biologically rich systems through research-based design and adaptive management.

Melanie Fessel, an architect, urban designer, and Director of Design at Terreform ONE, is founder of ONE (Open Network Ecology) Odyssey, an interdisciplinary research enterprise that draws on philanthropic design principles to integrate ecological values into urban environments. Previously she was an associate with the Cooper Union Institute for Sustainable Design. Melanie has worked as an architect in Germany, Switzerland, Spain, and the U.S. Additionally, she has taught architecture studio at Rensselaer Polytechnic Institute, Lawrence Technical Institute, and ONE Lab: NY School for Design and Science.

Pablo Garcia is an artist, architect, and Assistant Professor in the Department of Contemporary Practices at the School of the Art Institute of Chicago. His recent work has evolved from design-for-hire to internationally exhibited artworks, provocations, and research studies. From 2004-2007, Garcia worked as an architect and designer for Diller Scofidio + Renfro.

Alexandra Daisy Ginsberg is a designer, artist, and writer who seeks new roles for design by developing experimental approaches that help us imagine alternative ideals around technology. Director of Studio Alexandra Daisy Ginsberg, she collaborates with scientists, engineers, artists, designers, social scientists, galleries and industry around the world. She is also the lead author of *Synthetic Aesthetics: Investigating Synthetic Biology's Designs on Nature* (MIT Press, 2014), based on a Stanford University/University of Edinburgh initiative to develop discourse between synthetic biology, art, and design.

Dr. Jessica Green, Associate Professor at the University of Oregon, and external faculty at the Santa Fe Institute, is an applied and theoretical ecologist whose overarching aim is to understand the forces that organize heterogeneous ecological systems, and to apply this understanding to inform conservation policy and management decisions. Green is the founding director of the Biology and Built Environment Center at the University of Oregon, which applies theoretical, computational, and empirical approaches to study microbial systems in a wide range of environments.

Omer Haciomeroglu (MFA) is an Industrial Designer at Cliff Design, a Swedish Design Consultancy providing highly competent design works for clients such as Volvo, Electrolux, Saab, Atlas Copco, etc. He holds an Advanced Product Design Master's Degree from Umea Institute of Design, Sweden, and is a lover of nature and a believer in sustainable technology.

Victor Hadjikyriacou, who received his MA in architecture from University College, London in 2012, is an Architect at Vakis Associates in Cyprus. Previous to his current position, he worked for Foster + Partners and Paul Davis and Partners in London.

Doug Jackson is an architect who works on the potential of creative use-transformation of architectural form and space with the intent of making the physical environment more engaging and relevant to contemporary digital–and network–culture. He is the director of the Doug Jackson Design Office (DJDO), a small, full-service architecture and design practice focused on preserving and expanding architecture's unique ability to re-assemble the everyday material of the world into a new and inhabitable one.

Marcin Jakubowski, farmer/technologist, is the founder of Open Source Ecology, an open collaborative of engineers, producers, and builders who are developing the Global Village Construction Set (GVCS), a DIY tool set of 50 different industrial machines needed to create a small civilization with modern comforts. His goal is to create an open-source economy that optimizes both production and distribution while providing environmental regeneration and social justice.

Dr. Natalie Jeremijenko, artist, engineer, and Professor in Visual Arts at NYU, is the director of the xdesign Environmental Health Clinic, which develops and prescribes locally optimized and often playful strategies to effect remediation of environmental systems, generates measurable and mediagenic evidence, and coordinates diverse projects that bring about effective material change. Her research centers on structures of participation in the production of knowledge and information as well as the political and social possibilities (and limitations) of information and emerging technologies–mostly through public experiments. In this vein, her work spans a range of media from statistical indices, to biological substrates, to robotics.

Alex Kaiser teaches the art of architectural drawing and digital painting at the Architectural Association in London and l'École Spéciale d'Architecture in Paris, and offers workshops for architects and designers at Drawing at Work in London. He researches trans-media methods for design through drawing and painting, while taking line beyond the representational into fields from architecture and industrial design to bio-mimetics and beyond.

Dr. Lydia Kallipoliti, an architect, engineer, theorist, and Assistant Professor at Syracuse University, focuses on recycling material experiments and the intersection of cybernetic and ecological theories. A recipient of a Marvin E. Goody award for the creative use of materials, she is also the founder of EcoRedux, an online open-source educational resource documenting the history of ecological experimentation in the twentieth century.

Markus Kayser is a furniture and product designer, currently studying media matter at the MIT Media Lab. He is experimenting with hybrid solutions that link technology and natural energy to question current manufacturing methodologies and test new scenarios of production. Drawing on science, art, and engineering, his work engages in discussion about opportunities to produce design that involves new as well as forgotten processes and technologies.

Magnus Larsson, a writer, artist, and architect, runs Ordinary Ltd., a London-based experimental architecture, design, and research studio that explores novel ways of living in the material world. Devoted to the development of alternative building materials, he is exploring the potential of engineered wood, synthesized silk, and sandstone produced by bacteria.

Dr. Ferdinand Ludwig is a pioneering architect in the field of Living Plant Constructions, who works on projects that combine growth processes of living plants with engineering methods. He is coordinator and co-founder of the Research Group Baubotanik at IGMA, University of Stuttgart. While working on his PhD, he developed multiple horticultural construction techniques and analyzed botanical rules of growth to deduce rules for living plant constructions.

Greg Lynn is an architect distinguished both for his innovative application of digital technology to design and for pioneering the fabrication and manufacture of complex functional and ergonomic forms using CNC (Computer Numerically Controlled) machinery. His background in philosophy and architecture has led him to combine design and construction with writing and teaching. He holds concurrent academic posts at the University of Applied Arts in Vienna, UCLA, the Yale School of Architecture, and the European Graduate School (EGS). Greg Lynn FORM, his Venice, CA-based firm has received multiple awards, and its works are included in permanent collections of architecture and design museums worldwide.

Andrew Maynard is an architect, designer, and director, along with Mark Austin, of Andrew Maynard Architects in Melbourne. His conceptual and built works have been featured in many publications as well as international competitions. He has been the recipient of multiple awards, and in 2013, his HOUSE was named the "House of the Year" at the World Architecture Festival.

Dr. Oliver Medvedik is a biotechnology consultant and currently the Sandholm Visiting Assistant Professor of Biology and Bioengineering at The Cooper Union, where he is teaching courses in molecular and cellular biology and serving as Assistant Director of the Maurice Kanbar Center for Biomedical Research. As part of his doctoral work, he used single-celled budding yeast as a model system to map the genetic pathways that underlie the processes of aging in more complex organisms, such as humans.

Azadeh Mohammadi holds a Masters in Architecture from the University of Toronto, and is currently an intern at Archinect, an online publication/resource founded in 1997 to establish a more connected community of architects, students, and designers with the goal of making architecture more open and bringing together designers from around the world.

Dr. Anil Netravali is the Jean and Douglas McLean Professor in Fiber Science and Apparel Design in the Department of Materials Science and Engineering at Cornell University. His main research lies in the field of Fiber Reinforced Composites and Green materials, and he is working towards developing Green resins from plant-based proteins and starches to fabricate environment-friendly composites for a variety of applications.

Dr. Marc J. Neveu is an architect, architectural historian, and Assistant Professor at the College of Architecture and Environmental Design at Cal Poly. His areas of specialization are eighteenth-century architectural history and theory and the history and theory of architectural pedagogy. He is currently executive editor of the *Journal of Architectural Education*.

Zbigniew Oksiuta, architect, artist, and Lecturer at Rensselaer Polytechnic, experiments with the possibility of designing biological structures. His research concentrates on reducing space to a minimal physiological existence based primarily on verifiable physical and chemical parameters that put aside historical, social, urbanistic, and aesthetic factors. Oksiuta works with new soft technologies and biological materials that enable the development of new kinds of living habitats in the biosphere and space.

Enrico Pieraccioli and Claudio Granato founded Lash-Up, a multidisciplinary studio in Florence, Italy, that operates in the fields of architecture, design, and research, and encourages reflection on space and time in architecture. Claudio Granato investigates issues related to parametric-generative design; Enrico Pieraccioli details experiences about the visual arts.

Carlo F. Ratti, architect, engineer, inventor, educator, and activist, practices in Italy and teaches at MIT, where he directs the Senseable City Lab, a research group that explores how new technologies are changing the way we understand, design, and ultimately live in cities. He is a founding partner (with Walter Nicolino) of Carlo Ratti Associati in Turin, Italy, which develops innovative design projects that merge high-profile architecture and urban planning with cutting-edge digital technologies to create smart and "senseable" cities and buildings.

Aurora Robson is a multi-media artist known predominantly for her transformative work intercepting the waste stream. A recipient of a Pollock Krasner Grant and a TED/Lincoln Re-Imagine Prize, she has exhibited internationally and has had her work featured in many art magazines. Robson is also the founding artist of Project Vortex, an international collective of artists, designers, and architects who work with plastic debris.

François Roche, architect, theorist, Professor of Architecture and Urbanism at the European Graduate School (EGS), is the founder of New-Territories, a site dedicated to: Research as Speculation/Fiction as Practice/Practice as LifeSpan. He is also co-founder of the architectural firm, R&Sie(n), which periodically changes its name in order to illustrate its hybrid character as well as the need to destabilize the figure of the architect. Roche's work has been widely published and exhibited and is featured in Antonino di Raimo's *Francois Roche: Heretical Machinism and Living Architecture of New Territories* (ebook).

Phil Ross is an artist, inventor, and Assistant Professor at the University of San Francisco, whose sculptural artworks combine natural and technologically advanced materials and are literally grown into being, at once highly crafted and naturally formed, skillfully manipulated, and sloppily organic. Ross is also co-founder of MycoWorks, A Silicon Valley-based design and material engineering firm that creates sustainable design solutions with advanced biomaterials.

John Rhett Russo, architect and Associate Professor in Architecture at NJIT is inspired by the transmissive capacities of matter and the ecology of form that are part of the natural world. This approach parallels his interest in alternative modes of craft and its role in the development of complexity within the discipline of architecture. His work has received many awards and, along with his writings, has been widely published.

Jenny E. Sabin is an architectural designer, artist, and Assistant Professor in the School of Architecture at Cornell University, whose work investigates the intersections of architecture and science while applying insights and theories from biology and mathematics to the design of material structures. She is principal of Jenny Sabin Studio LLC, and co-founder (with Peter Lloyd Jones) of Sabin + Jones LabStudio, a hybrid research and design network devoted to developing, analyzing, and abstracting dynamic systems through the generation and design of new tools.

Dr. Nina Tandon, a Senior TED Fellow in 2012, has a PhD in Biomedical Engineering and is currently a Staff Associate in the Laboratory for Stem Cells and Tissue Engineering at Columbia University and adjunct faculty at the Cooper Union. She studies electrical signaling in the context of tissue engineering, with the goal of creating "spare parts" for human implantation and/or disease models.

Dr. Ioanna Theocharopoulou is an Assistant Professor of Interior Design at Parsons School of Design, whose research focuses on urbanization and sustainability as well as the history and theory of sustainable design. She has taught in the Cooper-Hewitt MA Program as well as at Columbia (GSAAP), where she initiated and co-curated ECOGRAM, a series of public events on sustainability in architectural design.

Skylar Tibbits, architect, internationally exhibited designer, and computer scientist, focuses on developing self-assembly technologies for large-scale structures in the physical environment. He is a Research Scientist in the Department of Architecture at MIT, where he also directs the Self-Assembly Lab, as well as the founder and principal of SJET LLC, a multidisciplinary research-based practice crossing disciplines from architecture and design, fabrication and computer science to robotics.

Jason Vigneri-Beane, architect, industrial designer, and project designer at Billings Jackson Design, has been instrumental in founding a number of celebrated design-research practices that concentrate on multi-disciplinary relationships among digital design, new media, infrastructure, and social organization. He also teaches and directs the Master of Science in Architecture program at Pratt Institute.

Chris Woebken is an artist and co-founder (with Elliott P. Montgomery) of the Extrapolation Factory, an imagination-based studio for design-led futures that develops experimental methods for collaboratively prototyping, experiencing, and impacting future scenarios embodied as artifacts in familiar, present-day contexts. Woebken uses futuring practices to create props, narratives, and visualizations that investigate the impacts as well as the aesthetic and social potentials of technologies.
BIOS Studios/Firms

Architecture Research Office (ARO), a New York-based firm led by Stephen Cassell, Adam Yarinsky, and Kim Yao, is as much a laboratory as a design practice. Through investigation, analysis and testing, ARO creates designs that unite the conceptual and the pragmatic within a strong, coherent vision. This research-driven process enables the firm to operate on a wide variety of projects and to craft elegant solutions to seemingly intractable problems, always in an effort to achieve the greatest aesthetic impact while using the fewest natural and financial resources. Among its current projects is the new home of the Division of Applied Mathematics at Brown University, and a chicken coop with radiant floor heating in a refurbished farmhouse in East Hampton, New York.

AUDC was founded by Robert Sumrell and Kazys Varnelis in 2001 as an experimental architectural collaborative with the mission of using the discipline's tools to research the role of the individual and the community in the contemporary urban environment. Inspired by the conceptual work of radical architectural groups such as Archizoom, UFO, and Haus Rucker Co, AUDC constructs realities, not objects, through multimedia experimentation to immerse viewers in the subject matter. Working with existing conditions instead of imposing new ones, AUDC reveals rather than masks reality. AUDC has exhibited widely in venues including the Wind Tunnel at the Art Center College of Design and Andrea Zittel's High Desert Test Sites, and has published its work in *Cabinet*, *Perspecta*, *Textfield*, *Verb*, and *306090*.

BIG (Bjarke Ingels Group), founded in 2005 by Bjarke Ingels, is a Copenhagen- and New York-based group of architects, designers, builders, and thinkers operating within the fields of architecture, urbanism, research, and development, and is involved in multiple building projects worldwide. BIG's architecture emerges out of a careful analysis of how contemporary life constantly evolves and changes. The firm aims for a pragmatic utopian architecture that steers clear of the petrifying pragmatism of boring boxes and the naïve utopian ideas of digital formalism. It engages in a kind of programmatic alchemy, creating architecture by mixing conventional ingredients such as living, leisure, working, parking, and shopping. A recipient of many awards, BIG is currently engaged in the design and construction of 2 World Trade Center in New York City.

Bittertang is a small design firm founded in 2005 and run by Antonio Torres and Michael Loverich who strive to bring happiness into the built environment by referencing the pleasurable world surrounding us. Its work explores multiple themes including pleasure, frothiness, biological matter, animal posturing, babies, sculpture, and coloration–all unified by *bel composto*. The firm has created anamorphic and neotenous projects ranging from living aquaculture orbs to stuffed animals, piñatas, and sukkahs. Bittertang received the Architectural League Prize for Young Architects and Designers in 2010.

Clouds AO, founded by Masayuki Sono and Ostap Rudakevych in 2010 in New York City, focuses on the potential of the immaterial, the experiential qualities of architecture, and the ways in which form and material can elicit lasting emotional or cognitive revelation. To achieve this end, Sono and Rudakevych pay careful attention to the unique parameters of each project, distilling research and analysis, making relevant facts materialize, and creating conditions that allow their design to synthesize ideas and result in a resonant experience. The firm was nominated for the 2014 Iakov Chernikhov prize, and in 2015 received an Honors Award from the New York Chapter of the AIA for its interior design of the new St. Mark's Bookshop.

ecoLogicStudio is a London-based architectural and urban-design practice that takes ecology as its conceptual as well as material paradigm. Founded in 2004 by Claudia Pasquero and Marco Poletto, the firm specializes in environmental design, urban self-sufficiency, and building integrated nature. Developing and applying a design method capable of exploiting the latest innovations in digital computational design, ecoLogicStudio deploys digital technologies to develop hyper-realities, regimes of intense exchange between the artificial and the natural, the designed and the accidental. Its work, which ranges from private villas and a public library to eco-roofs and installations at architectural biennials, is featured in *Systematic Architecture* (Routledge, 2012).

Elevator B was a collaborative project among five graduate students (Courtney Creenan, Kyle Mastilinski, Daniel Nead, Scott Selin, and Lisa Stern) in SUNY Buffalo's School of Architecture and Planning, the Department of Architecture's Ecological Practices Research Group, and Rigidized Metals, a Buffalo-based building material manufacturer. Its overall goal was to design and relocate a colony of honeybees occupying a building at Silo City, a dense cluster of grain elevators in Buffalo, NY. The project was an iconic gesture of the regeneration of Silo City, both naturally and economically. The material properties of the tower housing the colony of bees represent the cluster of material manufacturers now located around the site. Visitors enter the tower from below and look up, similar to the way in which they would experience the silos and bins of the nearby Marine A elevator.

Future City Lab is an interdisciplinary experimental design studio, workshop, and architectural think tank operating globally out of San Francisco, California and employing an adventurous team of designers, architects, technologists, digital craftspeople, urban ecologists, and more. Since 2002, founding principals Jason Kelly Johnson and Nataly Gattegno Ho have been collaborating on a wide range of award-winning projects that explore the intersections of design with advanced fabrication technologies, robotics, responsive building systems, and public space, while teaching, lecturing, publishing, and exhibiting their work internationally.

MY Studio, a Boston-based multidisciplinary practice founded by J. Meejin Yoon and Eric Höweler, operates in the space between architecture, art, and landscape. Believing in an embodied experience of architecture, the group sees media as material and its effects as palpable elements of architectural speculation. While its projects lie at the intersection of the conceptual and the corporeal, HYA/MYS is committed to both the practice-of and prospects-for architecture. From concept to construct, the studio is determined to realize the built idea and to test projects through the dynamic interaction between the construct and the larger public. Its work, which has been widely published, is featured in *Expanded Practice* (Princeton Architectural Press, 2009).

Hugh Broughton Architects is a London-based firm founded in 1995 with a portfolio spanning the commercial, institutional, cultural, and public sector. Built around a core of experienced architects, it is committed to the idea that architecture needs to respond to human needs, commercial reality, and environmental pragmatism in order to achieve physical meaning. Its approach requires that architects exercise their lateral thinking to the full in order to enter new territories, explore new forms of construction, and draw upon the full breadth of available technologies from a vast array of industries. This is epitomized by the firm's success in designing work for extreme environments, as exemplified by its award-winning scientific research facilities in Polar Regions.

Kokkugia is an experimental architectural research collaborative that explores generative design methodologies developed from the complex self-organizing behavior of biological, social, and material systems. Its agenda is to develop a non-linear architecture, one that emerges from the operation of complex systems and questions the established hierarchies that operate within architecture by encoding simple architectural decisions within a distributed system of autonomous computational entities or agents. Although Kokkugia's role is highly speculative–to imagine the future–its partners, Roland Snooks and Robert Stuart-Smith, direct separate architectural practices in London and Melbourne but continue to collaborate on strategic projects such as their recent Astana 2017 Expo scheme.

Land Art Generator Initiative (LAGI), co-founded and directed by Robert Ferry & Elizabeth Monoian, is a non-profit program that aims to implement sustainable design solutions by integrating art and interdisciplinary creative processes into the conception of renewable energy infrastructure. Its main goal is to hold competitions for and construct public art installations that distribute clean energy into the electrical grid and provide power for hundreds to thousands of homes around the world. Thus far it has initiated such projects in Abu Dhabi (2010), New York (2012), and Copenhagen (2014).

Lateral Office, a Toronto-based experimental design practice founded in 2003 by Mason White and Lola Sheppard, operates at the intersection of architecture, landscape, and urbanism. The studio is committed to design as a research vehicle for posing and responding to complex, urgent questions in the built environment while engaging in the wider context and climate of a project, be it social, ecological, or political. Recent work and research has focused on powerful design relationships between public realm, infrastructure, and the environment. Its projects have been exhibited in venues around the world and earned many awards, most recently Special Mention at the 2014 Venice Architectural Biennale.

MVVA, a Brooklyn-based landscape architecture firm founded by Michael Van Valkenburgh, creates environmentally sustainable and experientially rich places across a wide range of landscape scales, from city to campus to garden. Collaborating closely with urban planners, architects, engineers, and ecologists, MVVA subscribes to an integrated design methodology that ensures that its built landscapes grow from and are supported by integrated sustainability, outstanding environmental performance, financial resourcefulness, material resilience, technical innovation, and material expression. With projects such as the Brooklyn Bridge Park, and Maggie Daley Park in Chicago, MVVA's commissions have expanded to a scale capable of achieving "ecological urbanism."

Pneumastudio is a New York-based interdisciplinary design practice situated between architecture and landscape architecture. Much of its design work is experimental in terms of the exploration of new technologies, material and geometric systems, and engages in a variety of discourses related to contemporary design culture. To this extent, Pneumastudio's work relies heavily on the on-going academic involvement of its two principals, Chris Perry and Cathryn Dwyre, whose work and writings have been featured in many publications, most recently *Bracket 2: Goes Soft* (Actar, 2013) and *Post-Sustainability: Blueprints for a Green Planet* (Metropolis Books, forthcoming).

StudioKCA, a Brooklyn-based multi-disciplinary firm led by Jason Klimoski and Lesley Chang, combines the practices of architecture, interiors, industrial design and lighting design. Its group of designers, architects, and artists approach each project holistically, working to create environments that feel simple, connected, and complete. Whether designing a residence, commercial space, an art installation, or a light, they strive to tell a story and create a sense of place that resonates with the end user and the local environment. Among their recent installations is "Head in the Clouds"–53,780 plastic bottles strung together in an aluminum frame, which was on display at New York's Governor's Island in 2013.

Terreform ONE (Open Network Ecology) is a non-profit research group that promotes smart cities and serves as a unique multidisciplinary laboratory to advance the larger framework of socio-ecological design. Through creative projects and outreach efforts, its members–Mitchell Joachim, Maria Aiolova, Melanie Fessel, Nurhan Gokturk, Christian Hubert, and Executive Director, Vivian Kuan–aim to illuminate salient resolutions for the urban environment.

Zuloark, founded by Manuel Domina Aiolois is an open network of architects, designers, builders, and thinkers that redefines itself according to the platforms in which it collaborates. Since 2001, it has been working as an independent studio with renowned architects, other studios, and individuals in organization and project management to develop urban action through investigative and participative strategies. Recognized internationally, it won first prize in the XII Biennial of Spanish Architecture in 2014, and participated in MoMA's 2014 "Uneven Growth" exhibition.

About the authors

Mitchell Joachim, PhD, is a Co-Founder of Terreform ONE, a non-profit architecture and urban design research group in New York. Equally, he is an Associate Professor of Practice in Architecture and Urban Design at NYU Gallatin School of Individualized Study and holds joint appointments at the Tisch School of the Arts ITP and Tandon School of Engineering. Mitchell is a Co-Chair of Global Design NYU. Formerly, he worked as an architect at the professional offices of Frank Gehry in Los Angeles, Moshe Safdie in Boston, and I.M. Pei in New York. He has won many awards including: Fulbright Scholarship, R+D Award, AIA New York Urban Design Merit Award, Victor Papanek Social Design Award, 1st Place International Architecture Award, Zumtobel Award for Sustainability, Architizer A+ Award, History Channel Infiniti Award for City of the Future, and Time Magazine Best Invention with MIT Smart Cities Car. He is a TED Senior Fellow and has been awarded fellowships with Safdie Architects, and the Martin Society for Sustainability at MIT. Mitchell was featured in numerous articles: "The 100 People Who Are Changing America," in *Rolling Stone*, "The Smart List: 15 People the Next President Should Listen To," in *Wired*, "50 Under 50 Innovators of the 21st Century" by Images Publishing Group, "The NOW 99" in *Dwell*, and "Future of The Environment" in *Popular Science.* He co-authored the books, *Super Cells: Building with Biology* (TED Books) and *Global Design: Elsewhere Envisioned* (Prestel). His architectural work has been exhibited in numerous places including MoMA in New York, DOX Center for Contemporary Art in Prague, MASS MoCA in Massachusetts, The Building Centre in London, DAZ in Berlin, OCAD in Toronto, NAI in Rotterdam, and the Venice Biennale. Previously, he was the Frank Gehry Chair at the University of Toronto and faculty at Pratt, Columbia, Syracuse, Rensselaer, Washington (St. Louis), Parsons, EGS, and Cornell. He earned a PhD at the Massachusetts Institute of Technology, MAUD (Urban Design) at Harvard University, MArch at Columbia University, and a BPS from the University at Buffalo with honors.

Mike Silver, Assistant Professor of Architecture at University of Buffalo, pursues pioneering research in the fields of sustainable design, machine vision, high-performance computing and transformation optics. His work has been focused on the development of mobile applications for masonry construction (AutomasonMP3), on-site co-robotic systems, and a variety of new fabrication tools, including numerically controlled fiber-placement technology. Mike holds a Masters of Building Design from Columbia University, and is both a LeFevre '29 research fellow for The Knowlton School of Architecture in Col-umbus Ohio and a Sanders Fellow at the University of Michigan. He was the Director of Digital Media at the Yale School of Architecture from 2001-2004 and a design instructor at Harvard's Graduate School of Design. He is also the author of numerous books and articles on the relationship between technology and design practice, including *Pamphlet Architecture 19 Reading / Drawing / Building, AD's Mapping in the Age of Digital Media,* and *Programming Cultures* by Wiley and Sons. Mike is currently the director of Critical Systems Lab, a multidisciplinary design collective based in New York. In collaboration with mathematicians, computer scientists, and engineers, his office has worked at a variety of scales and has extensive experience in the production of furnishings, consumer products, web sites, and buildings. As an experimental collaborative, Silver's firm is deeply committed to the precise alignment of advanced technology, environmental design, poetic consciousness, architectural theory, academic scholarship, and the logistics of building construction. His work has been exhibited at the New Museum of Contemporary Art in Manhattan, the IDC in Nagoya Japan, the National Building Museum in Washington, D.C., the Architectural League in New York, and the Cooper-Hewitt National Design Museum. Mike built his first working robot arm using Scotch Tape and Spirograph parts at the age of 14.

Credits

EXTRATERRITORIALITY NEXUS: Melanie Fessel, Diana Agrest (thesis advisor)

LATERAL OFFICE & LCLA OFFICE: WEATHERFIELD: Mason White, Lola Sheppard, Luis Callejas, Matthew Spremulli, Alexander Laing

BJARKE INGELS GROUP (BIG): AMAGERFORBRAENDING: Partners in charge: Bjarke Ingels, David Zahle; Project Leader: Claus Hermansen; Project Architect: Nanna Gyldholm Mvid ZahTeam: Brian Yang, Jakob Ohm Laursen; Lise Jessen, Espen Vik, Narisara Ladawal Schrggton, D.C., the Architecturment of advanced teen, Ryohei Koike, Anders Hjortnaes, Henrick Poulsen, Annette Jensen, Jeppe Ecklon, Kamilla Heskje, Franck Fdida, Alberto Cumerlato, Gonzalo Castro, Chris Zhongtian Yuan, Aleksander Wadas, Liang Wang, Alexander Ejsing, Chris Falla, Mathias Bank, Katarzyna Siedlecka. Jelena Vucic, Alina Tamosiunaite, Armore Gutierrez, Maciej Zawadzki, Jakob Lange, Andreas Klok Pedersen, Daniel Selensky, Gül Ertekin, Xing Xiong, Sunming Lee, Long Zuo, Ji-young Yoon, Blake Smith, Buster Christensen, Simon Masson, Brygida Zawadzka, Zoltan David Kalaszi, Henrik Rømer Kania, Alexandra Gustafsson, Ariel Wallner, Ask Andersen, Balaj Ilulian, Dennis Rasmussen, Finn Nørkjaer, George Abraham, Helen Chen, Horia Soirescu, Jing Xu, Joanna Jakubowska, Johanna Nenander, Krysztof Marciszewski, Laura Wätte, Marcelina Kolasinska, Marcos Bano, Maren Allen, Matti Nørgaard, Michael Andersen, Niklas A. Rasch, Nynne Madsen, Øgaard, Mich Pero Vukovic, Richard Howis, Se Hyeon Kim, Toni Mateu.
THE DRYLINE: (BIG) Bjarke Ingels Group with One Architecture, Starr Whitehouse, James Lima Planning + Development, Project Projects, Green Shield Ecology, AEA Consulting, Level Agency for Infrastructure, Arcadis, and the Parsons School of Constructed Environments. Bjarke Ingels, Kai-Uwe Bergmann, Thomas Christofferson, Iben Falconer, Jeremy Alain Siegel, Daniel Kidd, Kurt Nieminen, Sun Yifu, Dammy Lee, Chooghyo Lee, Jack Lipson, David Spittler, Kenneth Amoah, David Dottelonde, Blake Smith, Hector Garcia, Ricardo De Palma, Daisy Zhang, Yaziel Jaurbe, Taylor Hewitt, Patricia Correa Velasquez

CLEAN: Azadeh Mohammadi

UNIVERSITY of GREENWICH: FUTURE VENICE: Rachel Armstrong, Neil Spiller, Martin Hanczyc, Christian Kerrigan, GMJ, European Center for Living Technology

P+G: HUMAN HERITAGE SITE: Enrico Pieraccioli, Claudio Granati

CLOUDS ARCHITECTURE OFFICE: AQUALTA: Ostap Rudakevych, Gretchen Stump

7°56'S-14°22'W: Charles Darwin, Sir Joseph Hooker

TERREFORM ONE: FAB TREE HAB, PLUG-IN ECOLOGY, BIO CITY MAP OF 11 MILLION, URBANEERING RESILIENT WATERFRONT, MYCOFORM SURFACE, IN VITRO MEAT HABITAT: Mitchell Joachim, Maria Aiolova, Melanie Fessel, Nurhan Gokturk, Oliver Medvedik, Christian Hubert, Vivian Kuan. Research fellows and collaborators: Amanda O'Keefe, Landon Young, Bahar Avanoglu, Ipek Avanoglu, Pedro Galindo-Landeira, Yinan Li, Brent Solomon, Jiachen Xu, Josef Schrock, Elisabeth Haid, Wagdy Moussa, James Schwartz, Jacqueline Hall, Greg Mulholland, Chloe Byme, Keith Comito, Adrian De Silva, Ian Slover, Daniel Dewit, Renee Fayzimatova, Alena Field, Nicholas Gervasi, Julien Gonzalez, Lucas Hamren, Patty Kaishian, Ahmad Khan, Laasyapriya Malladi, Karan Maniar, Ricardo Martin Coloma, Puja Patel, Merve Poyraz, Mina Rafiee, Mahsoo Salimi, Manjula Singh, Diego Wu Law, Eric Tan, Dylan Butman, Greg Mulholland, Shruti Grover, James Schwartz, Josue Ledema, Tania Doles, Philip Weller, Greg Pucillo, Shivina Harjani, Jesse Hull, Peter Zhang, Matthew Tarpley, Amanda O'Keefe, Bahar Avanoglu, Ipek Avanoglu, Brent Solomon, Pedro Galindo-Landeira, Yinan Li, Sophie Fabbri, Huy Buy,

Lara Greden, Javier Arbona. Consultants: Ellen Jorgenson, Genspace, Ezekiel Golan, TreeNovation, Greyshed. Sponsor: Ecovative. Photos: Micaela Rossato

ANDREW MAYNARD ARCHITECTS: CV08: Andrew Maynard

MAGNUSLARSSON: DUNE CITY: Magnus Larsson, Alex Kaiser

LAND ART GENERATOR INITIATIVE: HELIOFIELD: Myung Kweon Park, Yikyu Choe, Michael Chaveriat, Elizabeth Monoian, Robert Ferry

VINCENT CALLEBAUT ARCHITECTURES: LILYPADS: Vincent Callebaut

ICE FACTORY: Victor Hadjikyriacou

MVVA: ARC WILDLIFE BRIDGE: Michael van Valkenburgh

SQUARED DESIGN LAB: FILENES ECO-PAD: Meejin Yoon, Eric Howler, Franco Vairani, Josh Barandon, Jennifer Chuong, Cyrus Dochow, Nan Xiang, Dan Sullivan.

B+U ARCHITECTS: SKY CONDOS: Herwig Baumgartner, Scott Uriu, Nema Ashjaee, Aaron Ryan, Jack Gaumer, Ricardo Lledo, Anthony Morey

HUGH BROUGHTON ARCHITECTS: HALLEY VI: ANTARCTIC RESEARCH STATION: Hugh Broughton, AECOM, Billings Design, Galliford Try

BITTERTANG: MICROCOSMIC AQUACULTURE, GELATINOUS ORBS: Antonio Torres, Michael Loverich

PNEUMASTUDIO: SPIRABILIS: Cathryn Dwyre, Chris Perry, Justin Snider, Dave Mulder

STRANGE WEATHER: Pablo Garcia

SPLIT STUDIO: STRIPPED-DOWN VILLA: Jason Vigneri-Beane

DJDO: GROUND ELEMENTAL: Doug Jackson, Mark Neveu

KOKKUGIA and MITCHELL LAB @ TEXAS A&M: THE MICRO-BEHAVIOR OF MULTI-AGENT SYSTEMS: Roland Snooks, Ryan Wilson, Drew Busmire, Jacob Patapoff, Emily Knapp, Hong Bea Yang, Jose Padilla, Nick Gutierrez, Ashley Ricketson

FUTURE CITIES LAB: THEATER OF LOST SPECIES: Jason Kelly Johnson, Nataly Gattegno, Ripon DeLeon, Shawn Komlos, Ji Ahn, Fernando Amenedo, Matthew Clapham, Jonathon Payne, MACHINIC Digital Fabrication & Consulting

IGMA UNIVERSITOST SPECIES: BAUBOTANIK, LIVING PLANT CONSTRUCTION: Ferdinand Ludwig, Cornelius Hackenbracht, Jorge Cruz, Adrian Martinez, Cody May Gerd de Bruyn, Thomas, German Environmental Foundation (DBU), Oliver Storz, Daniel Sch Fabr

NEW-TERRITORIES/ R&SIE(N): "HE SHOT ME DOWN": Francois Roche, Stephanie Lavaux, Jean Navarro, Stephen Henrich, Marion Gauguet, Leopold Lambert, Andrea Koning, Igor Lacroix, Daniel Fernandez Flores

STUDIO KCA: HEAD IN THE CLOUDS PAVILION: Jason Klimoski, Lesley Chang

OPEN SOURCE ECOLOGY: Marcin Jakubowski

THE LIVING: AMPHIBIOUS ARCHITECTURE: David Benjamin, Mark Bain, Amelia Black, Natalie Jeremijenko, Abha Kataria, Jonathan Laventhol, Deborah Richards, Zenon Tech-Czarny, Kevin Wei, Chris Woebken, Soo-In Yang

B/a+p: ELEVATOR B, HIVE CITY: Rick Smith, Courtney Creenan, Kyle Mastalinski, Daniel Nead, Scott Selin, Lisa Stern, Brian Fentzke, Martha Bohm, Joyce Hwang, Christopher Romano, Philip Barr, Peter Grace, Marc Bajorek, Alex Poklinkowski, Yinang Zhang, Rigidized Metal, UB School of Architecture and Planning

ANIMAL SUPER POWERS: Chris Woebken and Kenichi Okada

BIOREACTORS, MEMBRANES AND ARCHITECTURE: Zbigniew Oksiuta

ECOLOGICSTUDIO: H.O.R.T.U.S ALGAE FARM: Marco Poletto, Claudia Pasquero

LIVING ARCHITECTURE SYSTEMS GROUP: RADIANT SOIL: Philip Beesley, Andrea Ling, Jonathan Tyrrell, Rachel Armstrong, PBAI Studio, Sue Balint, Eric Bury, Martin Correa, Pedro Garcia, Jonathan Gotfryd, Jayden Lee, Anne Paxton, Mingyi Zhou, Mariella Amodio, Martina Ferrera, Yonghan Kim, Brownyn Loucks, Sydney Morrison, Sarah Stephens, William Yam, Production, Jessica Anoche, Marjorie Artières, Olivia Aspinall, Jade Boyeldieu d'Auvigny, Lydia Chang, Polina Ershova, Fabio Latino, Hanaa Della Lama Taouzri, Rachel Trattles

SABIN+JONES LABSTUDIO: BRANCHING MORPHOGENESIS: Jenny E. Sabin, Andrew Lucia, Peter Lloyd Jones, Jones Lab members, Annette Fierro, Dwight Engel, Matthew Lake, Austin McInerny, Marta Moran, Misako Murata

CONCRETE RECYCLING ROBOT: Omer Haciomeroglu

YOUR ROTTEN FUTURE WILL BE GREAT: Phil Ross

GREG LYNN FORM: RECYCLED PLASTIC FURNITURE: Greg Lynn

UP-DROP: Aurora Robson

TRASH TRACK: Carlo Ratti, Assaf Biderman, Dietmar Offenhuber, Eugenio Morello, Tinauli, Kristian Kloeckl, Lewis Girod, Jennifer Dunnam, E Roon Kang, Kevin Nattinger, Avid Boustani, David Lee, Alan Anderson, Clio Andris, Carnaven Chiu, Chris Chung, Lorenzo Davolli, Kathryn Dineen, Natalia Duque Ciceri, Samantha Earl, Sarabjit Kaur, Sarah Neilson, Giovanni de Niederhausern, Jill Passano, Elizabeth Ramaccia, Renato Rinaldi, Francisca Rojas, Louis Sirota, Malima Wolf, Eugene Lee, Angela Wang, Armin Linke, Rex Britter, Stephen Miles, Tim Gutowski, Tim Pritchard, Jodee Fenton, Lance Albertson, Chad Johansen, Christie Rodgers, Shannon Cheng, Jon Dreher, Andy Smith, Richard Auger, Michael Cafferty, Shalini Ghandi, Jodee Fenton, Tim Pritchard

CASCADE FORMATIONS: LOW ENERGY-HIGH COMPLEXITY: Rhett Russo

bioMASON: BIOMANUFACTURED BRICK: Ginger Krieg Dosier

MICHAEL SILVER: CONSTRUCTION SITE AUTOMATION, GREEN MASONRY AND BIM: OSCR-4 TEAM: University at Buffalo - Mike Silver, Gary Chung, David Lin, Georine Pierre, Dylan Burns, Jia Jian Feng You, Evan Martinez, Christopher Vicente

EVAN DOUGLIS STUDIO LLC: GLASS WORKS: Evan Douglis

SOLAR SINTERING: Markus Kayser

REWILDING WITH SYNTHETIC BIOLOGY: Alexandra Daisy Ginsberg, Gemma Lord, Tommaso Lanza, Tom Mawby, Kent Redford, Nigel Dudley, Louise Carver

TISSUE CULTURE PROJECT: SEMI-LIVING VICTIMLESS UTOPIA: WILL WE EVER GET THERE?: Oron Catts, Ionat Zurr

SELF-ASSEMBLY LAB: MOLECULAR SELF-ASSEMBLY: Skylar Tibbits, Arthur Olson

ZULOARK: VERY LARGE STRUCTURE: Manuel Dominínguez

DECKER YEADON: nBOTS: SUSTAINING NANO-ROBOTIC ENVIRONMENT: Martina Decker, Peter Yeadon

XXL-XS New Directions in Ecological Design

Authors
Mitchell Joachim and Mike Silver

Graphic Design
Papersdoc SL

Cover design and concept
berger + stadel + walsh

Copyeditor
Irina Oryshkevich

Published by
Actar Publishers, New York, Barcelona
www.actar.com

Distributed by
Actar D Inc.

New York
355 Lexington Avenue, 8th Floor
New York, NY 10017
T +1 212 966 2207
F +1 212 966 2214
salesnewyork@actar-d.com

Barcelona
Roca i Batlle 2
08023 Barcelona
T +34 933 282 183
eurosales@actar-d.com

Printed and Bound in China

ISBN 9781940291871

Library of Congress Control Number: 2016938024

A CIP catalogue record for this book is available from the Library of Congress, Washington D.C., USA.